HIGH PERFORMANCE
Swimming

HIGH PERFORMANCE
Swimming

ALAN LYNN

THE CROWOOD PRESS

First published in 2008 by
The Crowood Press Ltd
Ramsbury, Marlborough
Wiltshire SN8 2HR

www.crowood.com

British Library Cataloguing-in-Publication Data
A catalogue record for this book is available from the British Library.

ISBN 978 1 84797 038 1

Disclaimer
Please note that the author and the publisher of this book do not accept any responsibility whatsoever for any error or omission, nor any loss, injury, damage, adverse outcome or liability suffered as a result of the use of the information contained in this book, or reliance upon it. Since some of the training exercises can be dangerous and could involve physical activities that are too strenuous for some individuals to engage in safely, it is essential that a doctor be consulted before training is undertaken.

Typeset by S R Nova Pvt Ltd., Bangalore, India

Printed and bound in Singapore by Craft Print International Ltd

Contents

Dedication

To Jackie and Cameron

Acknowledgements

The author and publishers would like to thank the following for their help in the production of this book: Stephen Brown of OMANBROWN (for the photographs); the University of Stirling, for the use of the National Swimming Academy pool (once again); and Stephen Binnie, for being such a patient and willing participant for the images.

Introduction

Competitive swimming is one of the world's most spectacular sports, with Olympic champions becoming celebrities and millionaires. Multiple winners such as Michael Phelps, Natalie Coughlin and Ian Thorpe transcend nationality, and are famous across the world for their aquatic exploits. In his fascinating book *Golden Girl*, US journalist Michael Silver lifts the lid on the world of élite swimming by describing the turbulent life and times of Natalie Coughlin as she became the most successful female swimmer at the Athens Olympics. In similar vein, P.H. Mullen writes about the hopes and dreams of Olympic medallist Tom Wilkens and his Santa Clara teammates as they attempt to qualify for the 2000 Sydney Olympic Games. These books, full of insights and written by sports journalists, examine the personal side of high performance swimming, detailing the relationships, challenges and human journeys involved in making it to the top of the sport.

This book, written by a coach, intends to guide the reader through the technical and scientific aspects of high performance swimming, providing information on the programmes and practices of élite coaches and swimmers. The first section, 'High Performance Swimming', will look at the crucial area of coaching the élite swimmer, drawing upon the author's research on the characteristics and development pathways of élite swimming coaches, including a look at the humanistic style of coaching. The second part of this section will look at things from the perspective of the élite swimmer, asking what they want of their coaches, and providing anecdotal information about how to get to the top – and then stay there! Finally, a look at the sport's professionalization and the worldwide competition calendar will lead into a short exposé of the threat of doping to one of the world's 'cleanest' sports.

The second section, 'Training', forms the largest part of the book, dealing with preparation for performance, and looking at the important area of periodization in the context of quadrennial planning. A unique element of this section is the information on specific event training, illustrating sample programmes and sessions from élite swimmers and coaches. Also in this section is another unique feature on 'special considerations', covering altitude training, the use of specialized equipment, and once more drawing on cutting-edge practices from leading experts.

The third section, 'High Performance Support Systems', looks at the myriad of support services available to today's élite swimmers. 'Developing Efficient Engines' scrutinizes the physiological aspects of performance, detailing best practice in test sets and protocols from across the world. 'Effective Techniques' examines the technical developments necessary to be the best, looking at stroke analysis and biomechanics. 'Technology and Tactics' takes this into the competition sphere, and details race analysis data and race strategies of champions. Finally, the controversial topic of 'Ergogenics' is discussed, with a look at swimsuit technologies.

Section 4, 'Competition', deals with psychology and those other factors involved in peaking for high performance that are often forgotten or coped with at the very last minute. 'Mind over Matter' will explain how to hone and develop mental preparation and skills development; 'Major Championship Meets' will look at travel and jetlag, and general coping strategies.

A final section gives information on how to find out more, and includes useful addresses, a glossary of terms and an index.

PART 1: HIGH PERFORMANCE SWIMMING

CHAPTER 1

Coaching

Before defining what is meant by élite swimming coaching, it is necessary to have an appreciation of the meanings implied by the term 'sports coaching', even if a precise definition cannot be agreed. Indeed, one of the defining characteristics of sports coaching is the breadth of the roles attributed to the coach. The term 'sports coaching' is used to refer to a variety of sport leadership roles and contexts. These range across all forms of sport, from participation sport, in which it is often used interchangeably with leader, teacher and instructor, to intensive performance sport, in which the coach may manage or orchestrate a team of contributing experts. The coaching role will vary enormously in the degree of direct (hands-on) intervention, long-term planning, control of the training environment, intervention styles, depth and form of interpersonal relationships, and technical knowledge. The athletes working with the coach will vary in their motives, intensity of commitment, skill levels, and perceived rewards. Organizational settings will be similarly varied.

Central to this enterprise is the coaching process. This has been defined by Lyle[1] as the 'purposeful and co-ordinated series of activities and interventions designed to improve competition performance'. It is most evident in the planned, co-ordinated and integrated programme of preparation and competition. However, it is perhaps useful to distinguish between three forms of coaching: participation, development, and performance (*see* Fig. 1). Each of these different forms of coaching has its own assumptions about the role of the coach, the completeness of the preparation for competition, the mix of participant and coach goals, and the extent and sophistication of the process. Although it may seem likely that the majority of questions about coaching and the coaching process can only be addressed satisfactorily in a performance coaching context, this can be overstated, and there is increasingly some attention being paid to research based on participation coaching.

Coaching is also a generic term, and there is extensive literature to support the use of coaching in its counselling/mentoring, training, preparation, and more general management function. There is ample evidence of the transfer of sport coaching 'principles and experience' to the corporate training industry. The term 'coaching' has a recognizable meaning in acting, dance, drama, examination preparation, and so on; in addition, it has come to be used for almost any guidance role that is intended to lead to 'improvement'.

THE DEVELOPMENT OF HIGH PERFORMANCE SWIMMING COACHES

Given the prominence of sport and the increasing visibility of high profile coaches, it is surprising to learn that relatively little is known about how one becomes a successful coach. Although coaching biographies and autobiographies are plentiful (notable in the world of swimming are Lawrie Lawrence's *Stories of Inspiration*[2], Don Talbot's *Nothing but the Best*[3] and a chapter on James 'Doc' Counsilman in Gary Walton's great book, *Beyond Winning*[4]), few studies have empirically documented the path to coaching success. The author has been researching this field using 'personal construct theory' (PCT) as a

Figure 1 Forms of coaching

Participation Coaching:
Largely to do with initiation into sport and with basic skills teaching. Some individuals, usually young people with greater levels of potential, will move quite quickly through this stage. Others will become more recreational or casual participants, often as they move into adulthood.

Characterised by:
- Lack of emphasis on competition goals
- Less intensive engagement
- Short term horizons and immediate satisfactions
- Absence of attention to components of performance
- Episodic rather than processual orientation
- Key skills are delivery/intervention based
- Less well firmed-up 'contract' between the coach and the sportspersons

Developmental Coaching:
This is characterised by rapid skills learning and a developing engagement with a sport specific competition programme. This is a key stage for talent identification. This stage is almost exclusively for younger persons in age group sport who are accelerating their way through the performance standards. It can be argued that 'instructors of adult sportspersons' who wish to improve but who do not satisfy the boundary criteria (for example golf instruction) should be included in this category.

Characterised by:
- Engagement in competition
- Identifiable performance goals
- Degree of co-ordination and planning, although perhaps episodic engagement
- Longer term goals
- Individuals have made a commitment to the sport
- Attention to basic components, e.g. physical conditioning, mental preparation
- Likely to be meaningful interpersonal relationship between coach and performer.

Performance Coaching:
Performers and circumstances come together to fulfil the majority of the coaching process boundary markers. Characterised by relatively intensive preparation and involvement in competition sport. Can apply to all ages and levels of developed ability. There may be some special cases, such as representative team/group coaches.

Characterised by:
- Intensive commitment to the preparation programme
- Intention to control performance variables in integrated and progressive fashion
- Clear competition goals, within recognised organisational/club/NGB structures
- Key skills in decision making, planning and data management
- More extensive interpersonal contact between coach and performer(s)
- Performance components individualized

means of determining how élite coaches became involved in coaching, how they were trained, critical incidents in their learning, and how they have become expert in their field.

The development of excellence in sport has received considerable research attention in recent years, and it is now evident that complex arrays of genetic and environmental factors interact to facilitate and nurture competitive sporting excellence. Perhaps the most consistent theme found across the literature is the critical role of the coach in developing sporting talent.

Although coaches' influence will vary across cultures, sports and stages of talent development, guidance from a competent coach is essential to becoming an expert performer.

Given the central or key role of the coach, it is ironic to discover that coach development has yet to be critically examined. The lack of a conceptual framework to explain coach development is even more surprising, given the comments of eminent scholars in sport psychology and education. For example, the learning elements required to develop excellence in coaching were identified almost twenty years ago (Gould, Giannini, Krane & Hodge)[5]. Furthermore, it has been more than two decades since Bloom[6] encouraged the scientific community to extend his work on athletic talent development to the interpersonal relations talent area, which clearly encompasses coaching.

Although a growing body of research exists on sports coaching, our understanding of coach development is limited. To better understand the development of coaches, it may be useful to adopt a lifespan perspective that focuses on developmental paths and activities. According to the ecological systems theory of Bronfenbrenner[7], coaching development would occur when coaches engaged regularly in social interactions and domain-related activities that became increasingly more complex over time. Several studies have shown the importance of past experiences as key sources of coaching knowledge. For example, Schinke, Bloom and Salmela[8] showed that the development of coaching competencies may be acquired through learning activities that take place in sport as an athlete, a coach, or outside the sporting arena, both in formal and informal educational environments.

Nevertheless, our understanding of how these different learning activities interact throughout development to eventually produce a coach have never been systematically analyzed. Questions to guide such research are: Have successful swimming coaches engaged in similar activities as competitive swimmers? How much time is invested in participation in swimming before starting to coach? Do successful swimming coaches have similar coaching developmental activity profiles (for example, the number and type of sports coached)? How much time is spent in coach developmental activities (training, practice, administration, coach education)?

Considering the number of times it has been mentioned, anyone involved in swimming coaching and the world of sport is aware that coaches play an important role, that coaching is complex, and that coaches

therefore need to develop a knowledge base that should include coaching knowledge and sport-specific knowledge. Recent research (Trudel & Gilbert, 2006)[9] has concluded that coaches learn to coach through two major ways: large-scale coach education programmes (acquisition); and experience (participation).

Using questionnaires and/or interviews, researchers were able to identify a number of specific events or situations (playing experience, mentoring, coaching courses, interactions with other coaches, Internet, and so on) as sources that coaches use to develop coaching knowledge and sport-specific knowledge. Considering that coaching certification is usually obtained only after successfully completing a formal coach education programme, we might expect that this source of learning would be the most important; however, many of the studies cited so far have instead shown that formalized learning venues are not valued by coaches as much as their day-to-day learning experiences in the field. This is perhaps an understandable finding when we consider the small amount of time a coach might spend in a formalized learning environment in comparison to the number of hours she or he spends in the swimming venue, coaching and interacting with swimmers, other coaches, and officials.

While the identification of coaches' learning sources is valuable, it can be argued that the investigation should not stop there. In fact, attempting to identify which sources are more important than others without looking at the coaches' learning process in these situations, may limit any initiative to provide the best learning environment for coaches. For example, at present there is difficulty explaining why there is little consensus among coaches regarding the relative importance of the sources.

Some coaches believe adamantly that past athletic experience is an asset, while others indicate that it is not very important. The mentoring process is, for many coaches, a key factor in learning how to coach well, and yet there is a danger in being limited to only one way to learn how to coach. Even the process of reflection, which is often cited as a way to learn from experience, may vary from coach to coach, depending on the presence of different conditions.

It is generally agreed that coaching is a process that primarily aids athletes achieve their peak performance in competition. To fulfil this objective the coach is engaged in a wide range of roles, and is required to apply a vast array of skills to a range of problems. Indeed, the complexity of the task is underlined by Jones et al[10], who identified thirty-seven standards to describe the coaching process, confirming the assertion that the requirements of effective coaching are both wide-ranging and specialized. Furthermore, it has become increasingly acknowledged that regardless of the level of knowledge and skill of the coach, it is the application of that knowledge and skill that separates the excellent practitioner from the average one.

So, how have élite swimming coaches been developed? Six élite coaches agreed to participate in a study conducted by the author. In order to collect meaningful data, repertory grids and qualitative interviews were completed to determine four aspects: (1) how the coaches became involved in coaching (initiation); (2) how they have been trained (education); (3) critical incidents in their development (experiential learning); and (4), how they have become expert (effectiveness).

They were categorized as élite coaches based on multiple criteria. First, they were actively involved in coaching at international level. Second, they had at least ten years of coaching experience, and have produced at least one international performer. Finally, they were each classified as a high performance coach by their National Governing Body of Sport (NGB). Each of the coaches was known to the author from his work as a coach and coach educator. All the coaches had been competitive swimmers at least to national level, and half of them had swum at international level; five of the coaches were male and one was female. All coaches

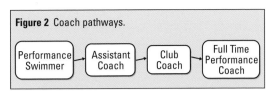

Figure 2 Coach pathways.

in the sample were employed full-time as performance coaches and/or swimming development officers. Fig. 2 illustrates the pathway followed by the coaches from swimmer to performance coach; this is in keeping with research on coaches from other sports.[11]

The reasons the coaches gave for becoming performance coaches were also fairly consistent with the existing literature. Fig. 3 lists these for this small sample and the wider research field. It is interesting to note that the distinctions between participation coaching made earlier (in Fig. 1) are just as clear in the motives for becoming coaches – that is, performance swimmers who have become performance coaches wished to stay involved in this environment. In determining the 'ideal' performance coach, one of the sample generated the list of constructs and contrasts shown in Fig. 4. What is clear from this list is that the coach had a definite view on the qualities of an effective coach, and that developing these would not be the sole preserve of formal coaching courses.

It is also fascinating to see the mix of ideas in what constitutes the ideal coach – for example, autocratic and intuitive, and so on. In terms of how this sample has developed their knowledge and skills, the responses were again in line with findings from other

Figure 3 Reasons for coaching.

General research	Swimming coach sample
Continued participation in sport	✓
Pride, achievement, success	✓
Fun & enjoyment	✓
Career pathway	✓
Fitness & health	X
Parental route	X
Helping others to improve	✓

Figure 4 Example of generated constructs from one coach.

The 'ideal' coach	Contrast
willing to learn	no new knowledge
totally reliable	unreliable
specific swimming background	no swimming background
shares knowledge	insular
respected by athletes	not respected by athletes
professional	hobby coach
highly organized	not organized
leader	follower
intuitive methods	scientific methods
highly experienced	little experience
good people skills	poor people skills
good communicator	poor communicator
fully qualified	no qualifications
coached a champion	no high level results
autocratic	democratic
approachable	hard to approach

Figure 5 Coach education and development.

Mentoring
Informal
Supportive
Non-regulated

Trial & Error
Compensating for knowledge gaps
Learning alongside swimmer development
Little or no external feedback available

Previous experience
Invaluable to understand sport
Technical insights
Empathy with swimmers

Coach education courses
Depends on quality of tutor
Good framework to work from
Great to share with peers

Training sessions
Squad-based
Very useful learning medium
Allied to mentoring

Books & videos
Depends on person & learning style
Not much available
Helped in early stages

Performance analysis
IT literacy crucial
Source of objective feedback
Increasingly essential at top level

Competitions
Learn at the 'sharp end'
Foreign experience invaluable
Contact with mentors appreciated

sports[12]. Represented by the illustration in Fig. 5, the coaches reported that they have experienced a multi-dimensional range of educational and developmental episodes. Critically, the key incidents in their learning are punctuated by occurrences outside the formal certification programme. For example, the influence of mentors is very highly rated by the group. This is most significant, as there is no formal coach mentoring programme in existence, thus these relationships must all have been established informally and in an unmediated fashion. Learning by 'trial and error' is another strongly featured component, with all the sample reporting that they had learned as much from their mistakes as they had from reinforcing successes. The implications of these findings for coach development and education are considerable.

HOW TO COACH

It has become increasingly clear that traditional instructional methods (telling an athlete what to do) are not the most effective way of supporting athlete learning and development. Coaches often report that they have to tell athletes over and over again the same things, and then under pressure of competition athletes go back to their old habits. Training sessions are frequently focused primarily on the knowledge the coach has to give, but this way of coaching can stifle the athletes' own potential, thinking, decision-making and creativity, and limit these to the extent of the imagination and experience of the coach.

The purpose of coaching is for athletes to learn about how things work best for them. First, this is about their individual physical and mental make-up, and where they are with technical and tactical development. Second, it is about being able to perform to their best when in competition or when challenged. A positive coaching philosophy has this purpose very clearly in mind: to develop independent athletes who are aware of what is theirs (ownership) in terms of performance. This ownership encourages them to be responsible for their performance, and this responsibility will enable them to repeat that performance as and when required, consistently and sustainably.

On deck this would lead a coach to provide, first, a planned and structured environment based on a shared set of goals; then to enable swimmers to 'do' the skill or 'set'; and then to ask questions about what the swimmer is noticing about their performance. The intended outcome is that in a competitive situation the swimmer will preferably just compete, be 'in the moment' and react, based on their self-awareness of the situation or movement. Part of the self-belief will be that the swimmer has an appropriate goal and knows that they can get back on track when something goes astray (see Part 4 of this book for more details on the psychology of swimming). The learning that happens at training should be about developing that skill – the skill of self-correcting or self-coaching, and of being the best that you can be on that day.

If the swimmer does find that they need to adapt, then they will be able to draw on focused attention learned in training situations. The focused attention may be about any of the following: What am I noticing? What would I like to do better? Where is the discomfort? Where am I now? Where would I like to be? How would I like it to be? This focused attention is noticed 'in the moment'. A judgement that is tinged with the emotion of looking at the outcome (after the moment – either good or bad) can take away the focus. Focused attention will enable the swimmer to avoid subjectively judging the performance, as that awareness enables them to focus on something identified as important: for example, with age group swimmers, almost immediately on touching the wall, the first reaction is to look at the electronic scoreboard for the finish time/place. This is a perfectly understandable response to the need for feedback, but it may cause a lack of focus on the performance itself

and only attribute positive or negative feelings to the outcome. By developing self-aware swimmers, coaches can get past this problem, and have them assess the mastery of performance first and the outcome second.

While the above description focuses mostly on coaches helping the swimmer find his/her own way, the approach does acknowledge that there will be times when coaches will decide it is necessary to give instructions. This can happen in particular when there is time pressure. The necessity to be directive is a signal for the coach that there is something that has not been learned in training and needs to be addressed at a future training session. However, as much as possible, it is advantageous for athletes and their performance if coaches attempt to move back into a humanistic approach. Coaches will need to develop their questioning skills to use this approach effectively. The GROW model below provides a sequence that coaches can use to develop the types of questions to ask:

The GROW Model

G What is your goal? (What are you wanting to achieve?).

R Reality (What is happening now?)

O Options (What options do you have?)

W What will you do now? (What are you going to do? Then loop round to the goal again: what did you notice now that you have had your turn?)

Humanistic coaching and its underpinning philosophy are equally relevant for team or individual sports, and for children, teenagers or adults. When a coach uses this approach, a swimmer has the opportunity to function as a complete, integrated human being, and this experience fosters the recognition that when performing, all aspects of the individual – physical, emotional, social and cognitive – are engaged (Lombardo, 1999)[13]. The purpose is to enable swimmers to be self-aware, and to involve them in the process of sport by learning, doing, thinking and feeling holistically (see Fig. 6). It is

Coaches' Code of Ethics

Respect the rights, dignity and worth of every individual athlete as a human being

- Treat everyone equally regardless of sex, disability, ethnic origin or religion.
- Respect the talent, developmental stage and goals of each athlete in order to help each athlete reach their full potential.

Maintain high standards of integrity

- Operate within the rules of your sport and in the spirit of fair play, while encouraging your athletes to do the same.
- Advocate a sporting environment free of drugs and other performance-enhancing substances within the guidelines of the World Anti-Doping Code.
- Do not disclose any confidential information relating to athletes without their written prior consent.

Be a positive role model for your sport and athletes, and act in a way that projects a positive image of coaching

- All athletes are deserving of equal attention and opportunities.
- Ensure the athlete's time spent with you is a positive experience.
- Be fair, considerate and honest with athletes.
- Encourage and promote a healthy lifestyle – refrain from smoking and drinking alcohol around athletes.

Professional responsibilities

- Display high standards in your language, manner, punctuality, preparation and presentation.
- Display control, courtesy, respect, honesty, dignity and professionalism to all involved within the sphere of sport – this includes opponents, coaches, officials, administrators, the media, parents and spectators. Encourage your athletes to demonstrate the same qualities.
- Be professional and accept responsibility for your actions. You should not only refrain from initiating a sexual relationship with an athlete, but should also discourage any attempt by an athlete to initiate a sexual relationship with you, explaining the ethical basis of your refusal.
- Accurately represent personal coaching qualifications, experience, competence and affiliations. Refrain from criticism of other coaches and athletes.

Make a commitment to providing a quality service to your athletes

- Seek continual improvement through ongoing coach education, and other personal and professional development opportunities.
- Provide athletes with planned and structured training programmes appropriate to their needs and goals.
- Seek advice and assistance from professionals when additional expertise is required.
- Maintain appropriate records.

Provide a safe environment for training and competition

- Adopt appropriate risk management strategies to ensure that the training and/or competition environment is safe.
- Ensure equipment and facilities meet safety standards.
- Ensure equipment, rules, training and the environment are appropriate for the age, physical and emotional maturity, experience and ability of the athletes.
- Show concern and caution toward sick and injured athletes.
- Allow further participation in training and competition only when appropriate.

Coaches' Code of Ethics (cont.)

- Encourage athletes to seek medical advice when required.
- Provide a modified training programme where appropriate.
- Maintain the same interest and support towards sick and injured athletes as you would to healthy athletes.

Protect your athletes from any form of personal abuse

- Refrain from any form of verbal, physical or emotional abuse towards your athletes.
- Refrain from any form of sexual or racial harassment, whether verbal or physical.
- Do not harass, abuse or discriminate against athletes on the basis of their sex, marital status, sexual orientation, religious or ethical beliefs, race, colour, ethnic origins, employment status, disability or distinguishing characteristics.
- Any physical contact with athletes should be appropriate to the situation and necessary for the athlete's skill development.
- Be alert to any forms of abuse directed towards athletes from other sources while in your care.

Figure 6 Humanistic coaching.

	DEFINITIONS (What does this mean for coaching?)	POSSIBLE COACH QUESTIONS (What do you want to achieve in this training session/ this season?)
ATHLETE-CENTRED	Develops independent, confident athletes able to 'coach' themselves Learners LEARN, coaches only help the process	What do you notice? What would you need to do about that? What is your goal for this season?
AWARENESS	Being in the moment. Helping athletes to be aware of what they are doing at the time rather than telling them what you think as the coach. Increasing focused attention	What are you noticing? What are you aware of? Is there anything you would like to do better? What did you focus on?
RESPONSIBILITY	Choosing to take action Choosing to work with the intensity level required to achieve the goal Choosing to work consciously while training	What are you trying to do? What happens now? What could you do to meet that goal? What will you do?
ATHLETE OWNERSHIP	The process belongs to the athletes. They are participating, performing, training because they believe in the cause.	Where do you see yourself at the end of this season? Where are you now? What could you do to get to that goal of this season? What will you do?
ANALYSIS	What the coach sees or the athlete thinks removed from the moment of doing. (Analysis can be initiated through video.)	What happened in the last 100 metres of the race?
EMPOWERMENT	An environment which consists of mutual visions, values or principles; the individual owns mutually established clear roles, responsibilities and boundaries, the individual is doing it for him/herself, but sees and owns the big picture (vision) and has self-determination (establishes values and strategies).	What are our goals? What strategies do we need to meet those goals? What values will you live by when attending to the strategies? What is our overall vision?

> **Working as a Coach**
>
> There are three basic ways of working as a coach:
> 1. Instructional mode (doing as the coach says): the coach talks, and the athlete listens and tries to do what the coach tells them (the athlete's body responds).
> 2. Analytical mode (creating analysis): the coach encourages analysis (either with or without technology), discussion, thinking and/or planning, for example about what worked or what to try next time (the athlete's mind responds).
> 3. Positive coaching (creating awareness): the coach helps the athlete to be in the moment and feel/notice what is happening (humanistic/holistic – mind and body respond together).

recognized that effective coaching requires the coach to vary their approach according to the needs of the athlete at that particular moment. There is a range of coaching styles, and coaches will shift within this range depending on factors such as the immediate needs of the athlete/group, time constraints, health and safety issues, and athlete receptiveness. Swimmers need to have self-belief to just 'do it'. So how does the coach help them to 'get there'?

The following two tables (Figs. 7 and 8) provide an overview of the characteristics of coach- and swimmer-centred coaches and swimmers respectively. This may be useful when discussing the athlete-centred coaching philosophy. These tables emphasize why the 'how to' of coaching significantly affects athlete learning. The characteristics in the swimmer-centred columns provide a focus for effective coaching approaches. A swimmer-centred coaching approach helps to develop talented people, who take responsibility for their own learning, regardless of the coaching community they participate in, or their stage of development. In addition to considering the coaching approach to be taken, it is vital that coaches at all levels adhere to a secure ethical framework.

[1]Lyle, J. (2002) *Sports Coaching Concepts: A Framework for Coaches Behaviour* Routledge, London.

[2]Lawrence, L. (1993) *Lawrence of Australia: Stories of Inspiration* Ironbank Press, NSW, Australia.

[3]Talbot, D., Heads, I., & Berry, K. (2003) *Talbot: Nothing but the Best* Lothian Books, Australia.

[4]Walton, G.M. (1992) *Beyond Winning: The Timeless Wisdom of Great Philosopher Coaches* Leisure Press, Champaign, Ill.

[5]Gould, D., Giannini, J., Krane, K., & Hodge, K. (1990) 'Educational needs of élite US national team, Pan American and Olympic coaches' *Journal of Teaching Physical Education* 9, 332-334.

[6]Bloom, B. (1985) *Developing talent in young people* Ballantine, New York.

[7]Bronfenbrenner, U., (1999) 'Environments in Developmental Perspective: Theoretical and Operational Models', in Friedman, S.L. & Wachs, T.D., eds. 'Measuring Environment across the Life Span: Emerging Methods and Concepts', American Psychological Association, Washington, 1999, 3-30.

[8]Schinke, R.J., Bloom, G.A., & Salmela, J.H. (1995) 'The career stages of élite Canadian basketball coaches' *Avante*, 1(1), 48-62.

[9]Trudel, P. & Gilbert, W. (2006) 'Coaching and coach education' in Kirk D., O'Sullivan M., & McDonald D., eds (2006) *Handbook of Research in Physical Education* Sage, London.

[10]Jones, D. F., Housner, L. D., & Kornspan, A. S. (1997) 'Interactive decision making and behavior of experienced and inexperienced basketball coaches during practice' *Journal of Teaching in Physical Education* 16, 454-468.

[11]Clark, V. (2005) 'The recruitment pathways of performance hockey coaches' Unpublished Masters thesis, University of Strathclyde.

[12]Irwin, G., Hanton, S., Kerwin, D.G., 'Reflective Practice and the Origins of Élite Coaching Knowledge' *Reflective Practice*, 2004, 5, 425-442.

[13]Lombardo, B.J. ((1987) *The Humanistic Coach: From Theory to Practice*. Charles Thomas Publishing, Springfield, Ill.

Figure 7 Humanistic coaching.

Coach-Centred Coach

- provides an environment of dependency
- expects the team to conform to his/her ways of doing
- speaks to rather than listens to the athletes
- tells athletes only what he/she thinks they need to know to suit his/her needs
- expects athletes to conform to values established by him/her
- has a 'winning at all costs' attitude, which promotes unfair or illegal practices
- does not actively discourage acts of cheating or unprofessional ways of seeking an advantage
- treats the team as one, rather than as individuals
- does not accept athletes' opinions
- insists that athletes abide by his/her rules
- is organized
- is inflexible and not open-minded
- makes the decisions for the athletes or team
- asks closed and redundant, or few, questions
- criticises mistakes
- uses threats or punishment to coerce athletes into following coach's expectations of behaviour
- provides feedback of what to fix
- is a disciplinarian
- insists on his/her way or the highway
- coaches to win, rather than to develop or educate athletes
- promotes fear of failure
- does not ask for athlete's evaluations of his/her coaching
- does not monitor or assess psychological and emotional experience as much as physical and technical ones
- fails to exercise a caring, athlete-centred approach
- stresses extrinsic rewards over intrinsic values
- promotes the role of sport as the most important aspect of athletes' lives
- promotes dictatorship and a 'one size fits all' philosophy.

Swimmer-Centred Coach

- provides a safe and confirming environment
- is empathetic and caring towards his/her athletes
- listens to athletes' and takes them seriously
- is honest and open
- reinforces values and morals through facilitation of teams' goals and the coach's own actions (role model)
- values all athletes' contributions equally, but accepts each athlete as a unique individual
- gives athletes responsibility to encourage accountability for their actions
- is purposeful and provides meaning to learning
- accepts athletes' opinions
- makes each athlete feel capable of succeeding
- through athlete responsibility, establishes reasonable limits for behaviour
- organizes and plans training sessions
- is flexible and open-ended
- provides athletes with appropriate choices and opportunities for decision-making
- assists athletes in establishing team and individual goals and values; goals should be multiple (outcome goals should NOT be the only ones)
- asks questions of his/her players; encourages problem solving and critical thinking
- provides information to players about their performance and other matters related to the team
- answers questions, encourages players to ask questions and seek knowledge
- assists players in analyzing their individual and the team's actions and feelings
- learns about his/her athletes, takes a personal interest in each one and 'gets to know them'
- promotes a healthy attitude toward sport and competition; stresses the intrinsic value over extrinsic rewards, the importance of respect for opponents, and other ethical values
- recognises the role of sport in a larger society, which should be democratic and egalitarian.

Figure 8 A comparison of characteristics of Swimmers who are coached by athlete-centred and coach-centred coaches.

Coach-centred Swimmers often:

- have their goals set for them
- feel as if they don't have a say in any direction
- lack enthusiasm
- are treated as a means to an end
- make no decisions
- talk back when they've had enough
- compete 'robotically'
- display anger and stubbornness
- listen to the coach's way
- have a disrespectful attitude
- are defensive when challenged
- get easily frustrated
- are not listened to
- feel that there is no respect or trust from the coach
- are encouraged to be individuals and therefore show uncooperativeness
- lack confidence and competence to make informed decisions.

Athlete-centred Swimmers often:

- set their own goals and have an intrinsic desire to reach them
- enjoy their sport
- show enthusiasm
- develop self-efficacy and confidence in their ability and are enabled to control results produced by their skill and effort
- understand that they contribute and take responsibility for their learning and direction
- are accountable for their actions
- are resourceful and innovative
- feel that they are important because of coaches' actions in understanding the athletes (e.g. listening, empathy)
- understand that there is a mutual trust and respect
- cooperate to enhance mutual goals and directions
- are more coachable because they have freedom and choice
- are highly committed to achieving levels of excellence
- are willing to engage totally in what they believe.

CHAPTER **2**

Swimming

THE DEVELOPMENT OF ÉLITE SWIMMERS

Any review of the literature covering studies on the development of expert performance suggests that several factors play a significant role in its evolution. The more common ones that are cited include the following, in no particular order: training; teaching/coaching; supportive parents; enjoyment; recovery; age; psychological skills and attributes; and innate abilities – all of which have received empirical support to varying extents. The author has coached several élite swimmers and has conducted research on the development of élite swimming coaches. The following short section is a distillation of this experience, punctuated with supportive examples of published research in this field.

Several factors seem to be important for the development and maintenance of expert swimming performance. It is interesting to note that some of these factors vary among the swimmers themselves, but many are consistent across the development pathways they all followed. For example, the context in which they were immersed generally influenced them in positive ways. Several resources, including family members, coaches and other athletes, were important to them. Parents are very supportive, however they were not as actively involved in the latter stages of development as swimmers moved away from home, and became more independent. For the most part, the swimmers I have coached have worked with just a few coaches during their development years (often the same person for many, many years).

This is a characteristic of the sport of swimming, where coaches invest significant time and energy assisting young swimmers to develop and refine skills and competition strategies. In their seminal study, Gould *et al*[1] found that members of successful international teams had coaches who instilled confidence and trust, and coped well with crisis situations. On the other hand, members of less successful teams had coaches who failed to develop trust and effective communication, and were not consistent in their behaviours, particularly in pressure situations.

Education is another important factor throughout a swimmer's career. Almost all the successful swimmers I have coached pursued tertiary education studies. Many of them were high achievers in both sport and school, and this was partly due to the fact that school was made a priority throughout their lives (by them, their parents and fully supported by me). Csikszentmihalyi *et al*[2] found that school was a valuable resource for talent development because in many cases, individuals had access to excellent teachers and coaches who created a positive environment in which they could develop skills and experience flow. My experiences suggest that education and sport can complement each other very well, and be pursued at a high level if athletes effectively manage their time (another attribute encouraged by the highly systematic environment created around competitive swimming).

The main personal characteristics manifested by swimmers at a high level are self-confidence and motivation. Swimmers who are confident about their abilities to succeed, and are motivated to train in order to become the best, will succeed more often than those who lack either of these attributes. Another couple of things I have found common in successful swimmers (and supported by research) are creativity and innovation. Usually characterized by a need to 'stay ahead of their rivals', this is again about building confidence and knowing that you are as well prepared as you can be. For an excellent example of this, see the training set devised by 400 IMer Lewis Smith in Chapter 6 'Specific Event Training', Fig. 35a.

Becoming a successful swimmer takes hours and hours of training. This confirms Ericsson *et al*'s[3] findings, that individuals must engage in extensive hours of deliberate practice to improve in their sport. For swimming, this involves pool training, land training (outside the pool – in the gym, weights room, and so on) and living a 'performance lifestyle' (eating correctly, not partying, and so on). Accumulating all of this deliberate practice (at least ten years according to the studies) is a long and dedicated process.

However, an important question remains to be answered: do athletes need as much deliberate practice once they reach the pinnacle of their sport? Krampe and Ericsson[4] investigated the role of deliberate practice in the maintenance of cognitive motor skills of young and older expert and accomplished amateur pianists. Their findings suggest that once élite levels of performance are attained, these levels must be actively maintained through regular, deliberate practice. However, it appears that the amount of deliberate practice required to maintain skills that have already been acquired is less than that required to initially acquire them. These findings could have important implications, because overtraining and staleness still appears to be prevalent at élite levels.

This raises the next important issue to consider, namely physiological tenets that limit performance. Swimming has long been known as 'a young person's sport', but this is changing. The author retired from swimming aged twenty (to complete degree studies at university), which was then very much the norm. But the average age of Olympic competitors is on the increase (circa plus five years in the last couple of decades, and rising), and long-held physiological concepts are being continually challenged. For example, if physiological capacity declines with age, why is US female swimmer Dara Torres (a forty-year-old mother) still setting world class and personal best times? Although younger than Torres, another US swimmer, Rachel Komisarz, set the second-fastest 100yd butterfly time ever in her thirties. The major implication of such examples may in fact be that programmes for young swimmers are much less intense, being focused more on enjoyment and mastery of skill, and less on winning and early success.

In addition to deliberate (physical) practice, mental preparation is very important in the early years, although this may not come in the form of structured 'training' sessions. Engaging in goal-setting, rudimentary visualization and positive self-talk are all strategies used by my swimmers from an early age (sometimes with encouragement from me, sometimes occurring naturally in the athletes themselves).

Orlick and Partington[5] found that goal-setting was one of the elements that distinguished successful from unsuccessful athletes. My experience would support the suggestion that it is an important skill to perfect in order to consistently perform at a high level in sport. There are other implications for sport psychology. The use of more traditional mental training skills and strategies appears to be important; however, it seems that less informal processes such as self-reflection and evaluation should also be encouraged prior to, during, and after training and competitions.

Linking mental training with other training activities appears to be another important point to reinforce when working with swimmers. For the swimmers who 'stuck with it', it is interesting that many of them adopted a particular mindset that allowed them to stay calm and focused on the tasks they needed to perform, and to minimize the stress and pressure associated with high profile events such as the Olympics or a World Championships. Even though they were getting ready for the biggest performance of their lives, they made an effort to keep things in perspective. This strategy has been strongly advocated by researchers in the field of sports psychology (Botterill, Patrick & Sawatzky, 1996)[6].

Recovery is another significant theme. Successful swimmers develop strategies to allow themselves to recover mentally and physically from their intense training and competitions. According to many researchers, the importance of recovery cannot be underestimated. Ericsson *et al* noted that because deliberate practice activities are mentally and physically effortful, they should be balanced with adequate recovery periods in order to prevent exhaustion or burnout. Morgan *et al*[7] revealed that athletes who do not allow their bodies to recuperate are at risk of being overtrained and of experiencing both psychological and physiological disturbances that could seriously affect their performance.

The issue of overtraining was also discussed in Gould *et al*'s study. These authors found that unsuccessful teams were overtrained, while successful teams took a number of breaks and were allowed to taper as the Olympics approached. It is interesting to note here that arguably the best swimmer the author has coached was significantly overtrained following a poorly conducted high altitude training camp with the national team, and took several months to regain full conditioning and resume normal training. Such findings have important implications for coaches who have the responsibility of closely monitoring the athletes' training and performances. Levin[8] reported that coaches should ask their athletes to share how they feel physically and mentally throughout their training season in order to detect any signs of exhaustion or overtraining (*see* Chapter 7 'Special Considerations' for more details).

Returning to the issue raised by the performances of Dara Torres and Rachel Komisarz, most élite-level swimmers achieve their best performances at an optimal age. But what constitutes the optimal age? It depends, in part, on what events they swim, according to research conducted by Dr Genadijus Sokolvas of US Swimming. Normally, swimmers reach peak performances at, or near the end of, their career training. To design a long-term training plan, it is important to know the 'age at peak performances' (APP) for various swimming events.

Another important factor in a long-term training plan is performance progression. If swimmers are progressing too fast, they may burn out before reaching their APP; but if they are progressing too slowly, they may not reach their individual potential at the end of their career. Long-term studies of élite-level swimmers reveal that there is an optimal rate of performance progression. Therefore when preparing a career training plan, coaches should ask three basic questions: (i) At what age should my swimmers reach peak performances? (ii) Is there an optimal annual rate of performance progression?; and (iii) Can we use performance progression to manage the workload volumes and intensities?

Normally, swimmers begin their long-term training at the age of six to eight years. If athletes begin swimming earlier, they may have more time until APP. The difference between APP and the beginning of long-term training creates what Sokolovas calls 'time reserve', for getting the maximum growth and development of the athlete's potential. By knowing APP and 'time reserve', coaches can design appropriate workloads in a career training plan. One of the methods to find APP is to calculate the mean age of the ten best swimmers in history for each event. At the time of writing, the average age of the current ten best swimmers in history for long course, metres events is presented in Fig. 9.

The oldest swimmers are in the men's and women's 50m freestyle (24.8 years). The difference between the average age of history's ten best swimmers for sprinters and distance swimmers may reach four to five years, and this pattern is similar in both genders. In most events, the age at peak performance for women is one to four years younger than men. It should be noted that there is greater variability in the age of peak performance in women as compared to men. Variability is slightly lower for longer distances. This kind of analysis indicates differences in age of peak performance between men and women, as well as among distances and strokes, although it does not explain them.

Event Men (Years)	Women (Years)
50 Free 24.8 ± 3.2	24.8 ± 5.3
100 Free 23.7 ± 2.5	20.9 ± 3.6
200 Free 23.4 ± 3.3	21.3 ± 4.3
400 Free 21.0 ± 1.4	19.1 ± 2.5
800 Free n/a	20.3 ± 3.8
1500 Free 20.1 ± 1.7	n/a
100 Back 22.4 ± 2. 7	19.4 ± 2.5
200 Back 22.4 ± 2.4	18.6 ± 2.0
100 Breast 22.7 ± 1.2	21.1 ± 3.0
200 Breast 21.5 ± 2. 7	20.0 ± 2.8
100 Fly 23.2 ± 3.0	23.8 ± 5.3
200 Fly 23.8 ± 4.0	21.3 ± 4.6
200 IM 20.4 ± 1.7	19.1 ± 2.4
400 IM 21.0 ± 1.9	18.4 ± 2.1

Figure 9 Average age of the current ten best swimmers in history.

In order to understand how élite-level swimmers were developed, the US swimming research team analyzed the long-term performance progression for world-best swimmers, including world record holders and Olympic medallists. They assumed that, if a swimmer was a world record holder or Olympic medallist, his or her career training plan was done correctly. For over twenty years, the individual performance times of élite swimmers during their entire developmental career were collected. From the data, the characteristics and differences of performance progression for both men and women were evaluated. The relationship between swimming time improvement and age is exponential. For example, the older the swimmer, the slower the rate of progression becomes.

After analysing more than 150 of the best swimmers' performance histories, distinguishing differences between sprinters and distance swimmers were found – namely, the longer the distance, the faster the rate of performance progression. Recall from Fig. 9 that the longer the distance, the younger the age at peak performance. In addition to this, women in some events have earlier APP and, therefore, their rate of progression may be accelerated. Typically, reliable data collection regarding career training is not feasible prior to the age of eleven, therefore the mathematical models begin at age eleven.

Based on the best swimmers' performance histories, optimal models for performance progression for each Olympic swimming event were calculated. The range of performance progression times is relatively wide at the age of eleven, but this gap is dependent largely upon the age at which the athlete begins career training. During the career training process, the gap and the difference between lower and upper levels is substantially reduced, reflecting a smaller and smaller portion of the swimming population.

The windows of performance progression are optimal models. Some élite-level swimmers may be slightly outside the models; however, these models cover about 70 per cent of élite-level swimmers. Coaches may use such models as tools to help in the management of individual career training plans. Optimally, coaches should have their swimmers try to achieve performances in the middle of the suggested time ranges, depending on age and gender. The volume and intensity should be adjusted accordingly, to where the swimmer fits within the time ranges. If the individual performance of the athlete is close to the lower level of the windows, then the coach should choose appropriate workloads that would ensure higher rates of performance progression the following year.

Corrections need to be made to the workload prescription at the beginning of each season, based on past performance and future performance goals. If the individual performance of a swimmer is close to the upper levels of the windows, then the coach should choose the correct workloads that would ensure optimal rate of performance progression. The goal should be to achieve the necessary level of performance with minimum workload intensity. Minimum intensity will ensure a higher rate of performance potential in the future. High intensity volumes are a tremendous stress on the human anatomy, and therefore should not be exhausted at the beginning of biological maturation.

THE GLOBALIZATION OF SWIMMING

Swimming is now a professional sport (some would argue that it always has been), and the measure of this may be the levels to which coaches and athletes will go in order to achieve success. The final part of this opening section of the book will look in detail at the threat of doping to our sport. First, however, it is appropriate to consider why there is so much at stake in swimming. As a key Olympic sport, swimming's ascent to global sports marketing giant follows the path of the Olympic Games in worldwide financial growth. A glance at the sponsors (partners is the preferred marketing term) of swimming organizations around the world (international and national) is like looking at the FTSE 100 Index or Fortune 500 listings.

With such exposure come raised expectations and stakes for success. Recent winners of the FINA World Cup Series (2007), Randall Bal (USA) and Thérèse Alshammar (Sweden) earned $100,000 for their efforts. This may not rival the earnings of élite soccer or basketball players, but in the pre-Olympic season, and in a series of events not really supported by all the world's leading swimmers, it is a tidy sum. World records set in the World Cup series earned a share of $50,000; there were five in total, which meant that Sweden's Stephan Nystrand ($20,000), Brazil's Thiago Periera ($10,000), Holland's Marleen Veldhuis ($10,000) and Natalie Coughlin ($10,000) of the USA also boosted their bank balances. With individual meets also guaranteeing a prize fund of $104,000 across the thirty-four races, the professional 'circuit' in swimming is alive and well. This fact is undoubtedly another contributory factor to the average age of competitors increasing year by year.

With swimmers also negotiating individual sponsorship and commercial deals (Michael Phelps is reputed to potentially earn $1 million in bonuses alone at the Beijing Olympics in 2008), the attraction of a lucrative career is obvious. Swimming can also lead to successful spin-off careers: thus US superstar Summer Sanders (Olympic gold in 1992) is a sports presenter on television, and 2004 Olympic 200m breaststroke champion Amanda Beard (hoping to defend in 2008) has been capitalizing on her good looks and athletic prowess with a modelling career.

One of the problems with all of this may be a temptation to break the rules in order to succeed (via state-sponsored doping in the cases of East Germany and China), or to take risks with individual circumstances (read later about disgraced Tunisian world champion, Oussama Mellouli) as the pressures of competing in a crowded competitive calendar take their toll. Fig. 10 (an early draft plan of the final Olympic cycle post-World Championships) shows just how busy the international calendar actually is for swimmers in the UK. This situation is replicated for swimmers across the world, and is a serious challenge to the planning and periodization of coaches and swimmers.

THE THREAT OF DOPING

'Doping' is the word used in sport when athletes use prohibited substances or methods to unfairly improve their sporting performance. 'Anti-doping' is the bid to eliminate doping from sport. If you've ever watched a swimming race, a game of football or another sport you love and have cheered on your favourite swimmer or team to victory, then imagine how meaningless that victory would become if your favourite athlete or team had used drugs to succeed. Sport is a major part of the spirit of all nations and generates positive role models for young people, but the most important thing of all is the way sport is played: it is crucial that across all sports there is a commitment to fair play.

Cheating is therefore unacceptable and contrary to the spirit of sport, and doping violates important values of fairness, camaraderie and human endeavour. For all athletes, it is important that their performances are true, without unethical practices. The use of doping substances or doping methods to enhance performance is fundamentally wrong, and is detrimental to the overall impact of sport. Drug misuse can be harmful to a swimmer's health or to others competing in the sport. It severely damages the integrity, image and value of sport, whether or not the motivation to use drugs is to improve performance. To achieve integrity and fairness in sport, a commitment from all athletes is critical.

The term 'doping' became current around the turn of the twentieth century, and originally referred to the illegal drugging of racehorses. However, the practice of enhancing performance through foreign substances or other artificial means is as old as competitive sport itself. Ancient Greek athletes are known to have used special diets and stimulating

Figure 10 Draft plan for Olympic macrocycle.

Event Dates	Event	Discipline	Venue	Country	Team/Squad
April 2007					
2nd–16th	Australian Age Championships	SW	Perth	Australia	Junior Women
May 2007					
6th–28th	Men's Camp/Competition (relay focus)	SW	Irvine	USA	GB
7th–21st	Men's 7 Hill Meet (including camp)	SW	Rome	Italy	GB
June 2007					
8th–10th	Seven Hills Meet	SW	Rome	Italy	GB
11th–21st	Men's & Women's Camp	SW	Sardinia	Italy	GB
9th–10th	Mare Nostrum Swimming Meeting	SW	Canet	France	GB
13th–14th	Mare Nostrum Swimming Meeting	SW	Barcelona	Spain	GB
July 2007					
18th–22nd	European Junior Swimming Championships	SW	Antwerp	Belgium	GB Juniors
23rd–27th	European Youth Olympic Festival	SW	Belgrade	Serbia	GB Juniors
27th–1st Aug	ASA Nationals	SW	Sheffield	GBR	GB
31st–4th Aug	US National Swimming Championships	SW	Indianapolis	USA	GB
August 2007					
2nd–5th	Paris International	SW	Paris	France	GB
8th–18th	World University Games	SW	Bangkok	Thailand	GB
8th–18th	Japan Osaka Training Camp	SW	Osaka	Japan	GB
21st–24th	Japan International Meet	SW	Chiba	Japan	GB
September 2007					
11th–25th	Training Camp	SW	Florida	USA	GB
15th–23rd	WC Development Male Event Camp	SW	Oviedo	Spain	GB Men's
15th–23rd	WC Development Female Event Camp	SW	Palma	Spain	GB Women's
15th–23rd	WC Development Female Sprint Camp	SW	Barcelona	Spain	GB Women's
TBC	Offshore Centre Camp	SW	Gold Coast	Australia	GB
October 2007					
4th–26th	Endless Summer	SW	Gold Coast	Australia	GB
27th–28th	World Cup Singapore	SW	Singapore	Singapore	GB

Figure 10 (Continued)

Event Dates	Event	Discipline	Venue	Country	Team/Squad
November 2007					
3rd–4th	World Cup Sydney	SW	Sydney	Australia	GB
3rd–16th	Endless Summer Group I	SW	Cairns	Australia	GB
3rd–16th	Endless Summer Group 2	SW	New Zealand	NZ	GB
3rd–16th	Endless Summer Group 3	SW	Canberra	Australia	GB
17 Nov–7 Dec	Endless Summer	SW	Gold Coast	Australia	GB
24 Nov–22 Dec	End of Year Tour - Female	SW	Singapore & Brisbane		GB Female
24 Nov–22 Dec	End of Year Tour - Male	SW	Perth & Brisbane		GB Male
December 2007					
13th–16th	European SC Swimming Championships	SW	Debrecan	Hungary	GB
15th–21st	Queensland Championships	SW	Queensland	Australia	GB Senior
TBC	US National Swimming Championships	SW	TBC	TBC	GB
TBC	Off Shore Centre Camp	SW	Gold Coast	Australia	GB
January 2008					
TBC	Training Camp	SW	Dubai or SA		GB
February 2008					
TBC	Training Camp	SW	Dubai or SA		GB
March 2008					
13th–24th	European LC Swimming Championships	SW	Eindhoven	Holland	GB
April 2008					
lst–6th	Olympic Games Trials	SW	Sheffield	GBR	GB
9th–13th April	FINA World SC Swimming Championships	SW	Manchester	GB	GB
27 Apr–3 May	Men's Camp	SW	Cyprus	GB	
27 Apr–3 May	Women's Camp	SW	France/Spain	GB	
TBC	Stage 1 Meet	SW	TBC	GBR	GB
May 2008					
TBC	Men's camp (2 weeks) & Competition	SW	TBC	TBC	GB
TBC	Women's camp (2 weeks) & Competition	SW	TBC	TBC	GB
June 2008					
10th–24th	Olympic Prep Camp	SW	Dubai		GB
25th–29th	ASA Nationals & Stage 3 Meet	SW	TBC	TBC	GB
July 2008					
10th–2nd Aug	Olympic Prep Camp	SW		Japan	GB
15th–28th	European Junior Swimming Championships	SW	Belgrade	Serbia	GB Juniors
1st–14th	2nd FINA World Youth Swimming Championships	SW	Monterey	Mexico	GB Youth
August 2008					
8th–24th	Olympic Games	SW	Beijing	China	GB
September 2008					
25th–5th October	Training Camp - Hawaii/World Cup Sydney	SW	Hawaii/Sydney		GB

potions to fortify themselves. Strychnine, caffeine, cocaine and alcohol were often used by cyclists and other endurance athletes in the nineteenth century. Thomas Hicks ran to victory in the Olympic marathon of 1904 in Saint Louis by help of raw egg, injections of strychnine and doses of brandy administered to him during the race! By the 1920s, however, it had become evident that restrictions regarding drug use in sports were necessary. In 1928 the International Amateur Athletic Federation (IAAF) became the first international sports federation to ban the use of doping (the use of stimulating substances). Many other federations followed suit, but restrictions remained ineffective as no tests were made.

Meanwhile the problem was made worse by synthetic hormones, invented in the 1930s and in growing use for doping purposes since the 1950s. The death of Danish cyclist Knud Enemark Jensen during competition at the Olympic Games in Rome 1960 (the autopsy revealed traces of amphetamine) increased the pressure for sports authorities to introduce drug tests. In 1966 UCI (cycling) and FIFA (football) were among the first international federations to introduce doping tests in their respective world championships. In the next year the International Olympic Committee (IOC) instituted its medical commission and set up its first list of prohibited substances. Drug tests were first introduced at the Winter Olympic Games in Grenoble and at the Olympic Games in Mexico in 1968. In the year before, the urgency of anti-doping work had been highlighted by another tragic death, that of cyclist Tom Simpson during the Tour de France.

Most international sports federations introduced drug testing by the 1970s. The use of anabolic steroids was becoming widespread, however, especially in strength events, as there was no way of detecting them yet. A reliable test method was finally introduced in 1974, and the IOC added anabolic steroids to its list of prohibited substances in 1976. While the fight against stimulants and steroids was producing results, the main front in the anti-doping war was rapidly shifting to blood doping. 'Blood boosting' – the removal and subsequent reinfusion of the athlete's blood in order to increase the level of oxygen-carrying haemoglobin – has been practised since the 1970s. The IOC banned blood doping in 1986 – however, other ways of increasing the level of haemoglobin were being experimented with.

One of these was erythropoietin (EPO), included in the IOC's list of prohibited substances in 1990 – but the fight against EPO was long hampered by lack of a reliable testing method. An EPO detection test, based on a combination of blood and urine analysis, was first implemented at the Sydney Olympic Games in 2000. In 1998 a large number of prohibited medical substances were found by police in a raid during the Tour de France, and the scandal led to a major reappraisal of the role of public authorities in anti-doping affairs. As early as 1963, France had been the first country to enact anti-doping legislation. Other countries followed suit, but international cooperation in anti-doping affairs was long restricted to the Council of Europe. In the 1980s there was a marked increase in cooperation between international sports authorities and various governmental agencies. Before 1998 debate was still taking place in several discrete forums (IOC, sports federations and individual governments), resulting in differing definitions, policies and sanctions.

One result of this confusion was that doping sanctions were often disputed, and sometimes overruled in civil courts. The Tour de France scandal highlighted the need for an independent international agency that would set unified standards for anti-doping work and co-ordinate the efforts of sports organizations and public authorities. The IOC took the initiative and convened the World Conference on Doping in Sport held in Lausanne in February 1999. Following the proposal of the conference, the World Anti-Doping Agency (WADA) was established in Lausanne on 10 November 1999.

Sport is governed by a set of anti-doping rules and guidelines called the World Anti-

Doping Code (the 'Code'). The Code is the basis of the World Anti-Doping Programme, and it aims to harmonize the rules and regulations governing anti-doping for all athletes, in all sports, throughout the world. A fundamental principle of the Code is to protect the rights of all athletes committed to competing in sport cleanly and fairly. The Code harmonized regulations regarding anti-doping across all sports and countries of the world, providing a framework for anti-doping policies, rules and regulations within sport organizations and among public authorities. Underpinning the Code is a set of four international standards that outline mandatory systems and processes for testing, the therapeutic use of prohibited substances or methods, the Prohibited List, and WADA-accredited laboratory processes.

It is generally accepted that the introduction of performance-enhancing drugs to swimming began in the early 1970s in the USSR and East Germany[9]. The inspiration for this approach came from successes in other sports, particularly track and field, cycling and weightlifting, with the doping programmes lasting until these two nations met their demise. The USSR relied heavily on its military for research into, and production of, performance-enhancing drugs[10]. There was an emphasis on products that would extend performance and serve both the military and sport. This Soviet scheme extended into other Eastern-Bloc countries, with the East German system slightly different. A centralized system was run by the state, and top sporting officials were made STASI[11] members, and from the top down coerced individuals who participated in sports. Effective secrecy was achieved through multi-tiered monitoring, the threat of severe punishments, and financial rewards for compliance. Exercise and medical specialists monitored programme implementations. The majority of programmes focused on power and speed events, with very few East German athletes excelling in endurance activities. It is now commonly known, and accepted by the perpetrators themselves, that East German swimmers since

1972 were subjected to systematic, state-led doping schemes[12].

In the 1970s there were only two positive drug tests. The first was the still controversial disqualification of Rick Demont (USA) for using the stimulant ephedrine to combat his asthma at the 1972 Olympic Games. This was more a case of ineptitude by USOC[13] officials, as the swimmer had declared the medication but the officials failed to follow through with the appropriate notifications. The second occurrence was the Soviet swimmer Viktor Kuznetsov at the 1978 World Championships, the first ever positive steroid test in swimming (incidentally, he wasn't banned for the offence). Meanwhile, other Soviet and East German swimmers were persisting with pharmacologically-enhanced training and competitive performances. Their ascendancy to dominance in the sport was protested by participants and coaches, but without 'evidence' (which now exists in abundance) could not be proved.

The testing capabilities of international sports bodies remained quite limited until the early 1980s. The sophisticated cheating of the Eastern Bloc nations remained far superior to detection capabilities and scope. Rumours emanated from the Los Angeles Olympic Games that positive drug tests were recorded, but there is no concrete evidence to substantiate the claims. During the 1980s there were only three positive tests recorded by FINA. East German and Russian swimmers always tested clean despite the widespread suspicion (and subsequent proof) of their performance-enhancement schemes. Rumours also escalated about other European swimming nations, particularly Eastern Bloc countries, using drugs that were undetectable.

In order to explain fully the continued threat of doping in swimming, we need to turn our attention to China (especially since the Eastern Bloc powers no longer exist and we know that their state-sponsored cheating actually did take place). None of China's swimmers made finals at the 1984 Olympic Games, then in the 1988 Olympic Games' swimming events, China improved to win three silver medals and one bronze among ten finalists. A third totalitarian regime was emerging as a swimming power. In 1990 three swimmers tested positive for anabolic steroids at the Chinese national swimming championships. In this one year, China matched the accumulated number of positive steroid tests in the history of the sport.

Testing capabilities still lagged well behind the deceptive practices and varieties of substances used by cheats in swimming. At the same time, prize money for major meets began to emerge, and nations started to offer 'significant' incentives for medals in major competitions (as discussed in the previous section). Conditions were ripe for an explosion in cheating by using drugs. The number of nations that had athletes test positive also expanded, and even Tunisia and Egypt, both non-traditional swimming powers, were involved. Incentives to cheat were clearly increasing dramatically. From 1990 to the 1992 Olympic Games a world total of eight positive tests was recorded.

At the 1992 Olympic Games, swimmers from the former USSR won six gold, and China four gold and five silver medals. As had become the consistent pattern, athletes from such nations emerged at Olympic Games to collect a high number of gold medals. But China's ascendancy in women's swimming was so rapid – no finalists to four gold medals in eight years – that it attracted significant attention. Not since the early 1970s, when East Germany emerged to dominate the World Championships in 1973 and the 1976 Olympic Games, had such an improvement been witnessed. The advent of China's swimmers on the world scene was startling, the eastern power moving from thirty in 1992 to ninety-eight in 1993 of top fifty performers in all events.

1994 has been called the 'year of drugs' in swimming. Four of China's swimmers tested positive in the first seven months of 1994[14]. At the Rome World Championships, China's women won twelve of sixteen events, dominat-

ing swimming in the manner of 1976 East Germans. Many head coaches from traditional swimming nations accused China of drug cheating[15], and the external signs of steroid abuse were evident in China's swimmers. Sadly, the official reaction by international sports bodies was less than effective, and both the IOC and FINA were swift to declare that China was 'clean'. However, within three weeks of the World Championships a further adverse doping finding shocked the swimming world, when two swimmers yielded positive results in out-of-competition testing in China. Prior to the start of the Asian Games in Hiroshima, five swimmers tested positive, and an additional seven to ten had high but borderline testosterone to epitestosterone ratios[16]. Having tested clean in Rome only three weeks before, these swimmers had now been caught because a new test for dihydrotestosterone (DHT) was introduced at Hiroshima, which had not been included in the Rome testing.

In 1995 China withdrew from the Pan Pacific Championships; this year also saw East Germany revisited. 1980 Olympic champion backstroker Rica Reinisch initiated a suit against her former coach and sports medicine physician for administering steroids and other performance-enhancing drugs without her knowledge or consent. The East German story was starting to come to light with other revelations and the investigation into East German sports by a German government panel. At the end of 1995 only ten swimmers from China ranked in the top twenty-five long course listings. No positive tests were reported for China's swimmers. Chinese male and female swimmers had recorded nineteen of the forty-one known reported positive drug tests in the history of swimming, those nineteen occurring since 1990.

1996 saw China's resurgence in swimming performance levels. After its National Championships and Olympic trials, China's potential women's Olympic team all recorded top twenty-five performances. The 1996 Olympic Games saw China win only one gold medal, a complete reversal of earlier performances in the year. Questions were raised as to whether China had finally acknowledged the existence of a doping problem. Ironically, it was a swimmer from a Western country who courted most controversy at the 1996 Atlanta Olympics: Irish swimmer Michelle Smith won three gold and one bronze medal in an unprecedented ascent to the top of the swimming world. Previously capable of no better than seventeenth at the Olympics, Smith shattered her lifetime bests in an astounding series of performances. Smith was subsequently 'caught' by the drug testers in 1998 in a bizarre scenario involving a whisky-tainted urine sample, and countless claims and counterclaims of misconduct.

The post-Olympic year of 1997 started quietly. Almost unnoticed was China's report of four steroid-related positive tests at an early season competition[17]. In October 1997 one of the most remarkable turnabouts in swimming history occurred. China's women broke the remaining East German drug-enhanced world records and recorded ten event times faster than winning performances at the Atlanta Games (including those by Michelle Smith!). A significant percentage of women had not been ranked previously in the top 150. No positive drug tests were recorded for swimmers, despite claims of extensive testing by the Chinese. Notwithstanding this, as teams arrived for the 1998 World Championships, the Australian Sports Drug Agency swooped down on incoming teams and performed up-to-date testing. At the same time a chance customs inspection at Sydney airport of one Chinese swimmer's bags revealed thirteen vials of human growth hormone.

The reaction in the swimming world was explosive, and the press started to attack; the extent of media and participant outrage had never been witnessed before in swimming. Eventually the offending swimmer was banned for four years and her coach for fifteen. One group of Chinese swimmers had arrived early in Perth. At the same time as the furore in Sydney was occurring, attempts to test the Perth contingent were initially thwarted. However, testing eventually did take place. Early during the championships it was announced that four of China's swimmers had tested positive for the masking agent Triamterene. Open calls for immediate total team expulsion were made, but China's swimmers completed the rest of the meet with many abysmal performances and few of high quality. The 1998 Perth World Championships was the first such international meet without a world record, and the drug controversy overshadowed some wonderful performances by swimmers from across the globe. Michael Klim was swimmer of the meet with seven medals, and a 15-year-old Ian Thorpe became the youngest-ever World Champion.

Since this time, the threat of doping has not gone away, and neither has the suspicion surrounding performances that seem to defy convention or world rankings. At the 2000 Sydney Olympic Games, China won no medals in swimming, although by the 2001 World Championships in Fukuoka, Japan, they had 'improved' to win two gold, two silver and three bronze medals – all in women's events. In Athens at the 2004 Olympics, China won one gold and one silver (both in women's events), and at the 2007 World Championships, they won one silver and one bronze medal – a far cry from their successes of the previous decade. The first seven years of the new millennium have yielded twenty-two cases of doping in swimming, and the fight continues.

A few weeks after the conclusion of the 2007 World Aquatics Championships in Melbourne, reports began to surface that Oussama Mellouli of Tunisia had tested positive for a banned substance at the US Open in November 2006. These reports surfaced because FINA, the international governing body of the sport, had discovered that Tunisian authorities had known about the positive test, and had only given him a warning. The rules state that when an athlete tests positive for a banned substance, he or she must be given a two-year ban from the sport. Accordingly, FINA took the case to the Court of Arbitration for Sport, demanding stiffer sanction.

Mellouli has since admitted that he took the medication Adderall, a stimulant and a form of amphetamine. In June 2006, a US national sports commentator wrote about how anecdotal evidence and some scientific studies showed rampant use of Adderall, Ritalin, and other drugs normally used for attention deficit disorder, instead applied towards all-night student 'cramming' sessions. Mellouli did not have a prescription for the drug, having received it from another university student shortly before the US Open meet. He argued that he took the pill in order to help himself with writing a term paper (to sustain or enhance his academic performance), and that the drug is not a performance-enhancing substance in competitive swimming[18]. However, Adderall is on the official banned substances list. On 11 September 2007, Mellouli lost his case before the court of arbitration for sport, and he was suspended for eighteen months, retroactive to 30 November 2006. As a result of this sanction, all his results from the 2007 World Championships have been expunged, and he will no longer be considered the first Arab world champion swimmer. However, he will be eligible to swim again by the time of the 2008 Summer Olympics in Beijing.

At the time of writing, another high-profile doping case is unfolding. Brazil's first ever Pan American swimming champion, Rebecca Gusmao, has tested positive for elevated levels of testosterone. The female sprinter has been conducting a spirited defence based on medical grounds.

Despite the protestations of many in authority, the lure of fame and glory, the ideologues of totalitarian regimes and the blatant stupidity of some individuals all conspire to put swimming as much at risk from the threat of doping as any other international sport, thus belying the myth of swimming as a 'clean' sport.

The Responsibilities of the Individual

Under the rules of the World Anti-Doping Code (WADC), you are ultimately responsible for any prohibited substance or method found in your system. You are responsible for those who you trust to take advice from about substances, medication and supplements, and you are accountable for those you entrust with access to your food and drink.

If you are an athlete, here are five key responsibilities:

1. Stay up to date with the latest prohibited list of substances and methods – www.wada-ama.org or www.100percentme.co.uk.
2. Check the status of any substance or method before using it by logging on to www.didglobal.com.
3. Inform your medical personnel that you must abide by anti-doping rules, and that any medical treatment you receive must not violate these rules.
4. If required by your sport, submit a therapeutic use exemption (TUE) for any prohibited substance or method you are prescribed.
5. If required by your international or national federation, provide accurate athlete whereabouts information for out-of-competition testing.

---

[1]Gould, D., Guinan, D., Greenleaf, C., Medbery, R., & Peterson, K. (1999) 'Factors affecting Olympic performance: Perceptions of athletes and coaches from more and less successful teams' *The Sport Psychologist* 13(4), 371–394.

[2]Csikszentmihalyi, M., Rathunde, K., & Whalen, S. (1993) *Talented teenagers: The roots of success and failure* Cambridge University Press, New York.

[3]Ericsson, K. A., Krampe, R. Th., & Tesch-Römer, C. (1993) 'The role of deliberate practice in the acquisition of expert performance' *Psychological Review* 100(3), 363–406.

[4]Krampe, R. Th., & Ericsson, K. A. (1996) 'Maintaining excellence: Deliberate practice and élite performance in young and older pianists' *Journal of Experimental Psychology*: General, 125(4), 331–359.

[5]Orlick, T., & Partington, J. (1988) 'Mental links to excellence' *The Sport Psychologist* 2, 105–130.

[6]Botterill, C., Patrick, T., & Sawatzky, M. (1996) *Human potential: Perspective, passion, preparation* Lifeskills, Winnipeg, Manitoba.

[7]Morgan, W. P., Brown, D. R., Raglin, J. S., O'Connor, P. J., & Ellickson, K. A. (1987) 'Psychological monitoring of overtraining and staleness' *British Journal of Sports Medicine* 21, 107–114.

[8]Levin, S. (1991) 'Overtraining causes Olympic-sized problems' *Physician and Sports Medicine* 19, 112–118.

[9]Rushall, B. S. (1998) 'A brief history of drugs in swimming'. *Australian Swimming and Fitness* March–April, 40–44.

[10]Kalinski, M. I. (2003) 'State-sponsored research on creatine supplements and blood doping in élite Soviet sport'. *Perspectives in Biology and Medicine, 46(3)*, 445–451.

[11]STASI – Ministerium für Staatssicherheit: East German state security police and intelligence agency.

[12]Leonard, J. (1995, September) Drug war . . . . ASCA Newsletter, 1, 6–7.

[13]United States Olympic Committee.

[14]Gendreau, E. (1994) 'Comments on the Use of Drugs in Chinese Sports'. An original posting from the internet bulletin board rec.sport.swimming.

[15]Haines, G. F. (1997) George Haines' Open Letter to Mustapha Larfaoui. One of swimming's greatest coaches speaks out.

[16]Rushall, B.S. (1998) 'A Brief history of drugs in swimming'. *Australian Swimming and Fitness* March–April, 40–44.

[17]Woollard, R., and Pasmos, E. (1996, January 29) 'Coaches "Expose" Cheating Past'. The *Hong Kong Standard*, Hong Kong.

[18]Rushall, B.S. and Jones M. (2007) 'Drugs in Sport: A Cure Worse than the Disease?' *International Journal of Sports Science & Coaching*, Vol. 2, No. 4, pp. 335–361.

PART 2 TRAINING

CHAPTER **3**

Training Principles and Methods

There are four general methods of pool training available to the coach and swimmer: swim (full stroke practice), kick (legs only), pull (arms only), and drill. However, adding this to the four strokes and the individual medley, and taking account of all the principles of training, the possibility of both short and long course swimming, environmental considerations such as altitude and/or warm weather training camps, plus the myriad of specialist equipment options on the market, and you have the ingredients for a challenging and complex recipe of training, stroke development and specific race preparation.

There are no easy formulas to the prescription of swimming training, and it is as much art as science – but there are some general principles of training that can assist in maximizing the preparation opportunities available.

INDIVIDUAL RESPONSE

Every individual is different, and will respond to training in a unique way. This may seem obvious, but research has shown that most swimming programmes are conducted on a group or squad basis, and that only performers of the very highest level have anything close to an individualized programme. There are many reasons for this (primarily concerning resources), but nevertheless, acknowledging the individual response to training is a fundamental tenet of designing and implementing effective training programmes. This principle should extend to age, gender, stroke, event and training status. Attempts to duplicate the programmes of champions will also result in

incorrect loadings of the work of training for most individuals.

The capacity to respond to training is related to the initial level of fitness and the physiological characteristics of each individual swimmer. The potential for improvement is greatest when the initial level of fitness is lowest, because when a swimmer is not fit, then performance improvements will be obvious and substantial with the onset of training. When a swimmer is fit, performance improvements will be small and relatively infrequent, because once maximum fitness has been achieved, it requires much less training to maintain performance than to gain it in the first place. Thus the response of an athlete will vary, depending upon the level of fitness and the training programme content.

THE PRINCIPLE OF ADAPTATION

Training has an effect on the human body – indeed the purpose of training is to have the desired effect on the body or more specifically, its processes. This (or these) effect(s) are governed by the principle of adaptation. Placing the systems in the body under stress will produce responses associated with the type of training performed. For example, an adaptation to aerobic training is a reduced sub-maximal heart rate for a given workload. Some adaptations take place in a matter of days, while others may take weeks or months. For effective training adaptations there must be (i) correct training; (ii) nutrients for growth and repair of tissues; and (iii) sufficient rest for the growth and repair to take place.

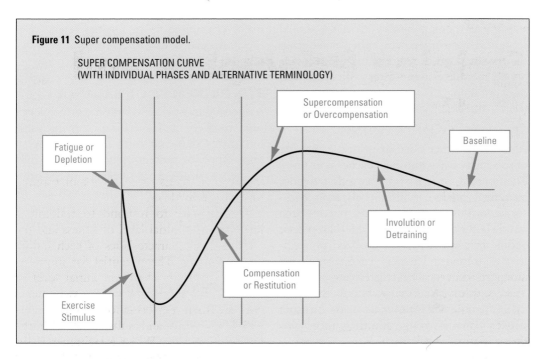

Figure 11 Super compensation model.

SUPER COMPENSATION CURVE
(WITH INDIVIDUAL PHASES AND ALTERNATIVE TERMINOLOGY)

Supercompensation or Overcompensation

Baseline

Fatigue or Depletion

Involution or Detraining

Compensation or Restitution

Exercise Stimulus

THE CONCEPT OF OVERLOAD

Probably the most important principle of all is the concept of overload in training; it is almost certainly the oldest of all principles. In order for adaptations to take place, the stress on the body's systems must be significant enough for physiological changes to occur – that is, they must be greater than 'usual'. The same stimuli will not provoke continued improvements, and therefore the principle of overloading must be applied. There is a danger in overloading, and it is the careful application of this principle that brings us to the next important principle.

SYSTEMATIC PLANNING

Often coupled with overload as a double impact principle, the use of a progressive or 'step-wise' approach to training prescription is the most obvious application of systematically planned training. Too much loading at once could result in overtraining or injury, and too little could result in no improvements being made. Swimming is a sport where it is easy to see the principles of progressive overload being used: for example, longer dis-tances, less rest, more repetitions, faster effort. The systematic treatment of training programmes in a structured and progressive manner is the result of careful and considered periodized planning by effective coaches.

REST AND RECOVERY

An often forgotten principle of training is rest and regeneration (recovery). Most training programmes are founded on the basis of **work** and the various categories and intensities thereof, and indeed this is a long-established tradition in physical training: but smart coaches also consider *recovery*-based training. Closely related to the individuality principle, recovery-based training allows the coach and swimmer to plan the training programme more accurately and appropriately. It could actually mean that the swimmer trains 'harder' because they have recovered fully, rather than having residual fatigue from too much, too often – although a better way to describe the outcome would be that swimmers can 'train smarter'.

The recovery time from heavy training or intense competitions is longer in some swimmers than in others. This is particularly the case with older swimmers – those with a substantial training history. Coaches should recognize these differences, either by reducing the training load or lengthening the recovery period in athletes who display the symptoms of overtraining.

SPECIFICITY IN TRAINING

Although another obvious principle, the use of specificity by swimming coaches is at times questionable. It is easy to note that regular basketball practice will not improve backstroke swimming performance, but research again shows that coaches are less than precise about their specific, individualized prescription of training. There is a mistaken belief amongst some coaches that freestyle is the 'training stroke', and that somehow the benefits of training will transfer across to the other strokes. This is wrong, and there is no evidence to support it!

Individual medley should be the cornerstone of all training programmes, and if anything is to be considered a 'training stroke', then it should be IM. Coaches should consider the following four aspects when applying the principle of specificity: (i) the event; (ii) the stroke; (iii) the target speed; and (iv) the energy system demands of these combined.

VARIETY IN TRAINING

As far as skill learning is concerned, the greater the range of opportunities given to swimmers, the greater the likelihood that they will improve. In training for physical capacity, the use of the variation principle can sometimes by overdone, and care should be taken to use variety as a motivational tool rather than simply an end in its own right.

THE PRINCIPLE OF REVERSIBILITY

Often simplified to 'if you don't use it, you lose it', this principle is more obvious after a period away from training, as swimmers discover how hard it is to gain fitness over a period of time, but how easy it is to lose it much more quickly. It is especially obvious in élite swimmers who may take a long break after a major championship or Olympics, and is as much associated with psychological as physiological parameters.

THE PRINCIPLE OF BALANCE

Associated most closely with the principles of rest, recovery and variation, this principle recognizes that you can't do everything at once. Applying training principles successfully requires as much art as science, and the principle of balance is where the coach can be creative in the design and implementation of training. Read on for information about balance in the training programmes of high performance swimmers.

LONG-TERM PLANNING

According to leading sports scientist and excellence researcher, K. Anders Ericsson of Florida State University, it takes ten years (or 10,000 hours) of extensive practice to excel in sports. Translating this into the language of swimming training, this is three to four hours per day of deliberate practice for ten years, and is supported by empirical and anecdotal evidence from successful swimmers. Refer back to Fig. 9 for details of the age of the top ten best performers in history. All these swimmers were engaged in extensive training programmes for at least ten years prior to achieving this level of performance.

Now, let's look at the different methods of training available.

KICKING

Whether it is taking full advantage of the 15m underwater off-starts and turns, or generating power from the legs on the last 50m of a race, the importance of kicking on swimming performance should not be underestimated. For example, Natalie Coughlin in setting her world record of 56.71 100m backstroke (short course) swam almost 60m underwater (4 × 15m per length). Perfecting this opportunity did not happen by accident, nor did it occur overnight: it was developed over time by careful planning and progressions, and no

Figure 12 Training principles.

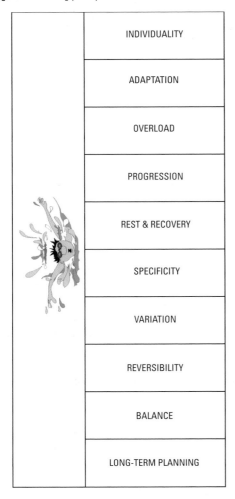

INDIVIDUALITY
ADAPTATION
OVERLOAD
PROGRESSION
REST & RECOVERY
SPECIFICITY
VARIATION
REVERSIBILITY
BALANCE
LONG-TERM PLANNING

Figure 13 Kicking with a kickboard.

Figure 14 Kicking with a stick.

A variety of options are available to coaches in designing kick sets and practices:

- With or without a kickboard? (Fig. 13)
- What size/shape of kickboard?
- With or without fins? (Fig. 14)
- What size/shape of fins? (Figs. 15a and 15b)
- Kick on the front, side or back?
- What distance, rest and speed to use?

PULLING

As with kicking, the aims and variety of pulling are varied. Some aspects of pulling are easier to perform than others due to the technique and flow of the strokes: for example, freestyle as opposed to butterfly with a pull buoy. Since the primary aim of pulling is to isolate and condition the arms, practices and training should be centred on this purpose. On butterfly, care should be taken to ensure that stroke mechanics are not compromised by pulling large distances

small amount of commitment by Coughlin and her coach Teri McKeever.

Kicking may be the slowest method of training, but this should not negate its impact on performance. A swimmer who improves their kicking ability is almost always a swimmer who swims faster. Kicking may not contribute greatly to 'direct' propulsion in all but the breaststroke, but enhanced body positions and reduced resistance as a result of effective kicking can significantly contribute to 'indirect propulsion' in the other three strokes. As a guide to kicking standards, if you can kick a 200m-long course under three minutes, that is a good start. The fastest swimmers (kickers) in the world will kick this distance in 2min 30sec or better.

Figure 15a Kicking with short fins.

Figure 16 Backstroke, pulling with a band.

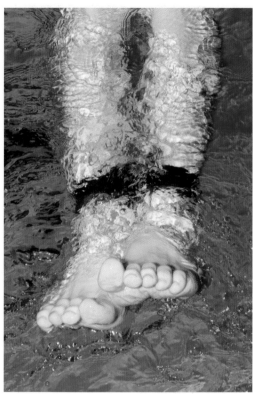

Figure 15b Kicking with long fins.

Figure 17 Variations in size and shape of hand paddles.

Figure 18a, b Hand paddles in use for freestyle pull.

with a pull buoy. All backstroke pulling should be done with a band only – no pull buoy should be used (*see* Fig.16). Paddle shapes and sizes are at the discretion of the coach/swimmer (*see* Fig. 17). Figs. 18a and 18b illustrate a couple of examples of freestyle pulling with different sizes and shapes of paddles. Breaststroke pull with a buoy, like butterfly, should rarely be done and never to the detriment of overall stroke mechanics (fly kick with breaststroke pull is a popular alternative). Freestyle pull probably offers the greatest variety in terms of

training options, but beware of over-using this method of training instead of improving full stroke swim.

A variety of options are available to coaches in designing pull sets and practices:

- With or without paddles?
- What size/shape of paddles?
- With or without pull buoy?
- What size/shape of pull buoy?
- With or without a band?
- What distance, rest and speed to use?

CHAPTER 4

Training Balance

There are many different labels given to swimming training, some of which differ in substance, and many others that do not and are simply known by their different names. In general, the three main areas of training emphasis coincide with the three energy systems, namely aerobic, anaerobic and alactic. Coaches, scientists and authors around the world have come up with countless labels for 'training zones', 'training systems', 'training categories' and so on, but they all came back to these three fundamental areas. Within each energy system there are different sub-types of training, and these generally give their names to the types of training that are common across most swimming programmes: aerobic sets, threshold sets, overload sets, lactate sets and so on.

I suggest that the simpler the system used, the better. Complicated zones and codified categories will do little to promote understanding by swimmers and coaches alike, and ultimately mean an overly complex system of planning, recording and monitoring. Fig. 19 illustrates a simple way of representing this concept, and also the principle of training balance. Too much training with high volume and intensity will result in overtraining, while too little training at too low an intensity will have no training effect at all.

The importance of energy zones in swimming is based on the existence of several different pathways to recycle energy in the muscle cells during exercise. The main pathways of energy recycling are non-aerobic metabolism (creatine phosphate), anaerobic metabolism (anaerobic glycolysis), and aerobic metabolism. Metabolism is the process of storing and releasing the energy. Energy for the body is stored in different forms, and pathways are

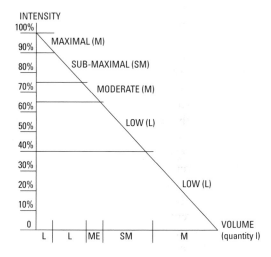

Figure 19 Balance of training.

used to convert these forms into accessible energy that an athlete can use to perform work.

There are no 'borders' to energy pathways in a body. At any given time, a number of pathways, not just one, may be engaged in energy production – although dominance of an energy source depends on the duration and intensity of the exercise (*see* Fig. 20). Usually workload is broken into several 'zones', based on the duration and intensity of the training. These training categories allow swimmers and coaches to develop a specific pathway of energy recycling, and to quantify, track and plan the physiological adaptations desired for their specific event. Swimming sets of different duration and intensity are supported by energy from different sources: therefore during high-intensity, short-term swimming bouts, most energy is recycled through the anaerobic pathway, a fast and non-oxidative way of energy recycling. During low-intensity, long-term

Figure 20 Interaction of energy systems with intensity and duration of exercise.

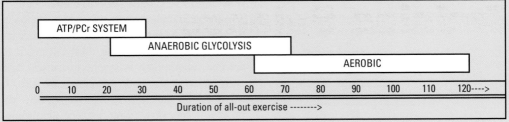

swimming bouts the energy is recycled mostly aerobically using oxygen: this is slower but more efficient than the anaerobic pathway.

A key aspect to remember is that the improvement of one energy system does not significantly influence another one. Thus when swimmers complete long distances they develop mostly aerobic energy sources; conversely, high-intensity swimming develops the anaerobic energy sources. Therefore, different swimming events require the training of different energy pathways. Fig. 21 details the relationship between energy systems and swimming events.

The preparation of competitive swimmers requires the evaluation of individual swimming intensities in each energy system. The same swimming intensity, or even heart rate, affects the energy recycling pathways differently when swimmers are at different stages of the season (that is, detrained or at peak performances). Adaptation in swimmers to the same swimming intensity depends on their current condition, types of muscle fibre, training history, and so on. Consequently it is important to test swimmers during the season, and select appropriate swimming intensities to train different energy zones. Details on test set protocols are contained in Part 3 of this book.

Adenosine triphosphate (ATP) is the only source of potential chemical energy in the body. It consists of one molecule of protein (adenosine) and three molecules of phosphate. Muscle cells always contain free ATP, which reduces to ADP (adenosine diphosphate) and releases the energy during the first few seconds of work (Fig. 22). The decomposition of ATP into ADP releases the energy and phosphoric acid, which increases the acid environment in the muscles. Then other energy storage forms are used to recycle ADP back to ATP through different pathways.

Figure 21 Relationship between energy systems and swimming events.

Competition times	Race distances	% ATP-CP	% Anaerobic metabolism	Aerobic metabolism	
				% Glucose metabolism	% Fat metabolism
10–15sec	25yd/m	50	50	Neg	Neg
19–30sec	50yd/m	20	60	20	Neg
40–60sec	100 yd/m	10	55	35	Neg
1.30–2min	200yd/m	7	40	53	Neg
2–3min	200yd/m	5	40	55	Neg
4–6min	500yd (400m)	Neg	35	65	Neg
7–10min	900yd (800m)	Neg	25	73	2
10–12min	1,000yd (900m)	Neg	20	75	5
14–22min	1,650yd (1,500m)	Neg	15	78	7

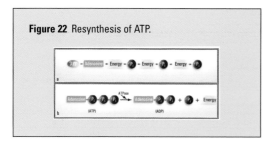

Figure 22 Resynthesis of ATP.

Working capacity in swimmers depends more on the rate of recycling ATP (from CP, glycogen, fats and proteins) than on the amount of ATP. With training, ATP-CP increases less than 20 per cent, while working capacity (swimming velocity) increases much more dramatically. There are three main pathways of energy metabolism (corresponding to the three broad categories of training, namely sprint, anaerobic and aerobic):

- creatine phosphate (immediate non-oxidative way of energy recycling);
- anaerobic metabolism (anaerobic-glycolitic non-oxidative way of energy recycling);
- aerobic metabolism (oxidative way of energy recycling).

The metabolism of creatine phosphate is the process of recycling ATP from CP. CP is stored in muscle cells, and it very rapidly recycles ATP from ADP. Usually after 2 to 3sec of high-intensity work, free ATP stores in muscle cells are depleted, and then CP phosphate is involved to recycle ATP. After 10 to 15sec of high intensity work, the rate of recycling ATP from CP is slowed down. Creatine phosphate has very high power, low capacity, and low efficiency. Examples of swimming sets designed to develop creatine phosphate metabolism feature short sprints (up to 25m) with maximum intensity and long rests, for example 2 × (8 × 20m) from the starting blocks on 80sec.

Anaerobic metabolism (anaerobic-glycolitic) is the non-oxidative process of recycling ATP from glycogen. Glycogen is stored in the muscle cells and fairly rapidly recycles ATP, though it is slower than from CP. Anaerobic metabolism produces lactate, and is the main energy system for exercise bouts of 30sec up to 2min;

when distances are longer, aerobic metabolism predominates. Anaerobic metabolism has high power, middle capacity, and low efficiency.

Aerobic metabolism is the oxidative process of recycling ATP primarily from glycogen; it is a slow process of recycling ATP. Glycogen for aerobic metabolism is stored in muscle, liver and blood; fats and proteins can also be involved in aerobic metabolism, but this process is very slow (long distance swimming). Aerobic metabolism is the main energy system for distances longer than 4min: the longer the distance, the more energy that is derived from aerobic metabolism. Aerobic metabolism takes place in a small, intracellular organelle called 'mitochondria'. Aerobic metabolism has low power, high capacity, and high efficiency.

Sources of energy in the body

Adenosine triphosphate (ATP)
Creatine phosphate (CP)
Glycogen (glucose)
Fats
Proteins (very limited capacity for exercise)

TRAINING (ENERGY) CATEGORIES IN SWIMMING

Based on the physiological responses of swimmers to different intensities, workload can be divided into the several energy zones. There are several classifications of workload; Fig. 23 shows one method of categorizing training with sample sets, and this illustration attempts to cover most of the variations in use across the world, with the author's preferred version shaded in the darker colour.

There are other forms of swimming used in training, such as warming up and swimming down. Fig. 24 shows the warm-up used by Ian Thorpe when he broke the world record for 400 Free (3.40.08) at the 2002 Commonwealth Games in Manchester, England, witnessed poolside by the author. The key thing to remember for warming up is that it is swimmer-, event- and context-specific: thus a male sprinter preparing for a heat swim will do something completely

Figure 23 Training categories.

Name	Explanation	Set length	Rest intervals	Weekly volume	Heartrate guide
Warm-up and Swim-down	Preparation for session (physical and mental) Recovery	600–1,500m (15–25min)	5–30sec max	min of 15%	Prog to 50 beats below max
Basic Aerobic	Slowest speed in training, technique work, long distance swims and drills	2,000–8,000m (25–I20min)	10–30sec, not full recovery	up to 45%	50–30 beats below max
Threshold	Improvements in aerobic capacity, without overstressing system	1,500–3,000m (25–40min)	10–40sec	up to 25%	30–20 beats below max
Overload	Just above threshold to stress improvements in VO$_2$ max	1,000–1,600m (15–25min)	1:1 work: rest ratio	up to 15%	20 below-max HR
Lactate Tolerance	Improving buffering capacity and pain of acidosis (passive rest)	300–800m (20–40min)	1- 5min passive recovery	up to 7%	Not relevant
Lactate Production	Improving ability to finish races as fast as possible (active rest)	200–600m (20–40min)	1–5min active recovery	up to 7%	Not relevant
Pure Speed	Fastest possible speeds in training (with and without aids)	200–600m (20–40min)	Full recovery between reps	up to 7%	Not relevant

Figure 24 Ian Thorpe's warm-up for his 400 Free world record.

Poolside chat with coach before going into water
400 loosen F/c
Quick confirmatory chat with coach
2 x 100 as 50 Pull / 50 Kick
200 as 100 Pull / 50 Kick / 50 pull
3 x 100 negative split on 1.45
8 x 50 drills including catch up & tempo
4 x 50 race pace (push-off on 60, turning to feet on wall) Times: 27.07 / 26.77 / 26.54 / 25.14
4 x 200 checking HR Total - 2500m
Race splits: 53.02 / 56.55 (1.49.57) / 55.86 (2.45.43)/ 54.65 (3.40.08)

different to a female distance swimmer preparing for a championship final.

As far as guides to swim-down go, Fig. 25 shows a swim-down protocol based on that used by the British swimming team. In a multi-event, heats finals and repeat days of competition format, it is vital that swimmers recover sufficiently between swims, between sessions and from one day to the next, including replacing energy. For more information on performance nutrition, *see* Crowood Sports Guides, *Swimming*, Chapter 16.

AEROBIC TRAINING

(To moderately improve oxidative capacity and the ability to use fats)

Variously known, basic aerobic training is the least intense training that swimmers do. It is also the type of training that covers the highest volume of work. Used mainly as maintenance and recovery training, 'base aerobic' work is simply that: low-intensity endurance training designed to improve sub-maximal cardiovascular efficiency and the use of oxygen in supplying energy to the working muscles. A season-long feature of training programmes, the traditional pattern of conditioning work sees a 'base' of aerobic fitness being built from the beginning and developed with higher intensity work as the season progresses. (The converse of this – that is, building speed first and then endurance – will be discussed later, in Chapter 6 Specific Event Training.)

Figure 25 Swim-down protocol.

Swimmers should attempt to keep moving as soon as they have completed a race; this includes moving the arms and legs in the water, and stretching and moving the arms and legs out of the water on the way to the swim-down pool. It is more important that you replenish your energy and recover from the race than you speak to anyone.

Remove (and replace with regular training suits) any special leg or body suits before the swim-down. Report to the swim-down pool within 3 minutes of the end of a race with a full drinks bottle and your choice of food. Replacement fluid should be drunk immediately and taken at every opportunity throughout the swim-down.

Swim a minimum of 200m easy

Swim 4 × 100m with up to 20sec rest, alternating Freestyle and Backstroke every 50m (*Breaststrokers may include own stroke*). The intensity should be steady, swum with good technique and the swimmer should breath frequently.

Swim 8 × 50m @ 50BBM, as 25 choice/25 race stroke (IMers do rolling medley) and focus on kicking the legs at a moderate level.

During the odd numbered repeats put in a fast burst of 2-3 strokes

Swim 4 x 100m @ 50BBM alternating freestyle and choice;

After 30sec rest: *If lactate is measured and* < 2mmol l-1 Swim-Down is completed *If lactate is not measured*: Heart Rate <100 beats per minute, then Swim-Down completed.

Otherwise

If La < 2.5 swim a further 200m <u>easy</u> (*Own Choice pace and stroke*)

If La > 2.5 swim a further 400m <u>easy</u> (*Own Choice pace and stroke*)

Monitor HR after 200m easy swims until <100 after 30sec rest

Base aerobic training can be done on all four strokes, although some swimmers may find it difficult to swim butterfly 'aerobically' at this low intensity. A very useful training aid on freestyle at this intensity is the snorkel (*see* Figs. 26a and 26b): by allowing all breathing to take place via the snorkel, the swimmer can concentrate on efficient stroke technique without the 'interruption' of breathing on the streamlined body position.

Three effects of basic aerobic training

Increased cardiac output
Increased blood volume
Improved blood shunting

Sample Basic Aerobic Training Set

(Early season for an eighteen-year-old male 400 IM swimmer)
500 free on 6.15
400 IM on 5.30
300 fly on 4.15
200 back on 3.00
100 breast on 1.35
Repeat × 4 (6,000m) with extra 60 sec between rounds

Guidelines for basic aerobic sets

- Minimum 20min long
- Maximum – as the session allows
- Short rests (5–30sec), according to repeat distance
- Repeat distances of 50m and upwards
- Low- to medium-intensity efforts

THRESHOLD TRAINING
(To improve oxidative capacity)

The term 'anaerobic threshold' is often derided by physiologists who say that it is a misnomer and that it (wrongly) implies the end of something (aerobic work) and the start of something else (anaerobic work). The acronym OBLA ('onset of blood lactate accumulation') is suggested as a more accurate alternative, and some swimming coaches do use the term. However, 'threshold' is very much a fixture in the vocabulary of coaches, and it is more important that the training it

Figure 26a, b Using a snorkel for aerobic training.

too much and the swimmer may struggle to cope with excessive amounts.

> ### Three effects of threshold training
>
> Increased use of VO_2max
> Increased removal of lactate
> Increased levels of mitochondria and myoglobin

> ### Sample Threshold Training Set
>
> (Mid-season for a sixteen-year-old female 200 fly swimmer)
> $3 \times (5 \times 200$ fly), with an extra 60sec between sets
> Set 1, as 50 fly–100 free–50 fly
> Set 2, as 100 fly–50 free–50 fly
> Set 3, all fly
> (3,000m)
> NB Establish stroke count and rhythm on Set 1, and maintain it through Sets 2 and 3.
> *The extra 60sec between sets is more psychological than physiological.
> This is an excellent indicator of a swimmer being able to swim fly aerobically.

> ### Guidelines for threshold sets
>
> - Minimum 20min long
> - Maximum 60min (for élite distance swimmers)
> - Short rests (10–60sec), according to repeat distance
> - Repeat distances of 50–400m
> - Medium intensity efforts

implies is done correctly, than arguing about the semantics of its name. In terms of simple concepts, it is more intense than basic aerobic work, but its physiological effects are very similar in generating cardio-respiratory and muscle cell adaptations.

Threshold training is used throughout the season and on all four strokes. It is also used as a reference point for prescribing other intensities of training, for example 'swim 2sec per 100 slower than threshold speed'. The blend of volume and intensity of threshold training is an important marker for the coach: too little and the adaptations will stagnate,

AEROBIC OVERLOAD
(To maximally improve oxidative capacity)

This is the highest intensity aerobic work possible and, as the name implies, is very taxing. One of its other names is VO_2max training, because it stresses maximal aerobic work. Overload sets cannot be repeated too many times in a week, and it takes good recovery strategies to be ready to 'go again'. Training benefits from overload work are mainly aerobic, but modest anaerobic advantages can also be gained. Swimmers should perform this work on their main stroke(s) to gain maximum benefits from the specificity of training principle. From the example of the butterfly swimmer above, the threshold training set of $3 \times (5 \times 200)$ probably ends with an overload effort in all but the most aerobically capable of fly swimmers.

Three effects of aerobic overload training

Increased VO_2max
Increased buffering capacity
Increased number of capillaries

Sample Overload Training Set

(Early season for senior male 400 freestyle swimmer)
20×100 F/c on 1.45
Holding the 'best average' times.
(2,000m)

Guidelines for Overload Sets

- 20 – 45min long
- 1:1 work:rest ratio for short repeats (close to this for longer reps)
- Repeat distances of 50–300m
- High intensity efforts

LACTATE TOLERANCE

(To improve buffering capacity)

Lactate tolerance training involves swimming at high intensity efforts over short repeat distances with a passive (and incomplete) recovery. By creating a build-up of lactic acid (lactate), one key training effect is improved buffering capacity of the muscles. This is a very stressful form of training, both physically and mentally, and is usually intro-duced into the training programme once a good level of conditioning has been reached. Recovery from this training takes around forty-eight hours, so two to three times a week are the maximum amounts possible. For maximum performance benefits, swimmers should do this type of training on their No. 1 stroke(s).

Allied to lactate tolerance training is 'lactate removal' training. As there is no active recovery during tolerance sets (the rest intervals won't allow this), the build-up of lactate needs to be removed immediately afterwards – hence the term 'lactate removal'. Essentially it is recovery work, but in the context of repeated training and competition swims, the ability to effectively remove lactic acid from the muscles becomes a very important part of the swimmers' arsenal against fatigue and under-performance. The example below shows a lactate tolerance set and a lactate removal set.

Three effects of lactate tolerance training

Improved tolerance of acidosis
Improved removal of lactate
Improved rate of anaerobic metabolism

Sample Lactate Tolerance Training Set
(Competition phase for senior male 200 butterfly swimmer)
4×25 fly on 40 prog effort, check speed and stroke count
4×50 fly on 1.00 prog effort 1–4
12×75 fly on 3.30 max effort (1,100m)
Twice through the following:
4×50 on 50 as free/25 form
2×100 on 1.45 as 50 free/50 form
1×200 free on 3.15
2×100 on 1.45 as 50 form/ 50 free
4×50 on 50 as 25 form/25 free
Checking recovery levels and concentrating on technique, not effort
(2,000m)

LACTATE PRODUCTION

(To improve glycolytic capacity)

Sometimes known as 'lactate power' or 'anaerobic capacity' training, the key difference between this and tolerance training is the presence of active recovery between maximal effort swims. Research has shown that doing this type of 'sprint' training can improve capacity by up to 20 per cent in just eight weeks. It has similar aims (and effects) to tolerance work in terms of improved buffering and energy release, but the active recovery elements mean that the physical and mental stress on the swimmer is slightly reduced.

It is possible for this type of training to be done every day because recovery time is less of an issue, but in practice coaches will usually prescribe it two to four times a week to balance out the other work being done. For maximum performance benefits, swimmers should also do this type of training on their No. 1 stroke(s).

PURE SPEED

(To improve alactic power)

Also known as 'power' sprint training, this is the fastest type of work done by swimmers – it can even be faster than race speeds with the assistance of paddles, fins or other devices such as tubing or towing machines. The scheduling of pure speed training is discussed later in this section, but it is best done when the swimmers are fresh and not suffering from the fatiguing effects of other forms of training. It can be done on all forms of training (swim, kick, pull or drills), and is thought to offer swimmers the best chance to transfer any strength and power gains on dry land into the pool environment. It can be done throughout the season, every day if desired, and (if done properly) does not deplete vital glycogen stores required for other training sets. Swimmers should focus pure speed training on their main stroke(s), and although it can be done faster than race speed, care should be taken to practise race stroke rates and patterns at all times.

Sample Pure Speed Training Set
(Taper phase for a senior female sprinter)
4 × 15m on 45
1 × 100 as 25 drill/swim on 2.00
4 × 20m on 60
1 × 150 as 50 swim/drill/swim on 2.50
4 × 25m on 1.15
1 × 200 as 50 drill/swim on 3.30
Repeat × 2 (480m speed work)

Guidelines for pure speed sets

- Approx 300–800m of 'speed' work
- Work: rest ratio of 1:6 with active or passive recovery
- Repeat distances of 10–25m
- Maximum intensity efforts
- Practice race stroke rates

CHAPTER 5

Training Sets

Most swimming training is done on an 'interval training' basis. First conceived in Germany in the 1930s, interval training has become the predominant form of training in most sports and is governed by the acronym DIRT. This has been modified over the years and different coaches have used the acronym to suit their needs, but it generally stands for D – the distance swum, I – the intensity of work, R – the number of repetitions to be performed, and T – the time (or interval) taken for each swim. Other acronyms have been used – including ANDFIR (by Madsen and Wilke in their seminal book *Coaching the Young Swimmer*), standing for Aim, Number, Distance, Frequency, Intensity, Rest – but the enduring appeal of DIRT is its simplicity and applicability. Within the 'interval training' framework there are a number of other training set types.

SLOW OR FAST INTERVAL SETS

Governed by the amount of rest in the set and the pace of the swims, these are the simplest and most common training sets. A 'fast interval' set would be 30 × 100m on a 2min turnaround; a 'slow interval' set would be over a longer distance, for example 10 × 400m on a 4.45min turnaround.

FARTLEK SWIMS

Literally meaning 'speedplay' and derived from *'langlauf* training' in cross-country skiing, fartlek swims are generally longer in duration and involve swims at varying speeds according to the stage of the season and design of the set. For example, this might involve swimming 4 × 800m with every sixth twenty-five fast on the first 800, every fifth twenty-five fast on the second 800, every fourth twenty-five fast on the third 800, and every third twenty-five fast on the fourth 800.

Coaches will often vary the strokes to be swum fast – for instance, in the above example swimming the 800s on freestyle with the fast twenty-fives on fly. A great way to use fartlek training is with a whistle, when the coach signals the faster portions by blasts on the whistle; this is particularly useful for controlling large groups.

OVER-DISTANCE SWIMS

Usually part of early season conditioning, over-distance swims are (as the name implies) longer than race distance, and used at a fairly low intensity to facilitate basic aerobic conditioning and recovery from higher intensity work. In the 4 × 800m example above, this could also be an 'over-distance' set for 100/200m swimmers (with or without the fartlek sections). Part 3 of this book illustrates this concept in a test set called 'double distance swims'.

PYRAMID SETS

Sometimes also known as 'Hungarian' sets, these are usually symmetrical in design and may involve manipulation of some or all of the DIRT variables. For example, 16 × 50 on 40, 8 × 100 on 80, 4 × 200 on 2.40, 2 × 400 on 5.20, 1 × 800 on 10.40, 2 × 400 on 5.00, 4 × 200 on 2.30, 8 × 100 on 75, 16 × 50 on 35. On the 'way up' to 800, the turnaround time is an average of 80sec per 100 and on the 'way back down' to the fifties it is an average of 37.5sec per fifty, except the last set on thirty-five. This done 'long course' was the author's favourite (and hardest) set as a swimmer!

PROGRESSIVE SETS

Again commonly used to vary the pace of swims, these sets are very popular in training and testing situations alike. For example, a set of 4 × (8 × 100 F/c) with each set even-paced, but faster than the previous one, could be used for conditioning and to monitor progress throughout the season – as the swimmers get fitter, the average times in each section of the set improve. Another way of designing a progressive set is to swim each repeat faster than the previous one, and repeat this cycle a number of times, for example 5 × (4 × 200 progress 1–4). The challenge is to be able to maintain the pattern, not just once, but five times. A further advantage of this type of training is that it covers a range of training intensities and therefore a number of physiological stimuli.

BROKEN SWIMS

Almost exclusively the preserve of race-preparation training, the concept of 'broken swims' is to provide an opportunity to practise race-pace swimming without performing the full race distance every time. For example, a common 'broken swim' for 200m events is to do 4 × 50m with 10sec rest between fifties.

There are several other variations of these themes, and of course if you add in the equipment possibilities described earlier (paddles, fins, kickboards, pullbuoys and so on), there are many possibilities for the innovative coach to design varied and challenging training programmes. The next section looks at this in relation to groups of events: 50s, 100s, 200s, 400s and 800/1500.

CHAPTER 6

Specific Event Training

By applying the *individuality* principle of training, we must recognize that every attempt should be made to provide specialized, focused training for swimmers relative to their age, event, gender and training history. The challenge for coaches is how best to do this, given the constraints of their programme and the complexities of each individual swimmer's training adaptations. There is no single way that is best, and every swimmer-coach unit will believe that their approach works; however, we can learn from what champion swimmers have done, and perhaps integrate their good practice into our own training programmes. After a brief synopsis on training periodization, this section deals with training for each of the events in turn and gives examples of training sets, sessions and cycles for successful international swimmers.

I have not used names of swimmers unless they have specifically given their permission for me to do so, but I would like to particularly thank the following national team coaches for their input to this section with ideas, and examples of programmes and sessions: Phil Potter, Ian Wright and Gary Paterson.

PERIODIZATION

Two of the most common features of the training programmes of swimmers are first, the periodization of training; and second, the transition from training to racing. Periodization can be defined in simple terms as the division of the annual training plan into smaller and more manageable phases of training. This approach permits one aspect of fitness to be the focus of training, while maintaining the others. In essence, a periodized training programme is really about being an organized and systematic coach.

The transition from training to racing is commonly referred to as the 'taper', and is characterized by a reduction in the volume of training and the refinement of race speed. Both periodization and tapering lead to the peaking of performance necessary for competition.

A fundamental principle of preparing swimmers is that periodization and tapering apply equally to all the different aspects of fitness such as endurance, speed, strength, flexibility and power. From a physiological viewpoint, there are several reasons for a periodized and balanced training programme leading up to major competition:

- Avoiding a high training load with excessive fatigue.
- Faster recovery and regeneration.
- Maintaining performances very close to their maximum for a long period of time.
- Correct peaking for the major competition of the year.
- Maintaining a basic level of fitness over a long period of training (or even a period of reduced training).
- A greater degree of specificity to be incorporated in training.
- A more efficient and effective taper.
- More complete adaptation to training without two or three parts of the programme interfering with each other when trained concurrently.
- Better planning for both major and minor competitions.
- More effective integration of sports science testing with the training programme.

A periodized swimming training and tapering programme is based on the principle of overload–recovery–peaking. This principle forms the basis of preparing swimming training programmes, with the aim of increasing the level of competitive performance. As discussed previously, the training programme must provide an overload (stimulus) to force the body to adapt to a previously unencountered level of stress. After sufficient application of the stimulus (in terms of magnitude and frequency), a period of recovery and regeneration will allow residual fatigue to disperse. If the processes of overload and recovery are managed correctly (that is, effective periodization), a period of super-compensation will occur so that performance is elevated to a higher level for important competitions. Most swimming coaches are familiar with the term 'periodization' and the various macro-, meso- and microcycles that are used to design a training programme. These terms are used to establish a sequencing of training within the overall programme.

MACROCYCLE

A 'macrocycle' refers to a long-term training phase lasting several weeks to months. In swimming, this usually represents the entire season in preparation for a major, annual competition (see Fig. 34 later in this section for an example of this). At senior level, there is commonly a two- or three-peak year, with emphasis on competitions every sixteen weeks or so – for example, the European SC Championships in mid-December, Olympic Trials in mid-April, and Olympic Games in late summer. The precise length of the macrocycle will depend on the specific training and/or competition objectives for the season and the individual swimmer's current fitness level. Some coaches will use the quadrennial between Olympics as their 'macro'-macrocycle, and deal with each year accordingly (see Fig. 33 for a version of this).

MESOCYCLE

The term 'mesocycle' refers to shorter training blocks within the annual programme; typically these are anything from seven to twenty weeks in length. A number of mesocycles combine to form a single phase of training: for example, the preparatory phase. Experience and scientific research has shown that after several weeks of intensive training, most athletes require some period of recovery. Hence the 'cyclical' nature of training over extended periods of time. Fig. 30 shows a fifteen-week mesocycle for a 100/200m swimmer.

There are many types of mesocycle, depending on the requirements of the programme, coach and swimmer. Some examples used by swimming coaches are the introductory cycle (general training, low volume – low intensity), preparatory cycle (transition from low volume – low intensity to higher volume training), specific cycle (more specialized, higher intensity training, with an emphasis on improving competitive speed), and the competition cycle (competitive performance on a single or repeated basis). In each case, the volume and intensity of work will vary according to the specific requirements of the programme for the swimmers.

Effective coaches are always aware of 'where they are' in the training programme. Getting bogged down and stale in a long and arduous training phase is not a very efficient approach to preparing for competition. Athletes should not struggle with their training for more than a few days without some intervention, or overtraining may occur.

MICROCYCLE

The term 'microcycle' refers to a short-term training block within a mesocycle. Most commonly, swimming training microcyles are planned around a standard seven-day training week. Coaches and swimmers are creatures of the modern working week, and most swimmers have to fit their training programmes around work, education and family commitments. However, coming in to important meets such as the Olympics, the training schedule takes precedence, and the day of the week, weekends and public holidays become less important. Microcycles represent the specific plans and strategies needed to achieve the broader objective of the training cycle – for example, to improve anaerobic capacity. Each microcycle consists of the individual (daily) workouts, and again these are based on the objectives of the mesocycle. Fig. 31 shows a microcycle for the swimmer featured in Fig. 29.

Periodization made easy

Plan strategic training in a macrocycle, broad outlines in a mesocycle, specific details for a microcycle, and fine-tune individualized training on a daily basis.

In most swimming programmes across the world, one of the fundamental principles that underpins the periodization of training is that the volume of training is increased before the intensity of training. Most coaches are familiar with the concept that a foundation of aerobic fitness is established easily in the cycle or competition season. After this initial period of increasing training volume to build endurance, the emphasis of training switches to the development of speed and anaerobic capacities. It is often observed that this base level of fitness can be re-established fairly quickly (in four to six weeks) in those swimmers with an extensive training background (although *see* Fig. 27 and the ensuing description of training for a counter-approach).

This has implications for older, more mature swimmers who are returning after a break. However, it is much more efficient for swimmers to maintain a basic fitness programme during the off-season. A reasonable level of fitness can be maintained on about 30 per cent of the full training volume: thus a swimmer who normally undertakes ten training sessions per week, should be able to maintain a base level of fitness for several weeks by just training three times per week. In this case, it is important to maintain some intensity in the work as volume and duration are reduced.

One approach that coaches find to be successful in certain situations is the use of three-day microcycles. The first variant involves two training sessions a day for the first two days, followed by a single session on the third day. In some circumstances in swimming, where three training sessions a day are used, the second variation takes the form of three sessions a day for two days, and then two sessions on the third and final day. In both versions, the first day is largely aerobic in nature, with a gradual decrease in volume and increase in intensity as the microcycle proceeds. The emphasis is on increasing speed from day to day, and athletes generally find this easier if the training volume is decreasing. Many swimmers (and coaches) like to finish each microcycle with a quality or speed session.

Another feature of training planning is the relationship between duration and intensity. Generally speaking, the lower the intensity of the cycle, the longer its duration. For higher intensity work, shorter two to four-day training cycles are used. Variation of training distance and intensity within cycles is important. Early in the programme, microcycles may involve higher intensity training for athletes already fatigued. The thinking is that this will provide a greater stimulus for adaptation. Later on, when the emphasis is on competition-specific speed, it is usually better to undertake high intensity training in a fresh condition in order to facilitate higher speeds.

SPRINTING (50/100M)

Despite the fact that only the 50m Freestyle is an Olympic event, the 50m Sprints are becoming a speciality in both short- and long-course swimming. The World, European, Pan Pacific Championships and Commonwealth Games all have 50m Butterfly, Backstroke and Breaststroke medals to be won.

Swimmers who dominate in these events last between 20sec (male 50m Freestyle, short course) and 30sec (female 50m Breaststroke, long course), and are the classic *fast-twitch fibre* specimens. Some of these outstanding athletes struggle to perform as well in the 'longer sprints' over 100m where the slightly greater aerobic demands make them more susceptible to fatigue. This is not to say that swimmers cannot 'cross over' from 50m to 100m events, and vice versa, but merely to recognize that where pure physiological capacity is at its most obvious – as in out-and-out sprinting – there is a high degree of specialization. This capacity for speed is even more evident in short-course 50m sprinting specialists, who find the transition to long-course 100s a distinct challenge.

Training for sprinters has probably undergone the most significant changes in recent years, with the influence of other sports (such as track and field athletics) most evident. In general, these 'new' approaches can be summarized as less time in the pool swimming at a low level aerobically, and more time in the gym working on strength and power. This doesn't mean a lack of quality or high-intensity swimming, but it does mean a much sharper focus on the work done in the pool improving tempo and racing skills.

Another difference in the 'modern' approach to training sprinters is the application of *reverse periodization*. Simply put, this is the development (and subsequent maintenance) of speed and anaerobic capacities first, rather than a traditional approach of building an aerobic base on which to build speed, and so on. Favoured mostly by coaches of sprinters in swimming, cycling and track, there is also some published empirical research to support this method of preparation (Rhea *et al*, 2003)[1]. Fig. 27 shows a reverse-periodization cycle for a British international female sprinter, and Fig. 28 shows a sample mid-season session for her.

Some detail about this plan: Week 32 until mid-Week 35 was a 'speed phase'. Having just swum a PB at the British Championships, the plan was to further improve maximum speed and alactic power in three key sprint sessions per week and with specific sets on starts/turns/finishes. Week 35 until the end of Week 38 was a 'production phase', attempting to maintain high speed over a longer period, with three key production sessions per week. The training volumes were still quite low per session, and Fig. 28 is an example of one key session during this phase. Again, there were specific sets on starts/turns/finishes.

Week 39 until the end of Week 41 was a 'tolerance phase' – swimming at speed/pace for longer and under extreme fatigue, aiming to maintain power output/efficient technique, with the training volume building throughout the phase. There were three key tolerance* sessions per week, with the focus on back-end speed and maintaining technique and speed under challenging conditions. Once more there were specific sets on starts/turns/finishes: the Mare Nostrum series fell in transition between tolerance and removal phases, with Canet, Barcelona and a training camp in Mataro straight after this latter meet. The purpose of this was to take the swimmer out of her comfort zone, with changed routines, no bodysuits in heats, and no rest between meets and camp. The swims at the meets weren't great, but a refocusing meeting was held during the camp.

Weeks 42 and 43 were a 'removal/VO2 phase' targeting increased maximal rate of lactic acid removal from working muscles under race conditions, and also to put more focus on developing the aerobic system at the same time as maintaining the previous anaerobic gains. There was a much higher training volume during this phase, which had three key removal/VO2 sessions per week. The likelihood was that speed would suffer from the high training loads.

The next two weeks (44 and 45) were similar to this, but with a higher volume and lower intensity. It was very important to maintain speed work throughout this phase, using combination and race prep sets.

The 'taper phase' then followed, namely Weeks 46 to 48. This was highlighted by initially a significant drop in volume, followed by small incremental drops. The main work was on combination sets, introducing broken swims without overdoing speed work, swim the first meet to assess progress, and then adjust accordingly for the next, main meet of the season. Overall the season was successful, and some good benefits were gained from the reverse periodization approach.

Figure 27 Reverse periodization for sprinting.

Wk#	WkCom.	Days to Go*			Competition/Camp	Emphasis	Target Volume
					Training and Competition Plan April–August 2007		
32	02/04/07	116	365	494		Speed Dev	25000
33	09/04/07	109	358	487	WC Dev Female Camp (10th–12th) Scottish Age Groups (13th/14th) 100/200 Fly/200 IM	Speed Dev	30000
34	16/04/07	102	351	480	4 day break(15th–18th)	Break/Speed Dev	20000
35	23/04/07	95	344	473		Speed Dev/La Production	30000
36	30/04/07	88	337	466		La Production	34000
37	07/05/07	81	330	459		La Production	38000
38	14/05/07	74	323	452		La Production	42000
39	21/05/07	67	316	445	Scottish Performance Weekend (25th/26th)	La Tolerance	45000
40	28/05/07	60	309	438	East District Open (2nd/3rd)	La Tolerance	48000
41	04/06/07	53	302	431	Mare Nostrum - Canet (9th/10th)	La Tolerance	50000
42	11/06/07	46	295	424	Mare Nostrum - Barcelona (13th/14th)	Removal/VO$_2$	52000
43	18/06/07	39	288	417	Camp - Mataro (15th–27th)	Removal/VO$_2$	55000
44	25/06/07	32	281	410	Scottish Open (28th–1st)	Aerobic	58000
45	02/07/07	25	274	403		Aerobic	58000
46	09/07/07	18	267	396		Race Preparation/Taper	50000
47	16/07/07	11	260	389		Taper	40000
48	23/07/07	4	253	382	ASA Champs (27th–1st)	Taper/Competition	30000
49	30/07/07		246	375	ASA Champs (27th–1st)	Competition	30000
50	06/08/07		239	368	World Student Games (9th–14th)	Competition	30000
51	13/08/07		232	361	World Student Games (9th–14th)	Competition/Break	
52	20/08/07		225	354	Break	Break	

*to start of ASA Champs (27/07/07)

*to start of Olympic Trials (01/04/08)

*to start of Beijing Olympics (08/08/08)

SPEED-ENDURANCE (100/200M)

Just as with the 'pure sprinters' competing in longer events, coaches will usually work on 'swimming down' to 100m or 'up' to 200m events. For example, double Olympic 100m Freestyle champion, Pieter van den Hoogenband (affectionately known as VDH) is also Olympic champion for 200m Freestyle and a bronze medallist for 50m Freestyle, demonstrating his versatility and ability to prepare for such a range of events. He is in fact the epitome of the 'modern swimmer', with thirty-seven medals across these events (and relays) in Olympic, World and European long course championships.

Periodization of training for these 'speed-endurance' races in all strokes takes careful planning. The fastest 100m event is the men's freestyle at 47.84sec, and the slowest 200m event is 2.20.54 (women's breaststroke); thus the physiological considerations are broadly between 47 and 140sec. Depending on how a swimmer 'swims the race', the training emphasis may differ between individuals and

Figure 28 Anaerobic session reverse periodized plan.

Workout Planning Sheet

Coach:		Date:	Friday 11/05/07	Time:	1800-2000
Session aims / objectives		*Lactate Production - #1 Swim*			
		u/w Kicking Skills			

#	Description			Total
1	Warm-up			2000
				(35mins)
		900 alt 200 FC/100 BK-5/7 DKs	+20	
		100 IM Drill		
		500 IM as 25 Kick/25 Swim		
		100 IM Swim		
		300 CH Kick as 50 Steady/25 Max		
		100 IM Swim BEST EFFORT		
2	Speed/Skills			1200
				(26mins)
		50 CH Swim MAX--} 15	1:00	
		100 FLY-BK - 11 kicks off wall	2:00	
		100 BR-FC - double pullout / 11 kicks off wall	2:00	
	2 x	50 on FRONT MAX↓} 15	1:30	
		50 CH Swim MAX--} 15	1:00	
		100 FLY-BK - 11 kicks off wall	2:00	
		100 BR-FC - double pullout/ 11 kicks off wall	2:00	
		50 on BACK MAX ↓} 15	1:30	
3	Lactate Production			1200 (360)
				(39mins)
		1 x MAX--} 20 FAD / 80 EASY	03:30	
		1 x MAX--} 30 FAD / 70 EASY	03:30	
		1 x MAX--} 40 FAD / 160 EASY	06:00	
		1 x MAX--} 30 FAD / 70 EASY	03:30	
		1 x MAX--} 40 FAD / 60 EASY	03:30	
		1 x MAX--} 50 FAD / 150 EASY	06:00	
		1 x MAX--} 40 FAD / 60 EASY	03:30	
		1 x MAX--} 50 FAD / 50 EASY	03:30	
		1 x MAX--} 60 FAD / 140 EASY	06:00	
4	Recovery			1100
				(22mins)
		100 Kick @ VO₂	+20	
		300 Swim @ AT		
		100 Kick @ AT		
		200 Swim @ A2		
		100 Kick @ A2		
		200 Swim@ A1		

approaches taken. Fig. 29 shows an example of an early-season mesocycle within the Olympic year macrocycle for a world-ranked 100/200m swimmer, and illustrates the division of the plan into more manageable segments, emphasizing basic aerobic development through to more quality work and a series of meets in November 2007. The key training objective for this period is shown on the right of the chart – Phase 1 'focusing on 100 return', that is, the second 50m of 100m races (note the swimmer performed a best 'in-season' time at the final competition, indicating that good progress was being made towards the overall objective). Fig. 30 gives more detail on the segments of this plan, with details of volume, training emphasis and test sets. The graph at the bottom shows an intriguing comparison between the planned and actual volumes completed.

On this point it is also interesting to compare this sheet with Fig. 27 for the sprinter. The average volumes are slightly more for the 100m/200m swimmer, but not significantly so.

Figure 29 Extract from Olympic macrocycle for 100/200m swimmer.

Week Beginning	WEEK No.	PHASE	MESO CYCLE	MICRO CYCLE	LAND (No)	LAND (Int)	EMPHASIS	COMP No.	COMPETITIVE SCHEDULE / Notes	Calender Month No.	
20-Aug-07	1			0	6		Building In		Land Only 60-90 mins evenings. Aviemore weekend	34	Phase #1
27-Aug-07	2		A	1	6	mh	Aerobic &		Inc: cross training [spinning/ rowing/ climbing/ walking/	35	General Conditioning on land.
03-Sep-07	3			2	5	mh	Strength		running/ camping	36	Intensive period focusing on
10-Sep-07	4			3	3	mh				37	100 return. [Speed/ Production]
17-Sep-07	5			1	3	mh	En1-3			38	
24-Sep-07	6		B	2	3	h	AT-V02			39	
01-Oct-07	7			3	3	m	Rec/Sp	1	ND Sprint Champs	40	
08-Oct-07	8	I		1	3	mh	En1-3			41	
15-Oct-07	9		C	2	3	h	AT-V02			42	Oct.
22-Oct-07	10			3	3	h	Rec/Sp			43	
29-Oct-07	11			1	3	vh	En1-3			44	
05-Nov-07	12		D	2	3	m	AT-V02			45	
12-Nov-07	13			3	3	m	Rec/Sp	2	REN 96	46	
19-Nov-07	14			1	2	mh	Transition	3	UDASC	47	
26-Nov-07	15		E	2	2	h	Transition	4	Sheffield Winter Meet [30th - 02nd Dec]	48	

Figure 30 Mesocycle for 100/200m swimmer.

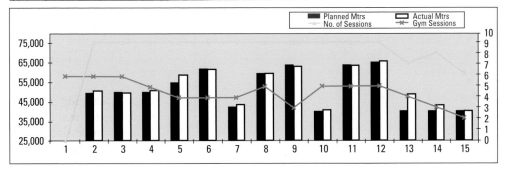

This may be more to do with the characteristics of each swimmer than anything else – that is, the 'sprinter' is capable of 'swimming up to 100' more than a *drop-dead sprinter* would be. Of course, the key difference between the two mesocycles is the 'traditional' versus 'reverse' periodized contrast. A specific microcycle from the speed endurance plan is shown in Fig. 31, and a lactate production session from that week is provided in Fig. 32.

Figure 31 Microcycle for 100/200m swimmer.

	Day	Monday	Tuesday	Wednesday	Thursday	Friday	Saturday	Sunday
	Date	08–Oct–07	09–Oct–07	10–Oct–07	11–Oct–07	12–Oct–07	13–Oct–07	14–Oct–07
AM	Main	Aerobic En1 - En2 Resistance Fc	Aerobic En3 Fc	Aerobic En1 Over Dist Fc-Bc		Aerobic En2 Resistance IM	Aerobic Recovery Speed Enhancement	
	Subset		Aerobic En1 No.1 Skills					
	Distance	6,600	6,550	6,300		6,550	5,750	
		Monday	Tuesday	Wednesday	Thursday	Friday	Saturday	Sunday
PM	Main	Aerobic En1 Be [3000m]		Aerobic En2 Resistance Fc - No.1	Anaerobic Threshold Fc-IM			Anaerobic Threshold Fc - No.1
	Subset	Lac. Prod No.1 - IM						
	Distance	6,200		5,800	7,300			6,450
AM	Land			Weights			Weekly Total	57,500
PM	Land	Weights			Pilates	Weights	Medicine Ball	
							Total Time	

% Work Done	
Aerobic (En1 ~ Rec)	Alactic (Spl)
Aerobic (En2 ~ capacity)	Lac. Prod (Sp2)
Aerobic (En3 ~ power)	Lac. Tol (Sp3)
Threshold (AT)	Skills (En1)
VO$_2$ Max (VO$_2$)	

Figure 32 Lactate production session for 100/200m swimmer.

Length of Session:	120 min		Date: 08th–Oct 2007			Time: 5.30pm Session No.:
	Cycle:	C		Week:	1	

Aim of Session:

1. Lactate Production No.1
2. Over Distance Be [Skills & Recovery]

Session Details:

W/up	3 x 200	Fc	DpS & Breath Control	3.00		600
	1 x 600	Alt 75's	Fc/ IM Form/ Fc/ Be	9.15		1200
En2	16 x 50	Alt	4 x Fc	Rhythm & Range	45	2000
			4 x IM	DpS	60	
Sp2	2 x 25	No.1	Walk Back		90 }	
					}	
	3 x 50	No.1	Max Speed	Racing Start	3.00 }	
					}	
En1	1 x 400	Alt Fc - IM		Recovery	6.00 } All x 2	3200
En1	8 x 75	Be	Even Pace & Hold SC		1.10	
En1 skill	4 x 300	Be	Hold Pace & SC from above		4.20	
En2	6 x 200	Be	Neg Splits		3.00	6200

Comments:

% Work Done			
Aerobic (En1 ~ Rec)	2600	Alactic (Sp1)	
Aerobic (En2 ~ capacity)	2000	Lac. Prod (Sp2)	400
Aerobic (En3 ~ power)		Lac. Tol (Sp3)	
Threshold (AT)		Skills (Enl)	1200
VO$_2$ Max (VO$_2$)			

SPEED-ENDURANCE (200/400M)

Looking at the next step up in distance, there are notable 200m/400m swimmers with some capable of 'swimming up' and others adept at 'swimming down'. For example, Ian Thorpe is an Olympic champion for 200m and 400m Freestyle and also held the 800 Free world record at one point in his career. On IM, most swimmers will compete in both 200m and 400m events, although the 200IM does attract more entries from other 'single stroke' specialists (most of whom are already trained as 200m swimmers anyway). For example, the top fifty swimmers in the 2007 world long-course rankings for 200IM featured at least 50 per cent of swimmers 'better known' (and better ranked) as single-stroke swimmers. Tom Dolan of the USA is a medley specialist and double Olympic champion on 400IM, he is also a former American record holder for 1650yd ('the mile'). Being a good IM swimmer requires versatility of skills and a range of physical capacities. Thus the 'physiological range' for speed-endurance is 1.43.86 (fastest 200m – men's freestyle) to 4.32.89 (fastest women's IM).

The example shown in Fig. 33 is of a four-year quadrennial plan leading up to the 2008 Beijing Olympic Games for a swimmer with the primary event of 400IM. Being successful at 400IM is the equivalent in swimming terms of the decathlon in track and field. Purists will value the champions on this particular event above all others because of their versatility and toughness. Note that Fig. 33 covers progressions through not just the 400IM, but also 200IM, 400 Free, 1500 Free, each of the form stroke 200s and the 100 Fly, because of their relevance for this most demanding of events. Keys to the 400IM are (i) a distance-based training programme; (ii) a very good breaststroke; (iii) a good sense of pacing; and (iv) effective stroke transitions. Fig. 34 is an extract from the quadrennial plan, showing the year 2006–07 seasonal plan. It is appropriate to highlight a specific set from this plan (Fig. 35a) to illustrate just how challenging the preparation for 400IM can be. This long-course set was devised by the swimmer to gauge progress on an annual basis. It involves swimming a 4000IM (that's 1000m on each stroke) on 56min, followed by 10 × 400IM on 5.30. Each column on this sheet shows the results for an individual swimmer with our featured swimmer the first column in from the left-hand side. Fig. 35b shows an IM analysis chart used by British Swimming to pinpoint strengths and weaknesses for 400IM.

ENDURANCE (800/1500)

There are 'out-and-out' distance swimmers who certainly struggle to 'swim down' to the shorter events, particularly 200m, but since Kieran Perkins of Australia demonstrated his complete range of freestyle prowess in the 1990s, there has been a tendency towards developing distance freestylers with a six-beat leg kick and an ability to swim long *and* fast. For example, current 800m and 1500m world record holder and double Olympic champion Grant Hackett is also the second fastest ever on 400m Freestyle, and was second in the 2005 world rankings for 200m Free behind Michael Phelps.

Jon Urbanchek's Formulas

Former University of Michigan coach, Jon Urbanchek, proposes the following formulas for quantifying the relationships between 200m, 400m and 1500m Freestyle times:

- hold 91.72 per cent of 200 time for 1500m
- hold 95.51 per cent of 200 time for 400m
- hold 95.95 per cent of 400 time for 1500m

Fig. 36 shows a year-long macrocycle for a world-class female distance freestyler. The key difference between this and the other plans is the predominance of aerobic work in all dimensions, and the significantly increased volumes on a weekly and seasonal average basis. Fig. 37 is a high volume–high intensity microcycle from the plan, with only the main

Figure 33 Quadrennial plan.

4 Year Olympic Training Plan
Target: Beijing 2008
Primary Event: 400 I.M.

Season	2004–2005	2005–2006	2006–2007	2007–2008
Sessions/week	10–11	11–12	11–12	11–12
Km/week	60–70	70–80	80–90	70–80
Hours/week	21–23	23–25	23–25	23–25
Weights	1–2 x 1 hr	2–3 x 1 hr	2–3 x 1 hr	2 x 1 hr
Land	3 x 1 hr	3 x 1 hr	3 x 1 hr	3 x 1 hr
Step Test	Back	Breast	Free	Fly
Training Emphasis	Aerobic capacity	Aerobic power	Stroke specific	Race pacing and strategy
Technique Emphasis	Bk rotation Brs kick	Fc timing Fly body position	Fc Timing I.M. switches	Refine all areas
GB representation	EJC final/medal	EJC Medal	Make World team	Olympic final/medal
Scotland representation	Make CG team	CG final/medal	n/a	n/a
400 I.M. Target	4:23 -> 4:21	4:19 -> 4:17	4:15 -> 4:14	4:12 -> 4:11
200 I.M. Target	2:07 -> 2:06	2:05 -> 2:04	2:03 -> 2:02	2:01 -> 2:00
400 Free Target	4:02 -> 4:00	3:58 -> 3:56	3:54 -> 3:53	3:51 -> 3:50
1500 Free Target	15:45	15:35	15:25	15:15
200 Fly Target	2:04 -> 2:03	2:02 -> 2:01	2:00 -> 1:59	1:58 -> 1:57
200 Back Target	2:06 -> 2:05	2:04 -> 2:03	2:02 -> 2:01	2:00 -> 1:59
200 Breast Target	2:22 -> 2:21	2:20 -> 2:19	2:18 -> 2:17	2:16 -> 2:15
100 Fly Target	59.0 -> 58.0	57.5 -> 57.0	56.5 -> 56.0	55.5 -> 55.0

Figure 34 Seasonal plan.

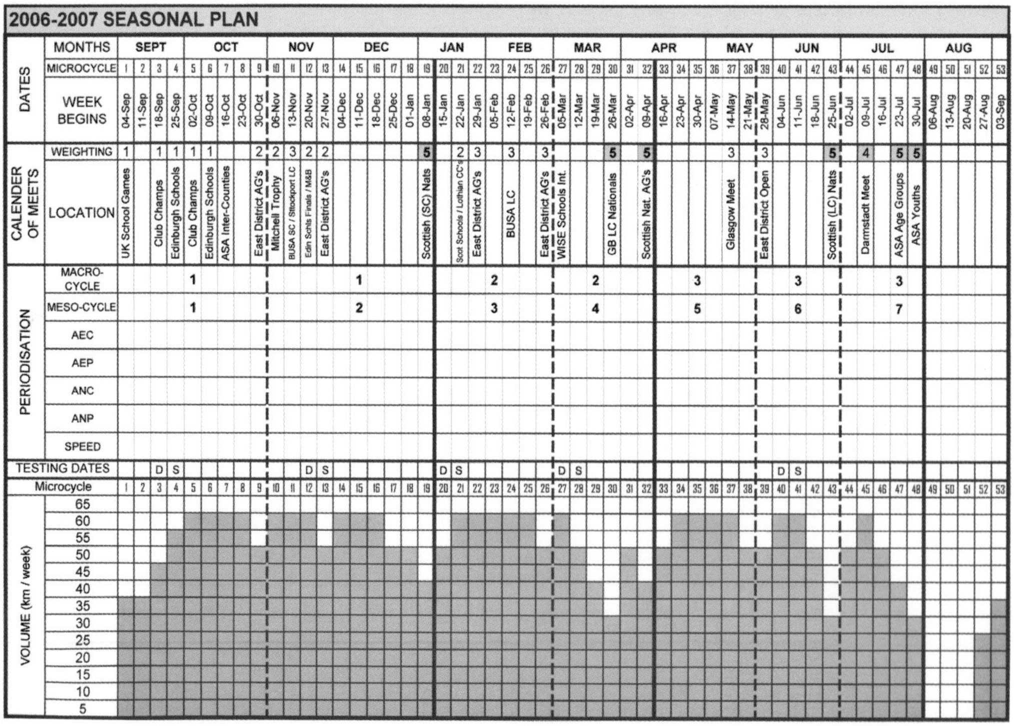

2006-2007 SEASONAL PLAN

Figure 35a Challenge set.

Calella Training Camp
4–12 June 2006
I.M. Aerobic Challenge Set ~ 9th June (AM)

4000 I.M. on:	56:00	56:00	59:00	60:00	62:00	62:00	62:00	62:00	62:00	62:00	62:00	62:00
Fly	12:59	14:49	13:22	14:23	14:31	15:32	15:19	15:57	15:22	14:57	15:32	16:59
Bk	13:02	13:10	13:22	13:46	14:44	14:36	14:54	14:23	14:39	15:47	14:43	14:20
Brs	14:49	13:10(Bk)	14:54	15:10	15:04	16:30	16:22	15:57	17:57	17:38	17:21	16:37
Fc	12:00	12:17	12:06	13:00	12:59	12:44	13:01	13:39	13:00	12:47	13:37	13:21
Total	00:52:50	00:53:20	00:53:44	00:56:19	00:57:18	00:59:22	00:59:36	00:59:56	01:00:58	01:01:09	01:01:13	01:01:17

10 x 400 I.M. on:	05:30	05:30	06:30	BRS on 6:30	06:30	06:30	06:30	06:30	06:30	06:30	06:30	06:30
1	5:17.0	5:23.0	5:23.0	5:47.0	5:42.0	6:12.0	6:11.0	6:07.0	6:07.0	6:28.0	6:11.0	6:12.0
2	5:14.0	5:23.0	5:24.0	5:37.0	5:43.0	6:25.0	6:09.0	6:02.0	6:12.0	-	6:12.0	6:16.0
3	5:07.0	5:23.0	5:22.0	5:39.0	5:44.0	6:26.0	6:00.0	6:01.0	6:16.0	~	6:08.0	6:18.0
4	5:10.0	5:16.0	5:19.0	5:30.0	5:52.0	6:25.0	5:58.0	5:55.0	6:11.0	6:30.0	6:05.0	6:24.0
5	5:09.0	5:12.0	5:18.0	5:34.0	5:46.0	6:24.0	5:56.0	6:02.0	6:08.0	6:22.0	6:00.0	6:28.0
6	5:07.0	5:12.0	5:17.0	5:52.0	5:40.0	6:13.0	5:51.0	6:01.0	6:07.0	6:10.0	5:50.0	6:34.0
7	5:09.0	5:16.0	5:16.0	5:34.0	5:44.0	6:12.0	5:49.0	6:02.0	6:02.0	6:07.0	5:50.0	-
8	5:06.0	5:16.0	5:14.0	5:23.0	5:34.0	~	5:42.0	6:01.0	6:00.0	-	5:43.0	-
9	5:04.0	5:15.0	5:12.0									
10	4:59.0	5:16.0	5:04.0									
Average:	5:08.2	5:17.2	5:16.9	5:37.0	5:43.1	6:19.6	5:57.0	6:01.4	6:07.9	6:19.4	5:59.9	6:22.0

Back

Figure 35b IM analysis chart.

Individual Medley strengths and weakness chart

	BF	BK	BR	FS	
100 and 200 best times for all strokes and differential	100 = 1:01 200 = 2:16 Diff = 15	100 = 1:03 200 = 2:13 Diff = 10	100 = 1:06 200 = 2:24 Diff = 18	100 = 56 200 = 1:59 Diff = 13	
Splits from their 400IM personal best time and difference between 100 PB and splits	1:03 2 seconds difference between splits for 400 IM and 100 PB time.	1:13 10 seconds difference between splits for 400 IM and 100 PB time.	1:15 9 seconds difference between splits for 400 IM and 100 PB time.	1:00 4 seconds difference between splits for 400 IM and 100 PB time	4:31.00 = Current 400IM personal best time
Actual 400IM splits as a % PB (100 + 6%) x 2 = goal time for 200	23.24% PB 100 +6% = 200 BF goal = 2:09.20	26.93% PB 100 +6% = 1:06.70 x 2 = 200 BK goal = 2:13.40	27.67% PB 100 +6% = 1:09.90 x 2 = 200 BR goal = 2:19.80	22.14% PB 100 +6% = 59.10 x 2 = 200 FS goal = 1:58.20	
PB 100m + 8% = target 400IM splits	1:05.80	1:08.04	1:11.28	1:00.48	4:25.60 = 400IM goal time
Target 400IM splits as a % 400 target time for each stroke = 200 goal time x 2 + differential between 100 & 200 best times	24.77% 400 BF Goal = 4:33.40 2:09.20 x 2 = 4:18.40 + 15 = 4:33.40	25.61% 400 BK Goal = 4:36.80 2:13.40 x 2 = 4:26.80 + 10 = 4:36.80	26.83% 400 BR Goal = 4:57.60 2:19.80 x 2 = 4:39.60 + 18 = 4:57.60	22.77% 400 Fs Goal = 4:09.40 1:58.20 x 2 = 3:56.40 + 13 = 4:09.40	
200 IM Target Splits 100 PB + 4% divided by 2	31.72 1:01 + 4% = 1:03 + 44 divided by 2 = 31.72	32.76 1:03 + 4% 1:05.52 divided by 2 = 32.76	34.32 1:06 + 4% = 1:08 + 64 divided by 2 = 34.32	29.12 56 + 4% = 58.24 divided by 2 = 29.12	2:07.92 = 200IM Goal time
200 Target based on target 400IM splits	200 BF/BK Goal = 2:13.84	200 BF/BK Goal = 2:19.32	200 BR/FS Goal = 2:11.76		

emphasis of each session shown; and Fig. 38 shows a specific long-course morning session from that week with a tough main set.

ERRORS IN TRAINING

A number of possible factors may influence a swimmer's readiness for competition. These factors relate specifically to the methods of training and the arrangement of the training cycles.

- An incorrect arrangement of micro- and mesocycles – quite simply the balance and emphasis of training, and if this is wrong, the wrong adaptations will occur (or none at all).
- A lack of sufficient recovery – ultimately culminating in an over-trained state.
- The demands on the athlete are made too rapidly – possibly leading to injury or the initial stages of over-training (usually known as over-reaching).
- Too high volume at maximal or sub-maximal intensity – related to both of the previous errors, and will eventually lead to a broken-down state.
- Too high submaximal intensity during endurance work – working at the wrong

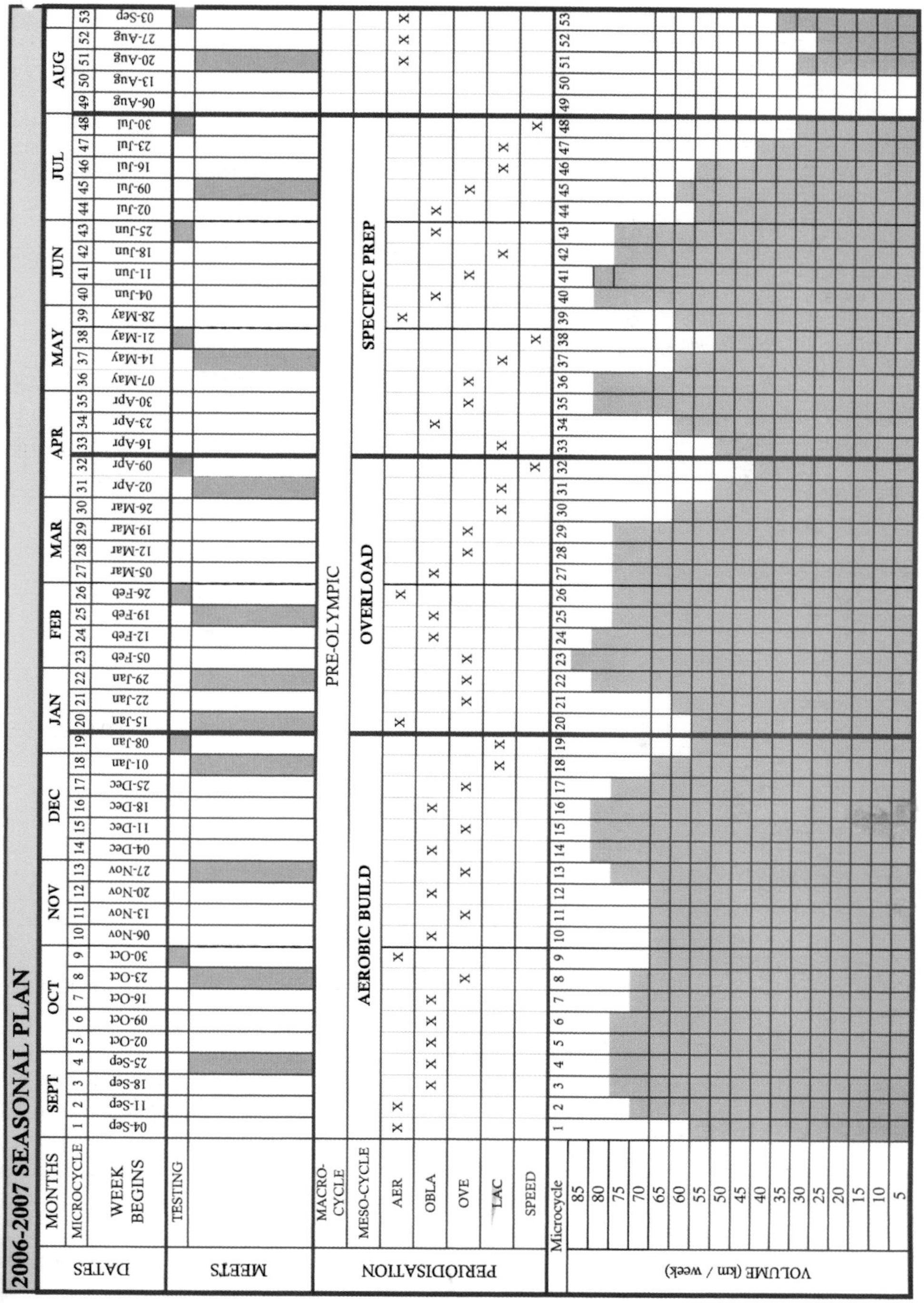

Figure 36 Macrocycle for distance swimmer.

Figure 37 Microcycle for distance swimmer.

TRAINING PHASE - overload mesocycle

DAY	MONDAY	TUESDAY	WEDNESDAY	THURSDAY	FRIDAY	SATURDAY	SUNDAY
DATE	05–Feb–06	06–Feb–06	07–Feb–06	08–Feb–06	09–Feb–06	10–Feb–06	11–Feb–06
A.M.							
[MAIN SET]	AER	OVE	AER	AER	AER	OVE	REST
Distance	7.2	8.0	6.2	6.0	8.0	7.8	
P.M.							
[MAIN SET]	OBLA	AER	OBLA	OVE	AER	AER	REST
Distance	7.4	6.6	6.0	7.8	6.2	7.8	
LAND	X		X		X		
DAILY TOTAL	14.6	14.6	12.2	13.8	14.2	15.6	0.0
							85.0

Figure 38 Set for distance swimmer.

Session Planning Sheet

Coach:	Date:	Tuesday 6/02/06	Time:	0600-0830 (LC)

Session aims / objectives: Overload Aerobic

#	Description		Total
1	Warm-up		
		8 x 200 Free on 3.00	
		as 50 Free, 50 Back, 25 Fly, 25 Brs, 50 IM order	
		last 4 faster than 1st 4	*1600*
2	Kick		
		400 on 6.45	
		300 on 4.55	
		200 on 3.15	
		100	*1000*
3	Pull	8 x 150 on 2.00	
		3 with paddles & buoys; 3 with buoys only; 2 with paddles only	*1200*
4	Main Set		
		7 x 500 on 6.15	
		Odds - neg split and progressively faster	
		Evens - hold stroke count & breathe hypoxic 5	*3500*
5	Swim-Down		
		14 x 50 on 50	
		1–5 Back	*700*
		6–10 Free	
		11–14 choice as 10m fast/40m easy	*8,000m*

intensity (especially too high) will not result in the correct training effects, and as with the previous three errors, can have very damaging effects.

- Excessive technical demands of complex skills – 'forcing' skill learning usually has the opposite effect from that desired, namely poorer techniques through an inability to complete the task. This error may also result in injuries.
- Excessive number of competitions – closely related to the factors controlling over-training, over-competing can have debilitating physical and mental effects (this is often a common error in young swimmers in their development years).
- Frequent changes in daily routine – change for change's sake is not a good justification for altered training plans. Adaptations will only occur when the training has had a chance to take effect.
- Exaggeration of one training method – staleness and/or over-emphasizing any one type of training are not conducive to improvements.
- Frequent failures due to over-ambitious training or performance goals – again, a combination of physical and psychological errors; swimmers need to experience both success and failure in order to develop their ultimate potential.

This list is by no means an exhaustive or complete one, and there are many other reasons why a swimmer may under-perform. What it does highlight however, is the complexity of the task of accurate training prescription.

[1]Rhea, M. R., Alvar, B. A., Burkett, L.N. & Ball, S.D. (2003) 'A Meta-Analysis to determine the dose response for strength development' *Med. Sci. Sports Exerc.*, Vol. 35, No. 3, pp. 456–464.

CHAPTER 7

Special Considerations

In addition to accurate and appropriate, 'traditional' forms of training, there are some special considerations for the high performance swimmer and coach to think about. The use of altitude training is as debatable and controversial today as it has been for the past thirty years; innovative technology to transfer land gains to the pool is expensive but arguably very beneficial; and the introduction of auditory cues to assist stroke technique and tempo has become increasingly popular in the past decade. Allied to which, the intricacies of tapering for performance are always worth discussing. Each of these opportunities is examined and discussed with practical examples provided.

ALTITUDE TRAINING

> High altitude training is a necessary training regimen in today's élite endurance sports. (Orjan Madsen, head coach German national swim team)

This proposition is not one shared by everyone in the fields of coaching or sports science, and there is a very clear division between those who support altitude training, and those who are opposed to its use with élite athletes. However, a closer examination of all the issues surrounding altitude training reveals a myriad of problems with conflicting terminology, the 'positivism of science', and the art of coaching. As you ascend to altitudes above about 1,000m (a little over 3,000ft), the amount of oxygen

that is carried by the haemoglobin (Hb) in the blood is reduced, resulting in less oxygen being delivered to exercising muscles. In endurance sports and events that rely on the availability of large amounts of oxygen, a decrease in delivery results in below-normal performance. However, this is mostly true only in low-speed endurance events, such as running, swimming, paddling and rowing. In high-speed endurance events, such as speed skating and cycling, the lessened air resistance experienced at altitude is more beneficial than is the loss of aerobic power, and performance is actually better at moderate altitude – for instance, in cycling, the world record for 1km (track) is some 2sec faster at altitude than the next best sea-level time.

With time spent training at altitude, the body makes some adjustments, and performance at altitude will improve over a period of several weeks. But regardless of the time spent at altitude, sea-level performances in slow-speed endurance events will never be matched at altitude. In fact, if previous sea-level times are matched at altitude, this usually means that sea-level times will reach new bests upon return to sea level. In as little as two weeks, altitude performance can be noticeably improved, and within about six weeks of altitude training, acclimatization will be quite complete. However, improvement in altitude performance may continue for much longer as you learn to compete in the unfamiliar environment of altitude. There are two distinctly different types of acclimatization taking place: a physiological one and a competitive one, with the latter type staying with you even after long periods of time back at sea level. You tend always to remember how to race at altitude – just ask anyone who has!

Any altitude at which you can perform quality training is useful, but moderate altitudes, in the range of 1,600–2,600m (5,000–8,500ft), are felt by most coaches and scientists to be ideal; for instance, Northern Arizona University's Centre for High Altitude Training at Flagstaff at 2,134m (7,000ft) elevation is certainly right in the middle of that range, and has become a popular destination for swimming teams from all over the world. At this altitude there are seldom any problems with altitude sickness, and normal amounts and relative intensities of training are generally easier to maintain.

Performance at altitude will probably improve about 4 per cent with adequate acclimatization. When returning to sea level, any improvement in performance is more a function of how much room the individual has for making improvements. There have been major improvements by some athletes, but when this is the case, it is usually a matter of the individual not being in top fitness prior to the altitude stay. Think of altitude training as just another type of training, and if you improve, then it was the right thing for you; if not, then, just like making a major change in weekly mileage, the change may have not been right for you at that particular time. Coaches and swimmers using altitude training in their annual and quadrennial plans should periodize and integrate altitude training in the same way they do every other form of training: it is not a quick fix, a magic pill or in any way an easy option.

Opinion on the benefits of high altitude training is extremely divided. Respected scientists, physiologists, coaches and swimmers on both sides of the argument make point and counter point about the usefulness and physiological effects of, and the individual response to, altitude training. Considerable research, academic papers and hundreds of thousands of observation hours by the brightest coaching minds in the world come to different conclusions. In debating these issues, the popular US-based journal, *Swimming Technique*[1], asks readers to reconcile these two items with the statement that follows them: (i) participants of USA Swimming's National Team Camp went to 13,000ft in October to participate in leadership and team building; and (ii) Chad Carvin trained with the Mission Viejo Nadadores in Colorado Springs for nearly three weeks in November and December. Three days later, unshaved and untapered, Carvin set an American record of 3:42.16 in the 400m Freestyle (short course). Yet now we have the statement:

> Although the field contains many studies, those which are definitive lead to the conclusion that altitude training is not an avenue for enhancing sea-level performances of highly trained swimmers. The practice of conducting altitude training camps for highly élite swimmers is not justified either on physiological grounds or performance benefits...

Thus write Professor Brent S. Rushall and colleagues at San Diego State University and the University of Canberra in Australia. Heresy or reality? the article goes on to speculate. Like the debate on lactate testing, opinion on this subject is clearly separated. Yet thriving businesses in many countries are based on the concept, as are training regimens by some of the world's best swimming coaches for their athletes. For example in 2007, some members of the German national team had spent almost three months at altitude by the end of June, all of this in a half-year that saw them tapering for the World Championships in the Australian springtime.

Altitude Training Top Tips:

Prior to Leaving for Altitude

- Two months before departure have a venous blood sample taken and analyzed for full blood count and ferritin levels.
- If results show low ferritin and/or low Hb, then take an iron supplement.
- A second blood sample should be taken two weeks prior to departure. If ferritin levels are still low, then there is no point in going to altitude and you will significantly increase the risk of getting ill.

Whilst at Altitude

- Initially reduce training intensity.
- Enhance rest and recovery strategy.
- Eat plenty of carbohydrate-rich foods.
- Eat plenty of iron-rich foods and take iron supplements.
- Check and maintain very good hydration.
- Protect yourself against the UVF rays with sun cream.
- Monitor blood counts at least weekly, if not more frequently.
- Monitor key parameters on a daily basis: CK, urea, urine osmolality, weight, resting HR.

Upon Return from Altitude

- Remember the first seven to ten days are crucial, so keep vigilant.
- Continue to eat a carbohydrate-rich diet.
- Enhance your rest and recovery strategies.
- Maintain good hydration.
- Use key training sets to monitor adjustment and therefore training loadings.
- Have a full blood count done within three days of returning.
- Continue with iron supplements.
- Within two weeks of return, perform an aerobic profile test.

The altitude training issue first surfaced in the 1960s in reports of European and Soviet aerobic research. The aftermath of the 1968 Olympics in Mexico City focused on the success of African distance runners. Meanwhile researchers in the 1970s, particularly in the Eastern Bloc, pressed on, resulting in some fairly clear messages to coaches and swimmers: that altitude affects physiology, individual response and preparation for competition; that management of the process is critical, especially in the transitional ascent and descent phases; and that whether and whom altitude training helps continues today as a lively issue of debate between the coaching and scientific communities.

The East-West divide in terms of altitude training philosophies exists to this day. The approach in the West is to consider classical scientific parameters (VO_2max, blood profiling and so on) in a 'before and after' scenario. In other words, did the exposure to altitude training have a beneficial physiological effect? The Eastern (European) approach is to consider this scenario from the opposite point of view, namely what are the requirements of the sport? How do we plan training according to this? And then finally, how will this be monitored? Very often this results in a more applied, rather than laboratory, setting.

Disagreement between coaches and scientists remains relatively subdued when the subject comes to elementary physiology. Exposure to altitude has been shown to affect nearly every physiological system in the human body, from ventilatory, cardiovascular, circulatory, central nervous, endocrine to muscular response. There is agreement that factors such as iron supplementation for everyone before, during and after altitude is a must; that weight loss is almost inevitable; that there is the likelihood of a decrease in testosterone levels; and probably most important of all, that staying hydrated is absolutely crucial. The author has conducted several altitude training camps, and can testify to each of these being highly significant. From a physiological standpoint, the body reacts to altitude with an acute increased ventilation of the lungs, increased Hb and enhanced oxygen extraction by the tissues. Response is immediate upon arrival, and varies from three to twenty-one days, based on the level of altitude attained.

The 1968 Olympic Games in Mexico highlighted the fact that the reduced density of air at altitude has beneficial effects on land-based sprinting performance. Drag is significantly reduced at altitude, resulting in (a) higher speeds for a given power output, and (b) lower energy cost to maintain a given speed. Performance standards, such as those by Bob Beaman in the long jump, were significantly enhanced, and records in these events stood for many years. However, the same reduced drag benefits are not possible in swimming due to the medium of water being of identical density to that at sea level.

In metabolic terms, there is considerable interest in the effects of altitude exposure on sprint performance. Events lasting less than one minute – namely all 50m and some 100m swimming events – are generally not impaired at moderate altitude. Such activities place minimal demands on the O_2 transport system and aerobic metabolism, leading some coaches and scientists to conclude that altitude training is an effective training mode for sprinters. However, other than a decrease in peak blood lactate accumulation at altitude, there is little scientific evidence to support this contention.

Most studies of altitude training have focused on endurance performance, for the likely reason that adapting to shortage of oxygen should enhance performance in events that are limited by ability to consume oxygen. In a controlled study, Martino et al[2] found major improvements in a 100m swimming test, and in peak and mean power of the upper body in a short all-out test. However, question marks surround the use of the control group in this study (Rushall et al, 1998)[3], and as yet the results have not been reproduced by other researchers. Mizuno et al[4] discovered that after an exposure to altitude, muscle buffering capacity increased, but they did not measure sprint performance. Further research in this area is needed to better understand these mechanisms. Although some scientific investigations have examined the effect of altitude on endurance athletes with direct measures of performance – for example, 5,000m time trials (Levine et al, 1992)[5] – many more studies have examined the effect of altitude exposure on maximal oxygen uptake (VO_2max). According to Wilmore and Costill[6], VO_2max is not affected by low-altitude exposure (that is, up to 1,600m), but decreases exponentially by approximately 11 per cent for every 1,000m of increase in elevation.

The most important physiological adaptations to living at high altitude are increased ventilation of the lungs, increased blood haemoglobin, and enhanced extraction of oxygen by the tissues. Several points are worthy of further discussion from this statement, allowing for the fact that adaptations will be altered at different elevations of exposure. Increased ventilation is beneficial at altitude, as it serves to increase oxygen delivery to the working muscles. This response is immediate upon arrival at altitude, more pronounced during the first few days, and stabilizes within six to ten days. The body attempts to move greater amounts of oxygen into the lungs by increasing respiratory rate, tidal volume or both. An increased oxygen transport capacity of the blood is the second stage of the acclimatization response to a decreased partial pressure of oxygen. Depending on the elevation, this could occur over the first few weeks of exposure. It is sometimes referred to as a natural form of blood doping.

It is commonly asserted that increased total blood haemoglobin should contribute to enhanced altitude performance. However, it has not been shown to improve performance on return to sea level. Additionally, there is evidence to support the fact that early increases in haemoglobin are due to a decrease in plasma volume, rather than improved manufacture of red blood cells. After four to seven days, 'real' Hb levels begin to increase at a rate of 1 per cent per week up to a ceiling of 12 per cent (Wolski et al 1996)[7]. To gain these benefits, athletes would have to undertake training camps of up to twelve weeks' duration, which are impractical and unlikely for many other economic and social reasons (although the German swim team mentioned previously do come close to this!).

The enhanced extraction of oxygen is a reaction that takes place in untrained individuals when exposed to altitude. Four main tissue-level changes occur: (a) increased muscle and tissue capillarization; (b) increased myoglobin concentration; (c) increased mitochondrial density; and (d) enzyme changes that enhance oxidative capacity. However, in highly trained aerobic athletes, oxygen extraction at the cellular level is already highly developed. To maximize O_2 transport at altitude, all links in the delivery, extraction and utilization phases of the aerobic mechanisms must be altered. If the term of altitude exposure is long enough, eventually all changes will be completed and maximal aerobic benefits will have occurred. However, oxygen delivery at altitude will still be less than it would be at sea level if aerobic fitness were fully trained prior to going to altitude.

The increased use of anaerobic metabolism at altitude as a substitute for reduced aerobic function is evidenced by the body's alteration in fuel use. Altitude exposure increases the utilization of blood glucose both at rest and in exercise, and skeletal muscle is the predominant site of glucose disposal at high altitude. Altitude acclimatization decreases reliance on free fatty acids as a fuel, and increases the use of blood glucose in both rest and exercise. These changes in fuel use indicate marked alterations in the metabolism underlying both exercise and recovery. It clearly has marked implications for a particular emphasis on nutrition control at altitude training.

During altitude training camps, total food intake and consequently CHO intake has been found to be decreased by anything from 10–50 per cent (Numela et al, 1996)[8]. There is also a greater reliance on CHO as a fuel for exercise at altitude, as it appears to be a more efficient energy source for work at reduced oxygen tension. Without effort on the part of the athlete to increase food and, in particular, CHO intake, there is likely to be a reduction in glycogen resynthesis after training sessions, and consequently an overall decrease in muscle glycogen stores. Insufficient replacement of CHO may lead to hypoglycaemia, altered protein metabolism (discussed later in relation to blood urea markers), central fatigue and ultimately exhaustion. Taking CHO supplements as glucose polymers has been shown to improve endurance at altitude, almost certainly due to improved muscle glycogen repletion.

Fluid requirements at altitude may be greater than those at sea level because of the low humidity of the atmosphere and the hyper-ventilation associated with altitude exposure. The higher the altitude the lower the humidity, and the quicker the sweat evaporates from the skin. This can lead to athletes thinking that they are sweating less than usual, which may lead to less actual consumption of fluid. An inappropriate thirst response, coupled with an increase in insensible water loss and the diuretic effect caused by altitude at the initial stages of exposure, can result in rapid dehydration. This has obvious health considerations, as the body copes with the elevated environment, and, combined with the previously discussed CHO intake, can quickly lead to an overtrained athlete. Athletes starting out at altitude with low body stores of iron may experience difficulty once the increase in red blood cell production is stimulated (Gore et al 1997)[9]. If appetite is depressed in any way, this may further restrict adequate intake of iron from food.

Prior to embarking on an altitude programme, it is essential that a complete biochemical analysis is done to highlight such issues. Simple supplementation with iron tablets can easily alleviate any identified deficiencies. In addition, vitamin supplementation may be necessary from such analysis, and quantities of vitamins C and E can help iron absorption and protect red blood cell formation.

Altitude training is just one part of the process of developing a swimmer to high performance. If the planning starts, as it should, with the career peak and works backwards, then altitude training becomes one constituent part of the process similar to strength training using weights. At a particular age and developmental stage, altitude camps are introduced and thereafter used systematically throughout the development of the swimmer. (Rushton, 1992)

This statement was made in a report by the then GB national team coach Clive Rushton, after visiting a series of altitude training camps conducted by the East German national swim team in 1992 (Rushton is now performance director for New Zealand Swimming). The use of altitude training by international swimming teams over the past three decades can be categorized into three main types:

- Live high/train high (LHTH): the classic format, where athletes live and train at altitude in purpose-built élite facilities. The US swimming base at Colorado Springs is an excellent example of this at moderate altitude.
- Live high/train low (LHTL): in recent years, attention in the scientific and coaching communities has focused on the live high/train low type of altitude training, either through the use of facilities at the top and bottom of mountains, for example Sierra Nevada/Granada in Spain, or through the use of regular sea-level swimming pools and by sleeping/living in simulated altitude chambers/houses/tents.
- Live low/train high (LLTH): the opposite of the previous example, mainly for residents of the areas where élite mountain-top facilities exist.

In terms of periodizing altitude training, there are generally three types, using the LHTH approach described above (shown in Fig. 39). Taking one of these as an example, the following structure and content of a Type B Camp is shown in Fig. 40.

In order to gain the optimum advantage from altitude training there are established guidelines for effective coaching practice that are followed in swimming:

- Swimmers must be in complete health prior to attending an altitude camp. Any minor ailments or problems may be exacerbated by the environmental conditions at altitude.
- High levels of fitness are required in order to maximize the benefits of the camp, and reduce the risk of overtraining.
- The work planned must be at the correct intensity, especially in the initial orientation period after arrival at altitude, and in the final regeneration period prior to returning to sea level.
- Special microcycle design is required to get optimal results from the camp.
- Nutritional requirements are crucial to the successful adaptations being sought. Adequate fluids, appropriate nutrients, and vitamin/mineral supplements must also be provided.
- Rest and contrasting activities must be planned to allow adaptations to occur.

Figure 39 Models of altitude training used in swimming.

Type	Aim	Duration	Within macrocycle
A	Improve general fitness, particularly aerobic capacity	10–14 days	Early season, first mesocycle, 3rd & 4th microcycles.
B	To prepare for high-intensity training following altitude.	21 days	After preparation phase, before hardest mesocycle of training.
C	Improve competition performance	15–21 days	In final major competition mesocycle, finish within 4 microcycles of final peak.

Figure 40 Training structure and content of a TypeB altitude camp for swimmimg.

HIGH ALTITUDE TRAINING CAMP																				
21 days duration																				
I	2	3	4	5	6	7	8	9	10	11	12	13	14	15	16	17	18	19	20	21
6 microcycles																				
2 days		4 days			4 days			4 days			4 days			4 days				3 days		
4 PHASES																				

2 days	7 days	10 days	2 days
-------	----------------------------	--	-------
ADAPT	BASIC TRAINING	SPECIFIC TRAINING	ADAPT
AI/2	AI/2	AI/2	AI/2
Land	Sp/Pwr	[T]	Land
	Dryland work	MVO$_2$	
		Lac Tol & Prod	
		Sp/Pwr	
		Dryland work	

A key element of planning for altitude training is the monitoring of training loads and responses. The British Olympic Association (Godfrey *et al*, 1997)[10] have produced a rationale for testing swimmers at altitude, including: (i) self-report questionnaires, including resting heart rate, completed daily by each swimmer; (ii) daily urine analysis to test osmolality; (iii) venous blood tests of full blood count, ferritin, testosterone, and cortisol; (iv) blood urea tests as a marker of physical stress from training; (v) creatine kinase tests to monitor recovery from intense training; and (vi) blood lactate and heart-rate tests to monitor training intensity and response levels. In Part 3 of the book, the issue of training monitoring and evaluation is covered in more detail, with examples of altitude training camps given.

TETHERED SWIMMING

Swimmers and coaches have always been on the lookout for innovative ways to improve performance. In the post-World War II era, 'tethered swimming' became fashionable and has progressed significantly from its early days of fixed ropes and cords. As the training method developed, more pliable materials have been used and rubber tubing of varying thicknesses and lengths employed according to the demands of the programme. More recently, even more ingenuous equipment has been invented to regulate and quantify this type of training, and support the efforts of all those determined to eke out precious hundredths of a second in the quest for major championship glory.

The oldest of these inventions is the 'Power Rack'©, where quite simply a vertical stack of discs or plates (usually associated with weight training) and a set of pulleys are attached to the swimmer by means of a cord and belt system. The swimmer swims a short distance (up to 15m/50ft) for a short period of time (6–8sec) against the resistance of the plates, and then swims easy back to the start, repeating this process in the manner of normal interval training, for example 10×10m on 60sec. A number of highly successful sprint programmes across the world have used this equipment, notably coach David Marsh at Auburn University, and one of his former swimmers, Bill Pilchuk, now a coach at the British Swimming High Performance Centre in Swansea. Many of the world's fastest swimmers are exponents of skilled and explosive performance on the Power Rack© and its descendants.

The next iteration of this equipment, the 'Power Tower'©, is credited to coach Frank Busch of the University of Arizona. As with the rack, the tower is mainly used in high intensity sprint training. Water buckets are attached to aircraft cabling, and the cable is attached to an adjustable belt, which is worn around the swimmer's waist. However, the tower differs from the rack in that it uses 25m (80ft) cables rather than the previous, shorter versions; it uses refillable water buckets instead of weights, resulting in a much lighter and more manoeuvrable set-up; it has a non-corrosive aluminium frame; and significantly it features dual buckets, cables and belts for two swimmers to train at a time as opposed to one. This also creates head-to-head training situations for competition and increased intensity.

As with the rack, the swimmer attaches the belt around the waist and then, in the water, pushes from the wall as if doing a normal sprint. The bucket in the Power Tower, filled with water, rises as the athlete swims away from the machine, creating resistance that can be overcome by the swimmer generating power. Unlike the rack, the more sophisticated tower can also pull the swimmers back, allowing them to swim at very fast speeds.

The most recent version of the tool is the Swim-Stack©, described by its creator Henryk Lakomy of Loughborough University as a 'precision-engineered weight stack attached to the swimmer in the water'. Like the rack and the tower, it is based around the concept of a resistance machine in the gym.

Figure 41 The Swim-Stack.

The complex pulley system offers swimmers and coaches flexibility and challenge (Fig. 41), particularly in their efforts to generate speed and power in the water. This most modern version of the traditional 'tethered swimming' form of training can also operate in two distinctive ways: resisted and assisted swimming (Figs. 42a & b illustrate both modes). When swimming away from the stack, the applied load resists the swimmer in the same way as the Power Rack. In contrast, when swimming back towards the stack, the swimmer feels the assistance of the load and can generate faster than normal speeds.

Each of these pieces of equipment should be located in line with, and up to 5m (16ft) from, the end of the lane or pool side; the best distance is around 2.5m (8ft) from the lane end, and ideally without the obstruction of

Figure 42a Resisted swimming with the Swim-Stack.

Figure 42b Assisted swimming with the Swim-Stack.

starting blocks directly in front. It is best if swimmers attach the belt when they are outside the pool and gently slip into the water (Figs. 43a & b); they should never dive into the pool whilst attached to the machine. The cord is placed at the back of the belt for freestyle, breaststroke and butterfly, and on the stomach for backstroke, when swimming against resistance. The position of the cord is reversed for assisted swimming; that is, behind the swimmer for backstroke and on the stomach for freestyle, breaststroke and butterfly.

In the resisted mode, the Swim-Stack provides specifically loaded resistance training for swimming, which is useful for both prescribing training and measuring improvements. The swimmer can swim up to 25m (80ft) against preset variable loads. As a consequence of the pulley arrangement, the actual resistance felt by the swimmer is one-tenth of the load lifted – so if the load lifted is 50kg

(110lb), then the resistive load to the swimmer is 5kg (11lb) or fifty Newtons (50N). This is useful for prescribing training loads, and is easily used in the application of the progressive overload principles of training, when early in the season, greater loads may be used, and during taper, very light resistance can be applied. As with the other equipment, the stack can be used not only to train the full swimming stroke, but also leg drive for starts and turns. It can also be used to develop power when pulling with the arms or kicking the legs in isolation.

In the assisted mode, the stack helps the swimmer to propel themselves at a greater speed than they can generate themselves. Additional assistance may also be provided by the coach 'pulling' the swimmer towards them, although care must be taken with this exercise. In order to benefit from the assistance of the stack, swimmers can either swim against the resistance for 25m (80ft), have a rest, then come back, or they can walk up the pool and then start (shown in Figs. 44a & b).

Coaches using any of the swim rack/ tower/stack devices have two main purposes in mind when programming work. Firstly, it is used to develop specific strength and power, assisting with the effective transfer of land training into swimming specific movements. Secondly, it is used to improve energy delivery in muscular contraction with sets targeting specific systems or capacities. Much like plyometric exercises on land, these machines act as a 'bridge' from conditioning work to swimming speed. Fig. 45 gives examples of the types of set that élite coaches use with these machines. They illustrate patterns and sequences for training. Coaches should adapt the loads and distances according to the ability of the swimmer. The Swim-Stack should be used up to three sessions per week as part of a specific strength/power development aspect within the programme. Just as with other sets, there should be a thorough warm-up/preparation followed by an effective swim-down. Figs. 46a-e and 47 give more detailed examples of sets that can be used with this equipment.

Figure 43a, b Using the Swim-Stack.

Figure 44a, b Walking along deck to use the Swim-Stack.

Figure 45 Training sets for the swim rack/tower/stack.

Swim Rep Duration	Number of Reps	Rest (s)	Work: Rest Ratio	Intensity
Basic Speed				
>10s*	4–6 Reps 2–3 sets	40–60s Active	1:6	Max effort
Lactate Tolerance				
>10s	4–6 Reps 2–3 sets	40–60s Active	1:6	Max effort
Lactate Production				
>10s	4–6 Reps 2–3 sets	40–60s Active	1:6	Max effort
200	None		None	Recovery swim

Always swim these sets focusing on CORRECT TECHNIQUE.

THE AQUAPACER

The Aquapacer, as it was first known, was invented in 1993 by coach Patrick Miley, and it was initially a low-key prototype until its international 'coming out parade' at the 1996 Olympics. Britain's Paul Palmer won silver and bronze medals in Atlanta in the 400 and 200m freestyles respectively, and attributed much of his success to his use of the Aquapacer in training. Following on from this, Peter Banks, US coach of double Olympic Champion in the 400 and 800 Free Brooke Bennett, working directly with coach Miley, saw the benefits of the Aquapacer as a way to contrast Bennett's training, improve her performance, and set her new challenges. With a naturally high stroke rate anyway, Bennett and coach Banks used the device to track her rate relative to speed and as an indicator of her training progress and race predictability. Nowadays the Aquapacer is known more commonly by the brand name of 'Tempo Trainer', and is in use by swimming coaches and teachers all over the world as they attempt to improve performance and skills at all levels.

The trainer itself is a two-part, battery-operated device: the base unit is a hand-held programmer with a numeric keypad (*see* Fig. 48). It sends variable frequency audio signals via an infrared link to a second battery-operated unit, which fits under a swimmer's cap or on a goggle strap (see Fig. 49), which was how the first-ever prototype was formed (attaching an old digital watch to a pair of goggles!). The base unit can store up to 120 split times, ninety-nine repeat swims, and up to sixteen programmes. The pacer unit can store as many as four programmes, and timing data can be adjusted to 1/100th of a second.

The early perception was that the Aquapacer was useful purely for stroke rate in the manner of an electronic metronome. In truth, the use of the device is only limited by a coach and swimmer's imagination.

Use the Aquapacer for:
- stroke times
- split times
- setting work/rest intervals
- distance per cycle variations
- pacing turns
- improving streamlining
- developing reaction time
- controlling pace on test sets

Fig. 50 is shown as an example of a training-based application for the Aquapacer. The easiest way to do this is to use a race in which a PB time was established (ideally the race will have been recorded by camera, and accuracy of stroke-rate data checked against this). Use

Figure 46a Distance-controlled Swim-Stack sets.

Swim (m)	Reps x Load (kg)	Rest (s)	Comments
8 x 25m	2 x 15	20	Maximum effort against
	4 x 20		resistance. Return to start after
	2 x 10		each effort-assisted swim
			recovery, then refer to 'rest' column
4 x 100	None	30	Swim fast for 25m concentrating on
			technique. Swim easy 75m
			again focus on technique
200	None	None	Recovery

Figure 46b Distance-controlled Swim-Stack sets.

Swim (m)	Load (kg)	Rest (s)	Comments
2 x 25	10	30	Maximum effort against resistance.
2 x 20	15	40	Return to start after each effort-assisted
2 x 15	20	50	swim recovery, then refer to 'rest' column
1 x 100	None	30	Free swim, best pace: focus on core
			stability and technique
3 x 200	None	None	Recovery, mixed strokes

Figure 46c Distance-controlled Swim-Stack sets.

Swim (m)	Reps x Load (kg)	Rest (s)	Comments
4 x 15	15	45–60	Maximum effort against resistance.
			Return to start after each effort-assisted
			swim recovery, then refer to 'rest' column
2 x 25	None No belt	45–60	Maximum effort: focus on technique
4 x 15	15	45–60	Maximum effort against resistance.
			Return to start after each effort-assisted
			swim recovery, then refer to 'rest' column
2 x 25	None No belt	45–60	Maximum effort: focus on technique

Figure 47 Time-controlled Swim-Stack set.

Swim (s)	Reps x Load (kg)	Rest (s)	Comments
4 x 5	2 x 25	30	Maximum effort against resistance.
4 x 7	4 x 15	40	Return to start after each effort-assisted
2 x 10	2 x 10	50	swim recovery, then refer to 'rest' column
2 x 10	2 x 10	50	Maximum effort against resistance.
4 x 7	4 x 15	40	Return to start after each effort-assisted
4 x 5	2 x 25	30	swim recovery, then refer to 'rest' column
200	None	None	As 25 hard, 25m easy throughout
200	None	None	Easy

Figure 48 The Aquapacer.

Figure 49 Inserting the Aquapacer.

Figure 50 Practical application of the Aquapacer.

Sets	Aquapacer setting	Comments
BASIC		
#1 stroke:		
4 x 50	Average race tempo	Hold race form
3 x 50	0.01 faster	Swim faster
2 x 50	0.01 faster	Swim faster
1 x 50	0.01 faster	Swim faster
ADVANCED		
#1 stroke:		
4 x 100	Average race tempo	Hold race form
3 x 100	0.01 faster	Swim faster
2 x 100	0.01 faster	Swim faster
1 x 100	0.01 faster	Swim faster

race performance. As an additional parameter you can record heart rates during these types of sets. This is covered in more detail in the next section on testing, but it is relevant to consider the value of this in the context of Aquapacer training, which in itself can be a very effective tool in controlling testing and monitoring situations. I prefer to use the 'Treffene' HR monitor for this purpose (*see* Figs. 51a & b).

In the initial stages of using the equipment, swimmers may feel that the pacer is too fast, but they will soon adjust to the auditory stimulus and become accomplished in its use. As with any and all equipment, maintaining stroke technique is of paramount importance with the Aquapacer. The temptation may be to cut the stroke short in order to stay 'with' the signal, but this should be avoided. Try to emphasize the propulsion of the stroke, and the speed/hand acceleration of the propulsive phase to stay with the pace for as long as possible. If the pace is lost, don't worry, set a target for the next rep of going a little further than before and you will soon be able to hold the stroke rate throughout each lap. The aim is to try and increase the stroke rate while maintaining stroke length. Each time a new PB is set, analyze the stroke rate again and adjust the Aquapacer sets accordingly. The Aquapacer was designed to give programmable lap splits combined with stroke rate, and many swim-

each segment of the race (25sec short course and 50sec long course) to note any changes on stroke rate; this will allow you to chart any decrements in stroke efficiency. In setting up challenging training sets, the Aquapacer can then be set for stroke rate, seconds per stroke, or individual lap times. Using slower stroke rates during training can be part of a progressive set building up to race pace or if the entire set is one of 'quality' you could even set more challenging stroke rates to develop improved

Figure 51a, b A 'Treffene' heart-rate monitor.

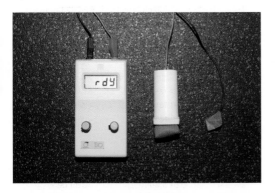

mers/coaches use them very successfully in both modes, notably diverse event specialists such as sprinter Dara Torres and distance swimmer Larsen Jensen.

TAPERING

Tapering is another important area of consideration for the high performance coach and swimmer. It is covered in much more detail in the Crowood books *Sports Guide – Swimming* and *Conditioning for Swimmers: A guide to land-based training*.

The coaching strategy of working swimmers hard and keeping them fatigued for many months was shown to be useful in the days when training usually did not fully stimulate or tax the physical capacities of individuals. As 'hard work' seemed to pay off, coaches logically assumed that if hard work produced desirable results, more and harder work would produce even better results. In swimming, and indeed in sports in general, that approach has been taken to extremes, and

is no longer supported by research evidence or the practices of very successful coaches and athletes. The British swimming team (when under the guidance of coach Bill Sweetenham) operated a strict set of guidelines for competition performances with targets set at 3 per cent, 2 per cent or 1 per cent above lifetime best according to training status, competition emphasis and cyclical planning. This ensured that even at their most tired, and in the hardest phase of training, swimmers had to perform very close to their best.

The underlying belief that has long been touted among swimming coaches is that, although swimmers are always tired and training hard, and that performances are not changing or are even getting worse, good things are still happening to them. That is a false belief. Better swimmers come from periodized programmes, with demonstrable training effects being derived from the judicious use of work and recovery throughout the year. However, there are still significant benefits to be gained from fine-tuning the preparation in the lead-up to the major competition(s) of the season, namely the tapering period.

There are two basic research findings that should govern the underlying considerations for developing a taper:

1 Many coaches fear a loss of conditioning and performance if training is reduced for a long period (at least two or three weeks) before a major competition. Research has clearly shown physiological gains achieved through extensive training are retained even when work volumes are reduced by amounts greater than one half. For some capacities, such as strength, the volume can be reduced to one tenth and the capacity level will still be retained. Even days off are helpful.

2 The major benefit from a taper is the recovery and restoration that it facilitates. The feature that actually influences the competitive performance is the quality and type of training that has preceded the taper. A competitive performance is best considered to be an indication of the training programme that

the athlete experienced, not some magical activity that occurred during the taper. The nature of long-term training governs the type and level of performance that will be exhibited in serious competitions. If that investment is not correct and ultimately specific, high-level performances will not ensue, no matter how effective the taper.

These two principles set the basic guidelines for tapering: they allow rest and recovery to occur fully without confounding the procedure with the fear that conditioning will be lost; and they perform specific performance tasks that will replicate the demands of the intended competitive effort.

A modern interpretation of why tapering works is that only neuromuscular and psychological factors recover – that is, there is little or no change in physiological status. What happens in a taper is that neural and cognitive capacities increase in use efficiency. Strength and power (neuromuscular functions) increase markedly, and the propelling efficiency of strokes (largely a cognitive recovery function) also increases. For these reasons, it is futile to attempt to get 'extra' physiological capacities during a taper. Its programming should allow neural and cognitive performance factors to recover and become more finely tuned.

A number of factors modify the actual length of a taper, all of which relate directly to the principles of training already discussed:

- Individuality in the tapering response. It should not be assumed that a planned taper will be appropriate for all swimmers. For those who recover very quickly during a 'group' taper it may be necessary to reinstitute several days of quality training to delay the peaked state. While that form of training is being followed by some, others might be working lightly as their slower recovery occurs. To accommodate individuality, a coach must be prepared to offer varied programmes for at least subgroups of swimmers so that peaked performances will occur according to the individual needs of athletes.

- The competitive schedule of the swimmer will also determine when a taper should start, and what are programmed as training items. For a swimmer who will compete in the most important event on the fourth day of a championship, the taper should start later than one who has to compete on the first day. However, the opportunity to do controlled convenient swimming is rarely afforded at championship meets. Thus, even though it seems logical to delay the late performing athlete's taper, the nature of the work that can be done over the crucial last three or four days at the competition site may require compromised planning. Usually, the commencement of the taper should be delayed even longer if quality work and volume cannot be fully exploited at the competitive arena because of the extended rest that will occur there.

- The length of time that a swimmer has been in hard training is proportional to the length of time allocated to a taper. When a season of training is uninterrupted, the taper will be longest. However, when interruptions occur – for example, a swimmer is selected for a trip abroad, goes on holiday, or is injured or ill – those interruptions should affect the length of a taper. Generally it can be assumed that the closer the interruption to a championship meet, the shorter the taper period.

After the optimal time a taper lasts (generally considered to be two to four weeks), performance potential gradually decreases due to the less than adequate volume of event-specific training. Performance standards can remain very high past this period, but the swimmer gradually loses important performance capacities.

> The general length of a taper should be two to four weeks, but certain events can intervene and warrant shortening its duration.

It is possible to extend the effects of a taper by alternating short bursts of intense training (actions that re-stimulate the specifically prepared physiological and biomechanical functions) with recovery. This occurs when there are a number of important swimming competitions in close proximity, for example in 2000 and 2004, the US Olympic Trials were held very close to the actual Olympics themselves. Apart from coping with the demands of travelling across the globe, the swimmers who took part in both competitions were able to sustain such a high level of performance that they were still breaking records on the final day of swimming each time. There are many reasons for these performances, not least of which are the excellent training and preparation programmes of the swimmers and their coaches – but it is also fair to say that without the judicious use of work and rest principles in the 'tapering' period between competitions, the ultimate performances may not have been possible.

> Taper effects can be extended by the judicious use of quality training stimuli on a maintenance training schedule.

The volume of work in a taper should be reduced to at least 60 per cent of that which existed during heavy training. However, for programmes that have had excessive volumes of training (for example, eleven sessions per week, 12km/7.5 miles per day), the reduction could be to a level even below this. The principle of individuality has to be considered as a major moderating variable for determining the appropriate length of the training volume reduction. Higher volume training in the immediate days preceding an event may be detrimental to performance, while a slow reduction in volume will have a beneficial effect on maximizing competition preparation.

Some form of consistent performance measurement on at least an alternate day schedule can be performed without any undue effect on competition performances. Times should be expected to improve gradually as the taper progresses.

> For a taper, training volume should be reduced to 60 per cent of normal heavy training volume.

The nature of the volume reduction should be by the session. Eleven training sessions a week should be gradually reduced to about half this number. It is wrong to continue an excessive number of sessions while performing smaller training session loads, however the mistake of removing all morning sessions from the schedule should not be made. Swimmers need to be able to swim fast in both morning (heat) and evening (semi or finals) races. Eliminating morning sessions would be a fundamental error in final preparations for a major meet (particularly as commercial demands have dictated that the Beijing Olympic finals will be in the morning to suit the US domestic television market).

Some reasons why sessions should be reduced are: (a) the sessions off allow for greater recovery and energy restoration, (b) the added rest time allows stresses from sources other than swimming to be tolerated, and (c) there is a greater potential for restorative sleep to occur.

> The number of training sessions should be reduced in a taper rather than reducing session loads, but balanced daily swimming should be a primary consideration.

The way the volume decrease should occur is not clear either from research or from the practice of successful coaches. Neither a stepwise nor a sudden decrease in volume appears to be any better than the other. It is suggested that tapering really only allows recovery, and that final performances are related more to the type of training that precedes it rather than what is done in the taper itself. It is hard to imagine how a few isolated events that occurred during a taper would be strong enough to override the conditioned strength of responses developed through very extended periods of demanding training requiring specific adaptations.

> The major purpose of a taper is to allow athletes to recover from various forms of fatigue.

The most important variable for influencing competition performance is the specificity of work that precedes the taper. That work should (a) be of the same pace as the anticipated performance level so that biomechanical patterns can be refined under varying levels of fatigue; (b) be of the same energy demand ratio (aerobic: anaerobic) to that demanded in each event; and (c) require the same psychological control functions that will be needed in each race. If a swimmer has several events, then each should be trained for specifically. A taper should continue specific training stimuli, and should eliminate all non-specific demanding training experiences.

Non-specific training – for example, slow swimming, kicking, use of swimming paddles, flippers, and so on – should only be used to provide variety and low-demand recovery activities. During a taper, the body should become highly sensitized to the specific qualities required for targeted events, and desensitized to irrelevant activities. That desensitization is important, because when a swimmer is tired in a race, the body has to determine which established forms of activity will be recruited to assist in performance maintenance. If there are slow-swimming patterns that are high in conditioned strength, they will be recruited and performance will suffer. If the body only knows fast-swimming patterns, then its selection options are limited to them, and consequently, fast swimming will be maintained. The activities programmed in the taper should always reinforce race-specific movement patterns and energy use.

If a swimmer intends to seriously contest several races, the demands of training (and subsequently of tapering) will be more complex as the set 'paces' of all events should be trained. The difficulty with meeting this criterion is that excessive training is possible when ideally the training load of the taper should be reduced incrementally. To compromise on this dilemma, any paces that are common to several events should be accommodated before a pace that is unique to a single event. Event preferences will also determine the importance of the selected specific training paces in the taper phase.

> The work performed in a taper should be either of race-specific quality or of a recovery nature.

A taper will allow the specific training effects that have occurred, particularly in the late specific preparatory and pre-competition training phases, to emerge. The continuing of only race-specific training will heighten an athlete's and the body's awareness of the qualities of race requirements, and that heightened sensitivity will increase the consistency of competition performance quality. Broken swims are a common way of ensuring that swimmers remain 'on task' during a taper.

Research tells us that improvements in performance during taper occur without changes in VO_2max, which suggests that the primary physiological changes are likely to be associated with adaptations at the muscular level rather than with oxygen delivery. Measuring VO_2max does not adequately reflect the positive effects of tapering in swimmers. Taper does not appear to affect sub-maximal post-exercise measurements (lactate, pH, bicarbonate, base excess) and heart rate. Blood measures have not been conclusively documented as being related to the taper phenomenon, and although not measured in swimmers, muscle glycogen and oxidative mechanisms have both been observed to increase in tapers in other sports.

> Improvement in power is probably the major factor responsible for the improvement in competitive swimming performance through taper.

If it is too late to attempt to correct any physically conditioned state or biomechanical flaw during a taper, and it is detrimental to institute a short period of intense quality training in the belief that a 'little more' physical capability will be developed, the only option for training during a taper is specific work that yields positive affirmations of a swimmer's readiness.

Psychological factors are the major ingredients of performance that *can* be changed and improved during a taper. Positive thinking, self-concept, self-efficacy and performance predictions should be developed to assist in developing a healthy approach to recovery and the impending competition. The development and refinement of mental skills are the major activities of tapering that will have the most direct transfer to the competitive situation. A large amount of time at training, and in particular at the competition site, should be spent honing mental control skills: for example, practising activities such as warm-ups for specific races, focusing, controlling simulated race segments, evaluating segment goals and rehearsing mental control content. A large section of tapering content should focus on psychological skills, specific mental control rehearsals, and the development of a group or team orientation. Part 4 of this book devotes considerable attention to these factors.

A number of other factors also moderate the effects of a taper and warrant adjustments in planning:

- Young swimmers require a shorter taper period than do older swimmers. Growing children and adolescents tire and recover more quickly than do mature adults, therefore adjustments in taper lengths should be made according to the developmental age of each swimmer.

- With the reduced load (energy demand) associated with tapering, swimmers have to reduce their food intake. If normal eating habits and volumes are maintained, weight gains are possible which, although minor, could have a slight detrimental effect on the swimmer.

- The first stage of a taper often produces a 'bloated' feeling because of extra water retention in the muscles. For every gram of glycogen, 3g of water is stored, and this often produces a feeling of being heavy or sluggish.

- 'Shaving down' has been shown to have mechanical and consequent physiological benefits, as well as the less tangible, psychological boost of feeling more 'sleek' in the water (see the discussion on 'Ergogenics' in Part 3 for more information on this).

- An increase in the number of high carbohydrate meals should occur, particularly as the competition occurs. This 'loading' should commence before travel and be maintained throughout the entire precompetition and competition period. High carbohydrate diets assist athletes to tolerate stress.

- Swimmers will usually increase their own internally generated pressures to improve performance. The more important the competition, the greater will be the level of self-imposed pressure. Since all swimmers have a limited capacity for handling pressure, it is usually wise to attempt to reduce external stresses – those emanating from parents, officials, the media, the coach – so that total pressure is manageable.

- An important psychological theme of a taper and competition preparation should be to remove uncertainty. This can be achieved if the coach increases his/her own level of planning and communication. The better a swimmer is made aware of what will happen and how things will be organized, the less stressful will be the impending travel and competitions. If the coach changes to a noticeable elevation in preparedness and communication, a positive model will be provided for athletes of heightened preparations and better forms of conduct as the competition approaches.

> If swimmers are expected to prepare better and pay attention to important details of their everyday life during a taper, the coach should model similar alterations and increases in attention to detail by planning better and communicating more frequently with swimmers.

- The main performance attribute that changes during a taper is power. Consistent measurement of power, by performing short-distance time trials, can be used to indicate the positive effects of a taper to swimmers.
- The pattern of daily activity that is established in the body, the circadian rhythm, through normal training, does not usually match the timing of activities at a serious swimming meet. Circadian rhythms significantly affect the ability of an individual to perform at a particular time, and adjusting training times to better match the timing of activity that will occur at the competition, as well as time changes that occur through travel, is something that should be programmed. When times for heats and finals are known and time adjustments made, training at those times is desirable before going to the competition – again the Beijing issue crops up, of heats in the evening, finals in the morning. (*See* the information on 'Travel and Jet Lag' for further specific details of this issue.)

> Circadian rhythms need to be synchronized with the demands of the competitive schedule for maximum performances to be achieved.

A taper period and competition preparation phase are stressful for athletes but often more stressful for coaches. Heightened self-monitoring by coaches of their decisions, programmes and actions should occur. Radical alterations in behaviour can signal panic to swimmers, which in turn could destroy their confidence and self-efficacy. To ensure that the coach is a constructive rather than inappropriate model, the following considerations should be contemplated daily:

With regard to the type of swimming that is being performed, to what is the swimmer's body adapting?

Non-specific work will have no value and can be counterproductive. Setting swims at 90 per cent intensity is meaningless to the body. The swimmer's mind may know that intention, but the body will only practise the neuromuscular patterns and stimulate the energy supply that facilitates performing at that less than race-pace speed. Only race-specific paces that require exact energy components and stimulate competition-specific mental control will have beneficial effects on performance. Any other form of swimming should be used for recovery purposes and should not be associated with serious intentions.

> Remove all non-specific training activities.

Are each swimmer's personal needs being accommodated?

Be prepared to rest swimmers at odd times, to programme separate activities, and to attend to personal requirements. The taper is too critical to persist with the convenience of group programming. Simply because it is easy for a coach to set a single programme for all swimmers to follow, this does not mean that it is best for all swimmers. During a taper and at competitions, coaches have to be prepared to work harder than normal, because individualized attention and programming are more demanding than single group control actions.

What assessment swims have been performed to detect lazy or over-eager swimmers?

Gradual recovery, with increasingly better levels of performance, particularly in activities that require a power component, should be expected. If changes are too rapid, then a slowing of the improvement might be achieved by increasing the daily training load. If performances are poor, even though increased rest has been programmed, malingering or outside-of-swimming intrusions should be investigated. Measurement is an essential feature for judging tapering progress. It will *not* consume a swimmer's potential to perform well in a race. A common means of doing this employed by swimmers and coaches is to perform short sections of key test sets used throughout the season to mark progress or race readiness, for example 2 × 400 or 3 × 200, measuring times/splits/stroke rates and finishing heart rate, etc.

Have the swimmers been prepared to do warm-ups, recovery routines and race simulations before travelling to the competition?

A coach should not be afraid to perform event simulations prior to important meets. If an athlete is not practised at performing between-event recovery routines prior to a competition, why should he/she be expected to be proficient at doing them under the stress of competition? There is a real programming need to perform these activities as part of normal training in the pre-competition and taper phases.

Since swimmers are asked to alter their behaviours and become more serious as a competition approaches, the coach should model those expectations by improved behaviours, planning, self-control and provision of individual attention.

The taper has traditionally been given more credit than it deserves for affecting performance. It is primarily a period that allows recovery, restitution, specific practice refinements, and planning of competition behaviours. What will be exhibited in races are the beneficial effects of the training that was experienced prior to the taper.

The psychological activity and state of the athlete becomes increasingly more important as the taper progresses, and should be the primary focus of the programme. It is incorrect to think that skills can be altered in any beneficial manner, or that extra physical condition can be gained by short bouts of intense training. When a taper is started, it is too late to consider any biomechanical or physiological changes to training. As the taper progresses, indications that performance is improving and that competition conduct activities are being practised will have beneficial effects on the athlete's psychological state. If events are predictable, practised, and accompanied by a self-efficacy of performance excellence, then a successful competition is likely.

The role of the coach as the model of seriousness, control, planning, and professional competence is important for swimmers to witness if they are expected to perform in a similar manner. Positive and constructive coaching exhibiting a capacity to cope with any problem in a competent manner will contribute to athletes believing that all conditions exist for them to perform well.

Finally, in relation to the use of land training within the taper: coaches when questioned about land training and individualization during tapering, report that different work is done both in and out of the pool, and some reduction in workloads is programmed – but is this enough? Physiotherapists involved in swimming have clear views that swimmers should stop weight training at least six weeks before a major meet. This may help to reduce any deep-seated muscle tightness – but what about the effects of de-training? Coach Alexyev Krasikov is credited with much of the success of Russian swimming and has clear views on the integrated effects of balanced tapers for swimming. In summary, they are:

Dry-land exercises will be more easily accepted by the swimmer's body if the exercises are administered in the following order: stretching, then strength, speed, or power and finally, relaxation.

Coach Krasikov believes that stretching and relaxation exercises during taper help develop quickness, and relaxed, flawless swimming technique. If muscles are too tense or swimmers can't effectively relax them, the amplitude of movements will be severely impeded during competition, especially when swum with a fast tempo. Consecutive actions of relaxation-contraction and stretching-relaxation are very important elements of every movement. At the beginning of the taper, dry land training has more specificity in its content, and becomes more oriented toward general maintenance during the end of the taper.

Thus the coaches and scientists seem to be at odds with each other once more. There is no empirical basis for this example, but it is undoubtedly part of a highly successful performance programme and coaching practice.

[1]Stott, M. (2001) 'High Hopes: Altitude training for swimmers'. *Swimming Technique*.

[2]Martino, M., Myers, K., & Bishop, P. (1995) 'Effects of 21 days training at altitude on sea-level anaerobic performance in competitive swimmers' *Medicine and Science in Sports and Exercise*, 27, S7 (Abstract 37).

[3]Rushall, B.S., Buono, M.J., Sucec, A.A., & Roberts, A.D. (1998) 'Elite swimmers and altitude training' *Swimming Science Bulletin*.

[4]Mizuno, Mizuno, M., Juel, C., & Rasmussen, T. (1990) 'Limb skeletal muscle adaptations in athletes after training at altitude' *Journal of Applied Physiology*, 68, pp. 496-502.

[5]Levine, B.D., & Stray-Gundersen, J. (1992) 'Altitude training does not improve running performance more than equivalent training near sea-level in trained runners' *Medicine and Science in Sports and Exercise*, 24, S95 (Abstract 569).

[6]Wilmore, J.H., & Costill, D.L. (1994) *Physiology of Sport and Exercise, Human Kinetics* Champaign, Illinois, pp. 268–278.

[7]Wolski, L.A., McKenzie, D.C., & Wenger, H.A. (1996) 'Altitude training for improvements in sea-level performance: is there scientific evidence of benefit?' *Sports Medicine*, 22, 251–263.

[8]Numela, A., Jouste, P., & Rusko, H. (1996) 'Effect of living high and training low on sea-level anaerobic performance in runners' *Medicine and Science in Sports and Exercise*, 28, S124 (abstract 740).

[9]Gore, C.J., Hahn, A.G., Burge, C.M., & Telford, R.D. (1997) 'VO2 max and haemaglobin mass of trained athletes during high intensity training' *International Journal of Sports Medicine*, 18, pp. 447–482.

[10]Godfrey, R., Ramsay, R., & Taylor, S. (1997) 'Physiology service provided to ASFGB altitude training camp: Public Report' British Olympic Medical Centre, Northwick Park, London.

PART 3 HIGH PERFORMANCE SUPPORT SYSTEMS

CHAPTER 8

Developing Efficient Engines

Fig. 52 lists the types of support mechanisms currently available to swimmers and coaches across the world. This isn't intended to be an exhaustive or complete list, merely an illustration of the range of services on offer to assist with preparation for high performance competition. These are all sophisticated resources, and not all of them will be discussed in detail in this section, but they do point to a very systematic coaching process in operation, and show how much attention is being paid to getting the very best out of what is available to our sport.

more easily administer to measure and evaluate the strengths and weaknesses of their swimmers. There are variations of these tests and test sets in common use around the world, so it is the main concepts that matter, not the specifics! Adapt these for use in your programme – you might use a different size pool – but stick to the basics and see your swimmers progress and improve.

Figure 52 Support systems for swimming programmes.

Service	Provider
Musculoskeletal Review	Physiotherapy
Injury Prevention	Physiotherapy
Injury Treatment	Physiotherapy
Sports Massage	Physio/Massage Therapist
Medical Review	Doctor
Blood Profiling	Doctor
Specialist referral	Consultant/ Surgeon
Starts/Turns/Finishes	Biomechanics
Underwater analysis	Biomechanics
Efficiency Test	Biomechanics
Performance Analysis	Biomechanics
Physiological Profiling	Physiology
Body Composition Assessment	Physiology/ Nutritionist
Altitude Training	Doctor/Physiology
Swim-Down Monitoring	Physiology
Assessment of food diary	Nutritionist
Hydration status assessment	Nutritionist
Mental Skills development	Psychology

The following tools are intended to give coaches a series of relevant tests that they can

The Principles of Monitoring and Evaluation

- Validity – ensure the test will measure what you want it to.
- Reliability – ensure that repeat testing is consistent.
- Specificity – particularly in terms of energy systems.
- Environment – check pool temperature, health and recovery status prior to each test.
- Safety – particularly if invasive blood testing is to be used.
- Administration – where possible use the same testers each time.
- Currency – interpret and use the results immediately.
- Clarity – keep things simple at all times!

These swimming test sets should be conducted on a regular basis, and they should form an integral part of the training programme. The tests are:

- Maximum heart rate (HRmax)
- Aerobic profile
- Aerobic capacity

- Aerobic range
- Double distance (DD)
- #1 kick
- #1 stroke efficiency

MAXIMUM HEART RATE TEST (HRMAX)

Warm-up

200m F/c build from easy to moderate pace on 3:15
200m rev IM on 3:15
8 x 50m choice as 25K, 25sw on 1.00
200m #1 stroke build each 50
10 × 50m as – odds #1 stroke 15m sprint then 35m DPS; evens choice drill, all on 60

Test set

200m #1 stroke increasing pace on each 50 to 200 pace
Rest 15sec and swimmers take their HR
3/4 × 100m max. effort, rest 15sec, check HR after each 100m
Minimum 600m recovery

Coaches can extend the 3/4 × 100m further if swimmers do not achieve HRmax (it may take some swimmers 3–4min to reach their HRmax). Heart rate will drop fast, especially in well-trained swimmers if the intensity is reduced or they do broken effort swims. Remember: achieving maximum speed is not the same as achieving maximum HR.

Some additional notes on maximum heart rate:

HRmax is influenced by factors such as the age, gender and genetic profiles of the swimmers (boys will generally have a maximum heart rate five to ten beats lower than that of girls). Resting heart-rate levels can be influenced by adaptations to endurance training, health status and the state of fatigue of the swimmers (suffering from the common cold may elevate your resting heart rate by ten to twenty beats/minute). The difference between the resting and maximum heart rate is the range in which different intensities of exercise are prescribed. Coaches should take care to use the results on HRmax tests in the correct way, with Fig. 51 the favoured method of most swimming coaches.

For example, a coach may (mistakenly) tell two swimmers to swim 15 × 200 holding a heart rate of 160 beats per minute. Why is this a mistake? Well, without properly applying the HRmax data, the swimmers may be working at completely different intensities.

Swimmer A: Maximum heart rate = 205
At 160 beats per minute they are working at 45 beats below their maximum heart rate.
Swimmer B: Maximum heart rate = 180
At 160 beats per minute they are working at 20 beats below their maximum heart rate.

These two swimmers will probably also have completely different resting heart rates, and will therefore be working at very different values above their resting heart rates. From the results of the HRmax test the coach should prescribe training sets based on heart-rate levels at 'beats below' the swimmers' maximum.

Swimmer A: Maximum heart rate = 205
At 30 beats below maximum heart rate they are working at 175 beats per minute.
Swimmer B: Maximum heart rate = 175
At 30 beats below maximum heart rate they are working at 145 beats per minute.

Both swimmers are now working at thirty beats below their maximum heart rate, but have to hold very different (individually relevant) levels.

Administering this test every two to three months during the season gives accuracy and individual relevance to training. Notes should also be kept by coaches of heart rates achieved on other high quality sets, in case the swimmer records a new maximum heart rate.

AEROBIC PROFILE

This test is used during periods of aerobic training to provide information on the endurance status of the swimmer, and to prescribe correct training intensities based on the results. The swimmer is required to perform five progressively faster aerobic swims, and the results are used to plot the aerobic profile of speed, heart rate, lactate, stroke efficiency and RPE data (*See* p. 97). This form of testing is often referred to as a 'step test'. It is important that the swims are even-paced (to demonstrate efficiency in the physiological production and use of energy), and that the test is not swum too fast at the beginning (otherwise it may be difficult to complete five in total).

There is great variation across the world in the distances used for such tests. I would recommend that a time of about 4min per swim is used as the guide (ensuring an aerobic effort), thus faster swimmers may be able to complete 5 × 400m, although others may do anything from 250–400m, depending on stroke and speed parameters. If training (and therefore testing) is to be specific, then the stroke swum on this test should be the swimmer's #1 stroke, i.e. a senior male breaststroker improving their aerobic profile test scores on 5 × 350m freestyle will be of virtually no value for anything other than perhaps indicating their ability to swim a 400m Free!

In terms of administering the test, splits and total times should be recorded, along with stroke rate and stroke data for at least the second portion of the swim (to check efficiency). At the completion of each repeat, heart rate, RPE (Fig. 53) and lactate measures should be recorded. These results can then be plotted, and an aerobic profile of the swimmer compiled for comparative purposes (Figs. 54a-f). In considering an individual's test results, we should be concerned with changes in certain physiological aspects against two main criteria: (i) comparison with the previous test; and, (ii) comparison with the swimmer's best ever test.

The aerobic profile test aims to assess important physiological changes in the swimmer. However, it should not be forgotten that it serves as a valuable 'test in its own right'. Coaches and swimmers should compare their times with previous tests, as they would do with their personal best (PB) times. If a

Figure 53 RPE Chart.

Rating	Description
6	No Exertion
7	Extremely Light
8	
9	Very Light
10	
11	Light
12	
13	Somewhat Hard
14	
15	Hard (Heavy)
16	
17	Very Hard
18	
19	Extremely Hard
20	Maximal Exertion

swimmer is faster throughout the test and records lower scores on all the physiological markers, there would be a great deal of confidence in their ability to swim fast in a 200–400m race on that stroke.

Before looking at some real results for this test, let me point out a common mistake with the use of this kind of data. Several books (and countless sports scientists) refer to the use of the V4 value (the velocity swum at a lactate of 4mmol/l of lactate) as a critical measure in determining not only aerobic potential, but also training speeds. This is a gross misunderstanding of the physiological mechanisms at work in each swimmer, and may lead to the same kind of inappropriate training prescription as that illustrated by asking all swimmers in a squad to swim at a heart rate of 160. Perhaps useful in writing up scientific papers where an arbitrary reference point enables inter- and intra-group comparisons to be made, it is far too general a concept to be of any real use to swimmers and coaches. The most useful implementation of the aerobic profile step test data is in gauging the changes in each swimmer's results from test to test. This can be done at any, and all lactate values, and indeed subtle alterations in these results may have major significance.

Figure 54 a, b, c, d, e, f Aerobic profile test results.

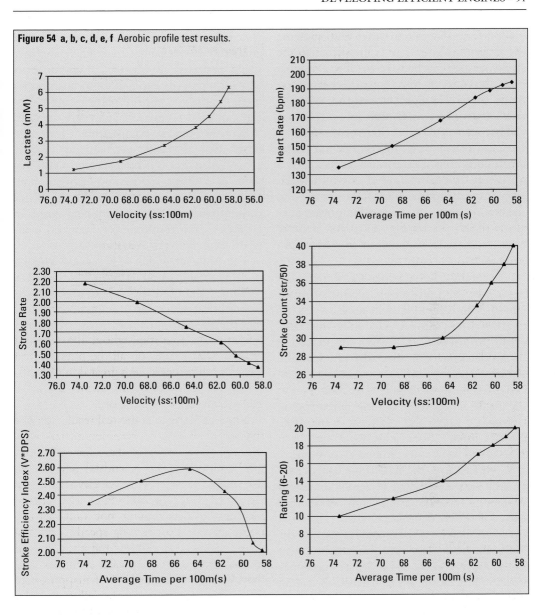

Changes in Lactate Values

Changes in the speed at lower lactate values can indicate changes in a swimmer's stroke efficiency, or an improved ability to mobilize fats as a source of energy. Improvements of these components are positive outcomes of the training process.

A change in the maximal lactate value achieved is also of interest. An increase indicates a greater contribution of energy supply from anaerobic glycolysis, a result that is important in the build-up to an important competition. A significant decrease in the maximal value may indicate either that the swimmer is glycogen-depleted, or that a training phase of primarily aerobic training has been conducted, thereby suppressing the production of lactate.

As described in the HRmax test, knowing the maximum heart rate is important to the swimmer and coach, as most of the training prescribed should be at intensities based on 'beats below HRmax'. Unlike the V4 'mistake' described above, velocity at HRmax (VHRmax – sometimes known as Vcrit or critical velocity) is a useful concept and can be determined from the aerobic profile. It is a good indicator of the speed at which maximum oxygen uptake (VO$_2$max) occurs, and therefore an estimate of aerobic power. It is also valuable in setting times for training levels to develop VO$_2$max or in performing 'overload or heart rate' sets.

The combination of stroke length (SL) and stroke rate (SR) provides a measure of stroke efficiency and has long been used by coaches to good effect (Figs. 54c, d, e show this). It is critical to measure and control this aspect, as stroke efficiency will affect the physiological responses, i.e. the heart-rate and lactate curves. A more efficient stroke will move the curves to the right irrespective of any physiological change. Of course this is a positive outcome, but we need to be sure what has been improved – technique, physiology or both?

In broad terms, the following changes may indicate an improvement in aerobic fitness or swimming economy: (i) shift downward and/or rightward of the lactate curve (Fig. 54a); (ii) a shift downward and/or rightward on the heart-rate graph (Fig. 54b); (iii) improvement in the lower portion of the lactate curve may indicate an increase in fat metabolism and an associated delay in lactate production; (iv) improvements at velocities greater than the 'OBLA' point may indicate enhanced lactate removal or improved buffering capacity; (v) a reduction in stroke count per 50m may indicate an improvement in stroke efficiency. It should also be noted that a non-linear increase in heart rate against stroke rate may indicate deterioration in the swimmer's stroke technique, masking changes in metabolic factors.

The following graphs demonstrate improvements in components of the aerobic profile

test. Fig. 55a shows improvement in aerobic endurance from one test to another; improvements in speeds are observed at all intensities above 2 mmol l-1. Fig. 55b shows an improvement in aerobic overload following a phase of threshold and overload training between tests. When the central components (heart and lungs) that contribute to endurance capacity are considered, it is not surprising to find that there is a direct relationship between both heart rate (HR – beats per minute) and oxygen consumption (VO$_2$) and swimming speed. In both cases, this relationship is linear (as is the relationship between HR and VO$_2$).

The point at which HR reaches a maximum has been found to be closely related to VO$_2$max, and used with some success in the prescription of aerobic training programmes and the prediction of performance. HRmax remains relatively stable throughout various

Figure 55a Improvements in the aerobic profile test.

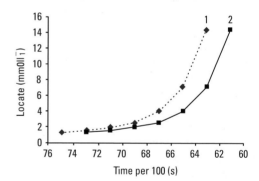

Figure 55b Improvements in aerobic overload shown in the profile test.

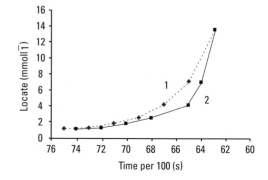

stages of training and periods during an individual's life. However, there is a gradual decline in HRmax as age increases, and the value will not be the same for all swimmers.

Once the test has been completed, the coach needs to be sure that the test has been conducted well and that the information gained from it can be used accurately to evaluate the training process. A number of questions can address this problem and may determine a 'good' or 'bad' test. If the quality of the test was poor, information will be of minimal value and consequently the test should be repeated within a week to gain a better reflection of the swimmer's true performance potential at that time. Illness, injury, poor pacing, fatigue (from a recent competition or training session) and glycogen depletion may impair the quality of the test.

The RPE scale was developed by Gunnar Borg in the early 1980s in an attempt to relate feelings of effort to physiological measures of intensity. The scale is a useful educational tool in allowing swimmers to pace swimming efforts during training. In the test situation, it can provide us with more insight into potential problems that the swimmer might be experiencing. For example, if the swimmer is suggesting a relatively high RPE after the first repetition, it may point to excessive stress on the body and indicate perhaps the onset of illness or muscle soreness from a recent weight-training session. If the final value (after repetition 7) is low, it may suggest that the swimmer is not capable of giving a maximal effort. In conjunction with the lactate levels, the information may indicate that the swimmer is glycogen-depleted or in an aerobic training phase and finding difficulty in sprinting. Comments should be sought from the swimmer in the following instances: (i) if the RPE is not <10 after repetition number 1; (ii) if the RPE is not >18 after repetition number 7.

The SEI is a product of the swimmer's stroke length and speed, and gives an indication of the stroke efficiency during the test. It can be used as a reference point for other tests, but also as a guide to stroke efficiency during different types of training. The higher the SEI value, the better the stroke efficiency. During the step test, the value can often increase as the swimmer swims faster; but on the last repetition, under fatigue, the value can drop as the stroke length shortens.

USING LACTATE TESTING – A HEALTH WARNING!

What do lactic acid measures actually show? Lactates are a partial measure of the amount of anaerobic work that is performed in exercise. In sports where fatigue is specific to the muscles being used, it is higher in some parts of the body than in others. When measures are taken in local-fatigue activities such as swimming, these measures are often less precise. Lactate measures are affected by many factors. Some of the more significant factors are i) diet and nutritional status; ii) state of long- or short-term fatigue; iii) movement efficiency or inefficiency; iv) mental state; v) task perceptions; vi) environmental (e.g. altitude, water temperature), (vii) training status; and (viii) muscle-fibre type, to name but a few.

The existence of these modifying factors will potentially decrease the value of the information that is generated by lactate testing. For accuracy, the control of these factors is very important and is one of the reasons why lactate measures remain popular in research laboratories (where influential variables can be controlled), and why coaches and sports scientists must attempt to control as many of these variables as possible for more accurate results.

In the best circumstances, lactate measures outside the laboratory are relatively gross measures of performance. They may be sensitive enough to measure obvious improvements in early exercise adaptation states, but are not sensitive enough for assessing the subtle changes that occur as the 'trained state' is nearing its maximum capacity. The fitter a swimmer becomes, the less valuable are lactate measures for assessing trained states. However, there is still value in using lactates to measure maintenance of this highly trained state, and for assessing anaerobic capacities via peak lactates, and so on.

Lactate measures do not provide sufficient evidence to make an alteration in an athlete's training programme when they are the sole index used. Coaches must ensure that heart rate, stroke efficiency and RPE data are collected – as shown in this example. Lactates cannot and should not be used to try and predict a swimmer's performance. They concern such a small portion of an athlete's total response that attempts to predict or diagnose performance from its values would introduce more error than accuracy into any forecast. Lactate values must be used with caution, and testing should be limited to simply describing how muscles adapt to different workloads, and whether an overall training adaptation is taking place.

Lactate accumulation is closely related to event and stroke specificity as well as individual differences in exercise response. Thus some races will produce more lactate than others. From the little research that there is on this subject, and the author's experience, the need for a strong buffering capacity is highest for 200m events. This suggests that lactate-tolerance training is very important for 200m swimmers. If similar physiological considerations are compared to other sports – that is, events lasting circa 2min in duration, such as 800m running, downhill skiing, track cycling – we see a comparable pattern of lactate accumulation.

Despite some of these cautionary notes, lactate measures do have some very real practical uses. In the last twenty years they have been used in a variety of innovative ways by progressive thinking coaches. For example, a female distance swimmer is given a set of 10 × 200m holding 800m race pace (2.12) on a turnaround of 3.30, and lactates, heart rates, RPE and stroke efficiency are taken for each swim. The pattern of times, physiological measures and responses can be used to determine much more than a change in training status, and may be a much better indicator of performance potential than a 'step test' alone. So the message is, understand the processes involved, control as many variables as possible, and don't be too restricted in your thinking about how to use lactate measures to improve performance.

AEROBIC CAPACITY

An alternative to the time-consuming and costly aerobic profile testing is to conduct a time-distance test. This is very much a 'field test' in that it only requires a stopwatch and the commitment of the swimmers to complete. The correlation between such tests and the more sophisticated step-testing protocols is actually very good - providing the swimmers are 100 per cent committed to a true and honest effort.

The options are to swim for a set length of time, for example 30min and record the distance swum; or to record the time taken for a set distance, for example 2,300m. Either is suitable, and coaches may vary the format to keep the swimmers motivated. The key outcome from the test is the average speed per 100m, which can then be used as a guide for training prescription. One weakness of this test is that it can really only be completed on backstroke and freestyle. Although there are some swimmers who can perform long distances aerobically on fly and breaststroke, it is not advisable for everyone, and so the profile test is much better.

As before, heart rate and RPE scores can be recorded, and the swimmers can do their own stroke counting on a regular basis, for example the last 25 or 50m of each 200m. Fig. 56a shows the result from a 3,000m test conducted at altitude, and Fig. 56b shows a 20 × 100 test conducted at sea level three weeks later (still on the same training camp).

AEROBIC RANGE

Another field-base test that can be incorporated into training sessions is that to measure 'aerobic range'. Similar in principle to the profile test, swimmers perform a set number of repeats at increasing intensities, and physiological markers are measured and recorded. My favourite version of this test is 3 × (10 × 100m), where each set of ten is a faster average time than the previous one.

Set 1 is a moderate intensity aerobic effort with even-paced times per 100, and corresponds to the lower portion of the velocity-lactate curve; Set 2 is around the OBLA pace – the middle portion of the curve – and should still be achievable in an aerobic sense; Set 3 is in effect a 'heart-rate' set of its own, and should see the swimmers following a best

average time format that is extremely difficult to hold by the last couple of swims.

Coaches should record all times, heart rates and RPE scores throughout, and if possible, lactate values on a regular basis during and especially after the set.

DOUBLE DISTANCE (DD) TEST

The double distance test should be administered following the aerobic profile test, ideally within three days, and certainly not more than five days after to give accurate and relevant comparative results. The swimmer performs a maximal effort swim (from a dive start), double the distance of their best event. The

Figure 56a 3000m aerobic capacity test.

Altitude Training Camp

Sierra Nevada, Spain ~ 16 January – 14 February 2007

Saturday 20th January (LCM)

3000m Fc Time Trial

	100s	500s	Total
100	01:04.8		
200	01:08.1		
300	01:08.5		
400	01:08.7		
500	01:09.1	05:39.2	05:39.2
600	01:09.7		
700	01:09.1		
800	01:09.5		
900	01:09.1		
1000	01:10.6	05:48.0	11:27.2
1100	01:10.5		
1200	01:10.2		
1300	01:10.5		
1400	01:10.3		
1500	01:10.4	05:51.9	17:19.1
1600	01:10.6		
1700	01:10.2		
1800	01:10.7		
1900	01:10.5		
2000	01:11.3	05:53.3	23:12.4
2100	01:11.5		
2200	01:11.4		
2300	01:11.2		
2400	01:11.3		
2500	01.10.2	05:55.6	29:08.0
2600	01:11.0		
2700	01:11.3		
2800	01:09.9		
2900	01:09.0		
3000	01:06.8	05:48.0	34:56.0

Figure 56b 20 x 100 aerobic overload test.

Altitude Training Camp
Sierra Nevada, Spain ~ 16 January – 14 February 2007

Monday 12th February (LCM) ~ SEA LEVEL
20 x 100 Fc Best Average on 2:00

	Swimmer A		Swimmer B	
	Time	HR	Time	HR
1	1:00.5	174	0:59.5	
2	0:59.9	190	0:59.5	
3	1:00.0	186	0:59.3	
4	0:59.2	187	0:58.9	
5	0:59.4	185	0:59.2	174
6	0:59.6	187	0:59.4	
7	0:59.9	189	0:59.2	
8	1:00.4	189	0:59.0	
9	1:00.5	186	0:59.3	
10	1:00.9	186	0:59.2	174
11	1:01.1	185	0:59.4	
12	1:01.5	194	0:59.6	
13	1:01.5	187	0:59.9	
14	1:01.6	194	0:59.0	
15	1:01.9	188	0:59.0	186
16	1:02.1	187	0:59.7	
17	1:01.8	193	0:59.0	
18	1:02.3	185	0:59.1	
19	1:01.9	185	0:59.0	
20	1:01.5	185	0:58.3	180
Average	**1:00.9**	**187**	**0:59.2**	**179**

coach records splits, heart rate, stroke rate and stroke count during the test, and if possible collects peak blood-lactate measures following the swim.

The values recorded should be compared with the final repetition performances of the five-step profile test, with the target being to achieve values as close as possible to those achieved. In particular compare the average time (per 100m) for the DD test to that for step 5. Distance swimmers (i.e. 1,500m swimmers completing 3,000m) are likely to be significantly slower in average 100m time.

However, this difference becomes a baseline, and the target is to close the gap throughout the course of the season.

#1 KICK

There are probably as many variations to field tests for kick as there are coaches! But in general, the rules for testing conditions are the same as for all other tests, and as long as each individual's results are compared with their own previous scores, then the actual format of the test is not important. My own preference is for the kick test to last

Figure 57 Kick test results.

Calella Training Camp
4 – 12 June 2006

Max Kick Set ~ Mon 5th June (PM)   4 x 200 No.1 Kick MAX On 5:00

Name	Stroke	1	2	3	4	Average Time
AA	Fc	2:53.0	2:52.0	2:52.0	2:52.0	2.52.2
BB	Brs	3:00.0	3:00.0	3:01.0	3:00.0	3:00.2
CC	Brs	3:04.0	3:01.0	3:01.0	2:59.0	3:01.2
DD	Fc	3:02.0	3:00.0	3:03.0	3:10.0	3:03.7
EE	Brs	3:07.0	3:11.0	3:15.0	3:04.0	3:09.2
FF	Fly	3:15.0	3:13.0	3:14.0	3:12.0	3:13.5
GG	Fc	3:15.0	3:18.0	3:17.0	3:17.0	3:16.7
HH	Bk	3:23.0	3:17.0	3:21.0	3:18.0	3:19.7
II	Fc	3:31.0	3:26.0	3:21.0	3:24.0	3:25.5
JJ	Fc	3.20.0	3:28.0	3:24.0	3:30.0	3:25.5
KK	Brs	3:27.0	3:30.0	3:22.0	3:27.0	3:26.5
LL	Bk	3:31.0	3:28.0	3:26.0	3:27.0	3:28.0
MM	Fc	3:33.0	3:39.0	3:40.0	3:36.0	3:37.0
NN	Brs	3:39.0	3:40.0	3:38.0	3:37.0	3:38.5
OO	Fc	3:46.0	3:40.0	3:44.0	3:45.0	3:43.7
PP	Fc	3:54.0	3:53.0	3:52.0	3:36.0	3:48.8
QQ	Fc	3:56.0	3:52.0	3:56.0	3:48.0	3:53.0
RR	Fc	4:35.0	4:21.0	4:10.0	3:58.0	4:16.0

800m in total, and then to use this (and its derivatives) to measure improvement: therefore start with 4 × 200 (sample test results are shown in Fig. 57), then do 400, 2 × 200, followed by 2 × 400, and building up to an 800m kick time trial. The aim is to complete an 800m kick under 12min.

#1 STROKE EFFICIENCY

The purpose of the 8 × 50m efficiency test is to progress through the set recording time, stroke count and stroke rates. Each swim should become faster by approximately 2sec. The target on the final 50m is to swim PB + 1sec, or faster. Descend 1–8, with the final swim being maximum effort. Plot the velocity (time in m per second) and stroke count for each swim on a graph (*see* Fig. 58).

The eight swims should get faster by approximately 2sec on each 50m swim. The 50s should be conducted on a comfortable interval of around 90sec turnaround. This test will establish critical information for training speeds, and for comparison to competition data.

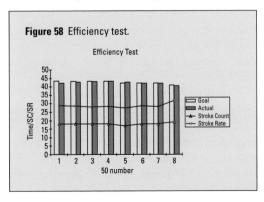

Figure 58 Efficiency test.

CHAPTER 9

Self Assessment

Giving a group of swimmers an identical training programme would not result in them all being equally fit. The same training regime may result in a strong training effect for one individual, but may impair the performance of another. Some of the reasons are that we all differ in (i) our current level of fitness; (ii) how fast we adapt to increased training; (iii) how fast we recover and regenerate from training sessions; (iv) how much stress we are under outside training; and (v) how much stress we can tolerate.

There is a very fine balance between a training load that makes you adapt and get fitter, and one that causes overtraining and a reduction in performance. This fine line is not only different between individuals, it can also change, in that during some periods you may be able to tolerate more training than others. Any increase in stress, even if it has nothing to do with training, will affect tolerance to, and recovery from training; if you have not largely recovered by your next session, then your ability to train hard is reduced, so you do not get fitter. What is more ominous is a progressive build-up of fatigue and damage, which not only reduces capacity to train for competition, but also reduces competitive performance. This extra stress could be illness or infection, poor diet, it could be stress at work, at home or studying.

The answer is daily monitoring of how swimmers feel, and a description of how hard and how much they are training: taken together, these can build up a very useful picture over the training year. Fig. 59 shows a very simple weekly training self-assessment sheet that can be completed by all swimmers.

We have already seen that the stress of training, and general stress in everyday life, can together affect the overall wellbeing of the swimmer. The stresses of altitude and heat must be added to this, and consideration given to their effects. In addition, when attending training camps, swimmers will also probably be doing more training than normal. When groups train at altitude or in a location where the weather is hot and/or humid, there is some simple information about the athlete that the coaches and support staff should keep track of. Hot climate and high altitude represent environmental extremes: they are not present in 'normal living', and when exposed to them, swimmers need a period of time to adapt. Fig. 60 shows data from an international swimmer on a warm-weather training camp, and is based on the type of information that can be collected via the chart in Fig. 59. In relation to each of the parameters in this and Fig. 61, the following explanatory details are offered:

Heart rate (before you get out of bed)
An elevated pulse in the morning can signify that you may be ill, or not recovered from previous training, or both! Only by taking your pulse regularly will you become aware of what is normal.

Weight (in kg, before breakfast)
Weight loss, if you do not intend it to happen, may mean something is not right.

Figure 59 Weekly training self assessment.

Weekly Training Self Assessment   Swimmer's name:

| | You this morning... | | | | | | | Your Training today... | | | | Other details |
| | Morning | | | | How would you rate your ... | | | | Swim | | Land | Intensity | Hydration |
Date	HR	Weight	Urine SG	PH	Sleep	Fatigue	Stress	Muscle soreness	Total distance	Total time	Total time	Score between	Volume drunk
	BPM	KG			Hrs	1 to 7	1 to 7	1 to 7	km	min	mm	1to7	litres

Urine analysis (in the morning)

Urine *specific gravity* (altitude and warm weather): the density of urine can be a good indicator as to whether or not you are dehydrated; being thirsty is often not enough. Dehydration is a problem both at altitude and in hot climates.

Urine alkalinity or p*H* (altitude only): the pH of urine can be used as a quick guide to how well an individual is coping with living at altitude. Both these tests use simple paper test strips on which you urinate; you can then read off the colour from a chart after a few seconds.

How you feel (on a scale of 1 to 7)

Asking the following questions is very important; it is also important to record the answers on a regular basis:

Did you sleep well?	1 well	7 insomnia
Feeling of fatigue?	1 none	7 very fatigued?
Stress?	1 no stress	7 highly stressed
Muscle soreness?	1 no soreness	7 very, very sore

Drinking volumes (end of the day)

If the density of urine suggests that you are dehydrated, it is useful to quantify roughly how much you have been drinking.

Training

How much and how hard? It is very useful to be able to keep track of the amount of exercise stress you are imposing on your body. A broad picture of how hard you train can be built up if you make an accurate daily record of your training distances, how long you spent training, and roughly how hard or how intense you felt the sessions were.

Training distance (in metres)

Distance covered in the pool each day.

Training time (in minutes)

Time spent on your main discipline. A very simple way of measuring your training load is by adding up the total time (in minutes) that

Figure 60 Daily stress and training.

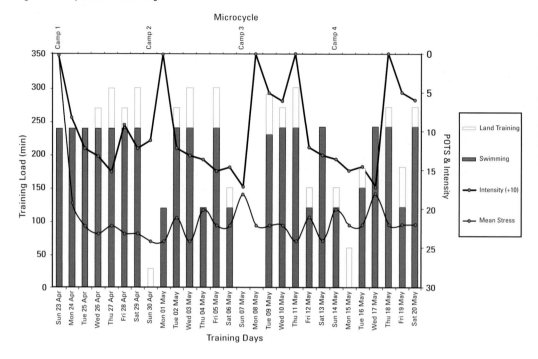

Figure 61 Weight, pulse and blood markers.

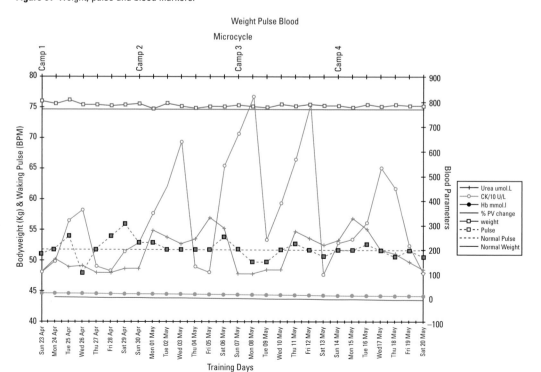

you spent in the pool, regardless of what the session was composed of.

Other training (in minutes)

Time spent on other active training – for example, circuits or weight training. Include the warm-ups, but not the flexibility sessions. Within any one cycle of training you may be doing a roughly similar mix of different modes of exercise. Therefore from week to week within this cycle the total time you have spent exercising is quite a good gauge of your training session.

Training intensity (scale of 1 to 7)

How hard do you feel you've worked? Recording these few simple things together, day by day, can go some considerable way to (i) ensuring you are imposing a *progressive overload* in your training programme, and *tapering* where appropriate; (ii) identifying what is too much training. For instance, if an increase in training volume or intensity has left you fatigued, sore and with an elevated morning heart rate, then we will have some idea of how much is too much for your current level of conditioning.

CHAPTER 10

Effective Techniques

Full details of the individual stroke techniques are contained in *Swimming–Crowood Sports Guide* (Crowood 2006) so there is no intention of repeating this information here. Although there are specific, individual differences in technique from swimmer to swimmer (and obviously faster swimmers are by definition 'better'), the basics of technique are common at all levels and, if maintained as swimmers develop physically, can be an important performance constant.

Speed in swimming requires the generation of strength, endurance and power, and the elimination of resistance, friction and drag. The faster you swim, the 'thicker' the water becomes: if you double your speed, you quadruple your resistance! Therefore, the faster you swim the more important it becomes to eliminate resistance. By balancing your body properly in the water, you can reduce resistance and save heartbeats to generate power and speed. US stroke guru and coach Bill Boomer has developed a body-balance concept, which involves counter-balancing the lower body's tendency to sink by extending the length of the body and applying downward pressure from the chin and sternum (pressing the 'T', as shown in Fig. 62).

In order to swim fast, you must generate power from the 'core' of your body (the hips and abdominal muscles), in the same way a baseball player swings a bat. A batter could never hit a home run by swinging the bat with just his arms: to create enough power to hit a home run, a batter must first open his hips, then drive the upper body around using his stomach muscles; the arms follow the hips, and transfer the hip power to the bat. Coach Boomer's concept of pressing the 'T' allows you to rotate from side to side, opening the hips so you can generate power from the abdominal muscles. The arms transfer power from the core (the hips and stomach) to the hands, rather than generating power.

The purpose of pressing the 'T' is twofold: (i) balancing the body reduces resistance and conserves energy; and (ii) it allows you to open the hips so you can generate power from the core of your body. It allows you to tap into the

Figure 62 Pressing the 'T'.

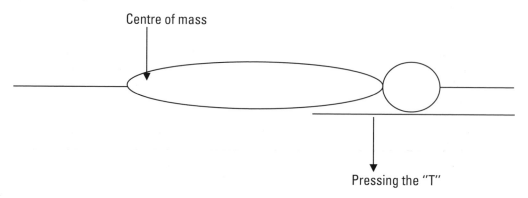

Centre of mass

Pressing the "T"

power of the 'engine' of your body (the hips and stomach), instead of limping along with just the use of the arms. When you are balancing your body pressing the 'T', you can generate rhythm, power and rotation from the hips and abdominal muscles. You increase speed by increasing the rhythm of rotation of the hips, not by 'revving up' your arms and 'spinning your wheels': this enables you to increase speed without decreasing distance per stroke.

Another benefit of rotating from side to side in freestyle and backstroke is that water flows over two surfaces (chest and back), rather than over just one surface (either the chest or the back). Cutting through the water on your side like this allows you to significantly reduce drag and resistance.

Swimming techniques, just like coaching and training philosophies, have underlying assumptions, too. For instance, what are the critical aspects of freestyle? What are the components you should never throw out, and what parts of freestyle are negotiable as you change speeds? Success is not an accident; the discovery of excellence doesn't just appear. Beyond looking for little tips here and there, you need to develop a rationale for how to construct your stroking patterns. One widely held assumption in freestyle swimming is the belief that the more force created at the hands and feet, the faster the swimmer will go. That is why so much time and energy is committed to strength training, for example. But perhaps this may not be entirely true. Perhaps the elimination of drag is just as important as the creation of force. Maybe as you swim faster, eliminating drag becomes much more important than creating propelling forces. Every time you double your speed, you create four times as much resistance; so the faster you get, the thicker the water feels and the harder it is to move through it. Therefore, given your limited ability to create energy, it may be better to spend more time on maximizing the energy you do have, by getting every drop of speed out of each effort. This means using creative body positioning to eliminate, as much as possible, the ever-increasing resistance of water as you increase speed.

This can be done by examining the natural tendencies of the human body in the water. It is very important to understand 'vertical balance', or the relationship between 'centre of mass' and 'centre of rotation'. The centre of mass is a point on or near the body, where all the weighted body parts, at any moment in time, are in gravitational balance. The centre of rotation (also called the centre of flotation or centre of buoyancy) is the single fulcrum point around which gravity pulls your centre of mass. The tendency for your centre of mass to rotate towards the pool bottom around your centre of rotation is called torque. Understanding and counterbalancing this torque without using excessive energy to do it, is to really understand the central issues for fast swimming. The underlying assumption here is that stroking patterns should be developed around the needs for balance (countering torque), eliminating frontal resistance (streamlining) and the development of stroke rate. These considerations are never thrown out as you attempt to create greater propelling forces at the hands and feet.

By positioning and shaping the body for a more balanced and streamlined profile, it will take less energy to push you through the water. The less energy you devote to keeping your body balanced, fighting the increasing frontal drag of poor streamlining, and having to use your hands and feet to correct errors caused by bad posture, the more energy you will have for fast swimming. Most stroking errors, as we know them, are caused by the swimmer having to use the hands and feet to compensate for their assuming that force creation comes before drag elimination.

Let's begin at the basics. What naturally happens to your body in the water when you hold your breath and do nothing, when you just hang there and float? Some people's bodies will assume a low hanging, almost vertical 'dead man's' float, and those positions in between are not very streamlined, as gravity pulls the heavier parts of the body downward. The most buoyant part of the body is between your armpits, and the heaviest part is somewhere around the belt buckle. You have a choice about what floats, and need to counteract the forces of gravity to bring your body into a relaxed, streamlined position, without using energy (kicking) to do it. Think of the body as a long lever arm like a seesaw. The length of the balancing line in the lever system of your body runs from the point of the extended finger tips to the extended toes, and includes the head and spine alignment. A seesaw is in balance when both ends are unsupported, stabilized and motionless. This equation does not require equal lengths and weights on both sides of the balancing point. To balance, you need equal products; the relationships between length and weight. These same conditions apply to the human body when trying to balance.

To accomplish this, the swimmer needs to be able to shift their centre of mass towards the centre of flotation. To do this they need to connect the product of the weight and length of the hips and legs on one side of the seesaw, to the following on the other side of the seesaw: (i) the product of the weight and length of the arms, (ii) the weight of the head, and (iii) a downward pressure on the head/chest unit ('T' – pressure). The closer these two points (the centre of mass and the centre of flotation) are, the less potential torque is in the system. Putting the centre of mass on the gravity line from the centre of rotation leaves you with no torque pressure on the body's lever system.

Creating and understanding this balanced system will eliminate the need to kick your body into a streamlined position. This balanced system also gives a more stable base or platform from which to freely direct the arms. In freestyle, this establishes a 'line' where the stroke rate and rhythm can originate at the hips. This condition is critical for being able to change speed in freestyle swimming, and most outstanding freestyle swimmers are very skilled at doing this. The same ability to shift and control the centre of mass in the short-axis strokes (fly- and breaststroke) creates the rhythm and momentum transfers that lead to higher average speeds in these two strokes.

An old-fashioned assumption is that to pick up the pace, you do it with the hands. This is wrong! If pace changes occur in the hands and feet, it will destroy the balance, rhythm and posture. Freestyle rhythm changes should occur at the hips, and they should never interfere with balance and posture. Swimmers need to evaluate the impact of any such change on the entire body – hips, head, legs, arms – as that change impacts on balance, rhythm and posture. All swimmers have a natural rhythm to their stroke, and that rhythm manifests itself along the balancing 'line', which includes the head and spine. It is critical that the head, the spine and the hips are connected, if the rhythm line is to be created. We can then marry the balance line to the rhythm line and direct all energies outward towards the hands and feet, the force transmitters. The hips won't bounce, the hands won't sweep out, and there will be no need to cross kick to compensate for the head every time a breath is taken.

Once a solid head and spine line is established and vertical balance is stabilized, swimmers and coaches can then examine ways to better position the body to decrease frontal resistance and redirect efforts towards forward streamlined propulsion. Horizontal balance is also important. Every time the head comes 'off line', the hips swing out or sink, and not only does it create drag, it forces the swimmer to counterbalance that action with their hands or feet to keep from swimming unevenly. In inefficient swimmers, too much hand motion is used for counterbalancing body errors, and is therefore not being used for propulsion.

Splayed hands, bobbing heads, ungainly recoveries, switching hips and strange shoulder dips are all stroking problems. Many coaches and swimmers look to each specifically and try to correct stroke errors at that point. But perhaps a more fundamental question needs to be asked: is a splayed hand or a switching hip the symptom, or the disease? Is it the problem, or the result of the problem?

Without a strong framework to operate from, without solid connected body parts acting as a single unit streamlined in the water, a swimmer will be like a Ferrari with flat tyres. It won't matter how powerful the engine is, you simply will not be able to swim as fast as you could if you took the time to correct these body imbalances. Coaches and swimmers should critically examine the strokes, evaluating assumptions and looking to see where the priorities lie in both training and stroke mechanics. Just as changing the tyres on the Ferrari can make the car run smoother and faster, it is also worth the effort to do the stroke technique equivalent in order to balance the stroke and become a better and faster swimmer. As a guide to assessing stroke technique, Figs. 63a–d are shown as examples, but developing your own is a good way of really understanding the principles of technique on each of the four strokes.

BUTTERFLY START, TURN AND FINISH
Start

The swimmer should be able to demonstrate complete control at the front of the block, i.e. no movement or rolling. A traditional 'grab start' controlled position is shown in Figs. 64a and b. The toes are curled over the edge, balance is maintained with the hips as far forward as possible and the head tucked in. The swimmer should have a fast response to the signal, and should thrust up and out from the starting block, achieving optimum height and distance. There should be a smooth entry led by the hands, then with straight arms the head in line, followed by the hips and legs, with the feet making a limited splash. There should be a

---

Figure 63a Butterfly evaluation checklist.

BUTTERFLY CHECKLIST

Score: 1 = Needs a lot of work; 2 = Fair, but can be better; 3 = Good, one of your strengths; 4 = National calibre technique

1.	BODY BALANCE				
1.1.	Good undulation	1	2	3	4
1.2.	Presses 'T' as arms catch	1	2	3	4
1.3.	Maintains good horizontal position from head to toes	1	2	3	4
1.4.	Head aligned with spine during catch (looking down)	1	2	3	4
2.	**LEGS**				
2.1.	Two kicks per arm catch	1	2	3	4
2.2.	One kick at hands entry and one at hands exit	1	2	3	4
2.3.	'Exit' kick is the 'big' kick	1	2	3	4
3.	**ARMS**				
3.1.	Hands enter in front of shoulders	1	2	3	4
3.2.	High elbow catch	1	2	3	4
3.3.	Elbows remain above hands throughout pull	1	2	3	4
3.4.	'Keyhole' pull pattern	1	2	3	4
3.5.	Hands exit at hips	1	2	3	4
3.6.	Symmetrical recovery	1	2	3	4
3.7.	Hands accelerate throughout pull	1	2	3	4
4.	**BREATHING**				
4.1.	Head lifts to breathe before arms exit water	1	2	3	4
4.2.	Chin stays near the water surface during breath	1	2	3	4
4.3.	Head re-enters water before the hands enter	1	2	3	4
4.4.	Head looks down during the catch/early pull phase	1	2	3	4

Distance per Stroke Count / 25m:_____

Figure 63b Backstroke evaluation checklist.

BACKSTROKE CHECKLIST

Score: 1 = Needs a lot of work; 2 = Fair, but can be better; 3 = Good, one of your strengths; 4 = National calibre technique

1.	BODY BALANCE				
	1.1. Horizontal body position	1	2	3	4
	1.2. Head aligned with spine	1	2	3	4
	1.3. Hips rotate with shoulders	1	2	3	4
	1.4. Body roll equal to both sides	1	2	3	4
	1.5. Head steady and still	1	2	3	4
2.	**LEGS**				
	2.1. Continuous strong, steady kick	1	2	3	4
	2.2. Correct hip/knee bend	1	2	3	4
	2.3. Toes pointed	1	2	3	4
	2.4. Feet stay underwater, but 'boil' the surface	1	2	3	4
3.	**ARMS**				
	3.1. Straight arm recovery over shoulders	1	2	3	4
	3.2. Pinkie first entry	1	2	3	4
	3.3. Hands enter in front of shoulders	1	2	3	4
	3.4. Deep, early high elbow catch	1	2	3	4
	3.5. Curved pull pattern ('W')	1	2	3	4
	3.6. Hands exit at thighs	1	2	3	4
	3.7. Hands accelerate throughout pull	1	2	3	4

Distance per Stroke Count / 25m:_____

Figure 63c Breaststroke evaluation checklist.

BREASTROKE CHECKLIST

Score: 1 = Needs a lot of work; 2 = Fair, but can be better; 3 = Good, one of your strengths; 4 = National calibre technique

1.	BODY BALANCE				
	1.1. Head stays aligned with body during catch	1	2	3	4
	1.2. Presses 'T' as arms extend out	1	2	3	4
	1.3. Good undulation	1	2	3	4
2.	**LEGS**				
	2.1. Heels together at beginning of recovery	1	2	3	4
	2.2. Knees not directly below hips at catch	1	2	3	4
	2.3. High heels at catch	1	2	3	4
	2.4. Ankles outside knees at catch	1	2	3	4
	2.5. Dorsiflexion of foot during kick	1	2	3	4
	2.6. Soles together at end of kick	1	2	3	4
3.	**ARMS**				
	3.1. Wide catch with hands outside elbows	1	2	3	4
	3.2. High elbow from catch to insweep	1	2	3	4
	3.3. Insweep in front of shoulders	1	2	3	4
	3.4. Palm down recovery	1	2	3	4
	3.5. Arms straight at end of recovery	1	2	3	4
4.	**BREATHING**				
	4.1. Head aligned with spine during catch (looking down)	1	2	3	4
	4.2. Head lifts during the insweep	1	2	3	4
	4.3 Head re-enters water as arms extend forward	1	2	3	4

Distance per Stroke Count / 25m:_____

Figure 63d Freestyle evaluation checklist.

FREESTYLE EVALUATION

Score: 1 = Needs a lot of work; 2 = Fair, but can be better; 3 = Good, one of your strengths; 4 = National calibre technique

1.	**BODY BALANCE**				
	1.1.	Horizontal body position	1	2	3	4
	1.2.	Head aligned with spine	1	2	3	4
	1.3.	Hips rotate with shoulders	1	2	3	4
	1.4.	Body roll equal to both sides	1	2	3	4
	1.5.	Head rotates when breathing - stays aligned	1	2	3	4
2.	**LEGS**				
	2.1.	Continuous strong, steady kick	1	2	3	4
	2.2.	Correct hip/knee bend	1	2	3	4
	2.3.	Toes pointed	1	2	3	4
3.	**ARMS**				
	3.1.	Relaxed bent arm recovery	1	2	3	4
	3.2.	Hands enter in front of shoulders	1	2	3	4
	3.3.	Both arms in front quadrant at entry	1	2	3	4
	3.4.	Early high elbow catch	1	2	3	4
	3.5.	Elbow remains above hand throughout pull	1	2	3	4
	3.6.	Curved pull pattern	1	2	3	4
	3.7.	Hands exit at thighs	1	2	3	4
	3.8.	Hands accelerate throughout pull	1	2	3	4

Distance per Stroke Count / 25m:_____

Figure 64a, b Grab start.

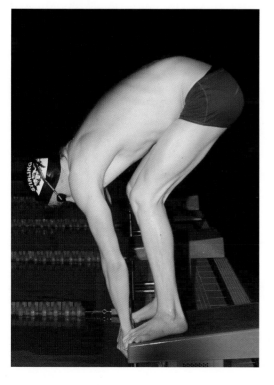

streamlined glide under the surface, with the hands and head directing the body towards the surface. The feet should start kicking almost immediately, and the arms should pull the body to the surface for transition to full stroke. The swimmer should not breathe during the first stroke cycle. The rules permit the swimmer to travel up to 15m underwater before starting to swim, and swimmers should be encouraged to take full advantage of this as they develop according to age, skill and fitness.

Turn

The stroke length should not change during the last 5m. The body should be streamlined at the touch, with elbows slightly bent, and there should be no extra glide. There should be a two-handed touch as allowed by the laws. There should be a good tuck and pivot action, with the head staying low. One arm should move over the water and the other below the water as both feet are placed on the wall with the knees bent. The arms should be placed above the head, under the surface of the water, as the feet and legs push. There should be a streamlined glide under the surface, with the hands and head directing the body towards the surface. The feet should kick just before the body starts to slow down. Both arms

Figure 66 Butterfly.

should pull for a smooth transition into full stroke at the surface. The swimmer should not breathe during the first stroke cycle.

> The technique for fly turn is identical to that for breaststroke and for breast-free in the IM.

Finish

The stroke length should not change during the last 5m. The body should be streamlined at the touch, with elbows straight and no extra glide. The finish should be positively registered with a two-handed touch as allowed by the laws.

Figure 65a, b, c Pivot turn for fly, breaststroke and breast-free.

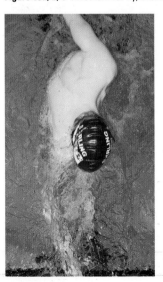

BACKSTROKE START, TURN AND FINISH

Start

The swimmer should adopt a comfortable position on the wall, with legs, arms and head ready to respond to the starting signal. The hands grip the bar outside shoulder width, the feet are one slightly higher than the other, and the body is held close to the wall ready to uncoil powerfully on the starting signal. The swimmer should have a fast response to the signal, pushing up and back with the feet and legs. The arms should swing beyond the head, clear of the water. The hands and arms should come together to form a streamlined shape. The back should arch and the whole body should be clear of the water. There should be a smooth entry led by the hands, then with straight arms, the head in line, followed by the hips and legs and pointed feet. There should be a streamlined glide under the surface with the hand and head directing the body towards the surface before the 15m marker. The feet should begin a dolphin, then flutter kick, and should continue until the start of the first arm pull. One arm should pull for a smooth transition into full stroke at the surface, with the legs moving to an alternate action without any hesitation. The head should break the surface before the 15m marker. As for butterfly starts, swimmers should be encouraged to take full advantage of the '15m rule' according to age, skill and fitness.

Figure 67 Backstroke.

Figure 68a, b, c Backstroke start.

Figure 69 Backstroke race start.

Turn

There should be no interruption of the stroke cycle during the last 5m. The flags should be used to check strokes, and the head should *not* turn to look at the wall. There should be a continuous strong kick. There should be a positive rotation on to the front at the appropriate distance from the wall, and a smooth fast forward flip to place the feet on the wall, before any momentum is lost. There should be a strong push from the feet and legs as the hands are placed above the head ready for the stretch to a streamlined position. There should be a streamlined glide under the surface, with the hands and head directing the body smoothly towards the surface. The feet should kick just before the body starts to slow down. One arm should pull for a smooth transition into full stroke at the surface. The swimmer should not breathe during the first stroke cycle.

Finish

There should be no interruption of the stroke cycle during the last 5m. The flags should be used, and the head should *not* turn to look at the wall, and there should be a continuous strong kick. The finish should be positively registered with one hand, lying flat on the back at full stretch.

Figure 71 Backstroke finish.

Figure 70a, b, c Backstroke turn.

BREASTSTROKE START, TURN AND FINISH

Start

The swimmer should be able to demonstrate complete control at the front of the block – no movement or rolling. Figs. 72a and b illustrate the 'take your marks' position for a track start on the blocks. Unlike the grab start shown in Fig. 64, the track start (as the name suggests) has one foot in front of the other. The front foot has the toes over the edge, as before, with the weight further back towards the rear foot. A vigorous pull with the arms initiates the flight after the starting signal. The swimmer should have a fast response to the signal, should thrust up and out from the starting block, and should achieve optimum height and distance.

A track start is characterized by fast reactions and a steeper flight/entry. There should be a smooth entry led by the hands, then with straight arms, the head in line, followed by the hips and legs, with the feet making a limited splash. There should be a streamlined glide under the surface, with the hands and head directing the body to a horizontal position. There should be one complete long stroke under the water, starting just before the body starts to slow down. As the hands are returned closely to the body to a position above the head, the feet are raised in preparation to kick to the surface. As the feet begin the first kick, the hands and head direct the body towards the surface. As the head breaks the surface, the hands begin the second arm cycle.

Turn

The breaststroke turn is almost identical to that on butterfly, apart from the different stroke techniques on the way in and out of the wall. The 'on the wall' and 'push-off' sequence shown in Fig. 65 is entirely the same for both strokes. The stroke length should not change during the last 5m. The body should be streamlined at the touch, with elbows slightly bent, and there should be no extra glide.

Figure 72a, b Track start.

There should be a two-handed touch as allowed by the laws. There should be a good tuck and pivot action, with the head staying low. One arm should move over the water and the other below the water as both feet are placed on the wall with the knees bent. The arms should be placed above the head, under the surface of the water as the feet and legs push. There should be a streamlined glide under the surface, with the hands and head directing the body to a horizontal position. There should be one complete long stroke under the water, starting just before the body starts to slow down. As the hands are returned, close to the body, to a position above the head, the feet should be raised in preparation for the kick to the surface. As the feet begin the first kick, the hands and head should direct the body towards the surface. As the head breaks the surface, the hands should begin the second arm cycle.

Finish

The stroke length should not change during the last 5m. The body should be streamlined at the touch, with elbows straight and no extra glide. The finish should be positively registered with a two-handed touch as allowed by the laws.

FREESTYLE START, TURN AND FINISH

Swimmers should use either of the two starting techniques explained previously for freestyle.

Figure 73 Backstroke finish.

Start

The swimmer should be able to demonstrate complete control at the front of the block, with no movement or rolling. They should have a fast response to the signal, thrusting up and out from the starting block and achieving optimum height and distance. There should be a smooth entry led by the hands, then with straight arms and the head in line, followed by the hips and legs, with feet making little splash. There should be a streamlined glide under the surface, with the hands and head directing the body smoothly towards the surface. The feet should kick just before the body starts to slow down. One arm should pull for a smooth transition into full stroke at the surface. The swimmer should not breathe during the first stroke cycle.

Turn

There should be no interruption of the stroke cycle during the last 5m. There should be a continuous strong kick, and the hand and head should lead down into the turning movement. There should be a smooth, fast flip, placing the feet on the wall with knees bent. The legs should provide a strong, powerful push as the hands, arms and body stretch to a streamlined position. There should be a streamlined glide under the surface, with the hands and head directing the body smoothly towards the surface. The feet should kick just before the body starts to slow down. One arm should pull for a smooth transition into full stroke at the surface. The swimmer should not breathe during the first stroke cycle.

The sequence of progressions for freestyle and backstroke turns are shown in Figs. 74a – e. Both turns have the same evolution, and at the appropriate point in the sequence of learning shown, a backstroke turning skill is completed before moving on to the freestyle version.

Finish

There should be no interruption of the stroke cycle during the last 5m. The swimmer should not breathe during the last 5m, and there should be a continuous, strong kick.

Figure 74a, b, c, d, e Freestyle (flip or tumble) turn.

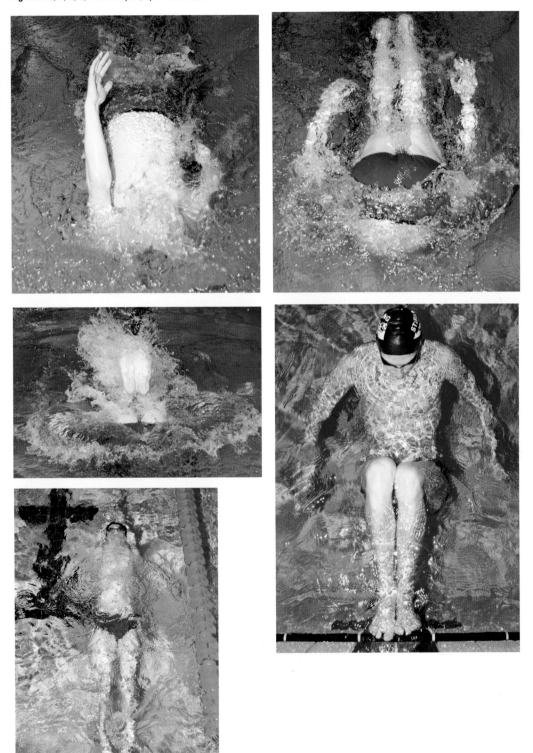

The finish should be positively registered, with the hand stretched out in front and the head still down (Fig. 75).

IM STARTS, TURNS AND FINISH

According to most leading coaches, the IM is the 'fifth stroke' of swimming, and should be considered as much in its own right as a combination of the four recognized strokes. Performed in the standard order of butterfly, backstroke, breaststroke and freestyle, the 'IM' is the most rigorous of swimming tests. As the focus of this section of the book is on racing skills, the illustrations that follow are concerned

Figure 76a, b, c, d Fly-back turn.

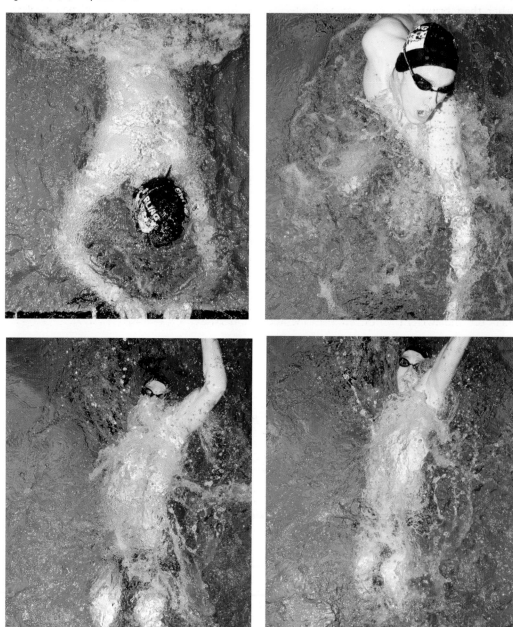

with the transitions from one stroke to another in the IM. All other technical information for the four strokes applies equally to the medley as to the individual stroke in question.

Fly-Back IM Turn

This is the easiest of the three IM transitions. As the swimmer comes in on their front and goes out on their back, there is little to do other than bring the knees up and effect a powerful push-off. The contact time between the hands touching and feet leaving should be as short as possible. Using the 15m rule on the backstroke should again be encouraged.

Back-Breast IM Turn

There are a couple of possibilities to switch strokes in the middle of an IM race. Some swimmers will use the simple 'swivel turn' shown in Figs. 77a and b. This is useful because a breath can be taken as the mouth clears the water during the 'on the wall' phase. A potentially faster turn is shown in Fig. 77c, with a 'back flip' performed as the hand touches. This may change direction more quickly, but the loss of a sustained breath may be crucial to the physiological demands of the race in its later stages. For this reason, most swimmers use the swivel turn on the 400 IM and the flip turn on a 200 IM race. Coaches and swimmers should practise both throughout the season.

Breast-Free IM Turn

The standard turn as described for butterfly and breaststroke, and illustrated in Fig. 65, is the turn used for the last stroke transition in IM. An important final point to make is that swimmers should 'settle' into the new stroke as quickly as possible after each change. This means that technique and stroke tempo should be established a few strokes into the new race segment. Swimmers who coast into and out of the transitions will lose valuable time, and will not maximize their performance potential.

VIDEO RESOURCES

There are a number of video resources available for swimmers and coaches to analyse these technical factors. Some are sophisticated (expensive) and require considerable skills to operate (*see* Fig. 78a), others are much simpler in concept and can be operated by the coach (*see* Fig. 78b). The former is a dual above- and underwater system that downloads the footage into a specific software package. The latter provides a remote live underwater CCD video feed to the capture

Figure 77a, b, c Back-breast turn.

Figure 78a, b Underwater camera (moving).

Figure 79a, b Underwater camera (fixed mount).

method of preference. The system operates by being attached to either a pole or a fixed underwater mount (which can be placed anywhere on the pool floor and is excellent for capturing footage of starts and turns) via a cable to a flat screen LCD monitor (*see* Figs. 79a and b). This allows the coach to instantly monitor the swimmer's stroke, and to analyze in real time those areas that may need attention. The coach can record directly on to another video camera or on to a laptop for storage and/or future use. It is very portable and relatively light, but what makes it so useful is the ease of use and the clarity of the images produced.

TECHNOLOGY AND RACING

The evaluation of race strategy beyond basic split times has been of interest to coaches for as long as athletes have been swimming. However, it wasn't until the early 1970s that researchers and coaches really expanded their analysis to include more variables than split times. Many techniques and technologies have been developed to offer scientists a method for comparing élite swimmers to average swimmers, and to allow coaches a better method of evaluating the strengths and weaknesses of swimmers' performances. 'Race analysis' is now commonly used across the world to assess competition performance.

The primary objectives in the continued development of race analysis systems are: (i) the collection of information that coaches and swimmers use every day to evaluate and improve performance; (ii) the creation of accurate and easy-to-use measurement tools; and (iii) the organization of information for long-term swimmer comparisons. The protocols for race analysis systems do vary according to the development process in each country, but the basic components are common to all. Information is collected by means of fixed video cameras, and processed by a software package to produce the basic performance data. The information measured during a race includes the following variables:

- **Breakout time** The time from the starting signal (start) or feet leaving the wall (turns), to the head breaking the surface.
- **Breakout distance** The distance from the wall that a swimmer's head breaks the surface, in metres.
- **Splits** The official subtractive split time for the distance measured (usually 50m).
- **Drop-off** The difference in seconds between the distance measured and the preceding distance, for example the first and second 50m of a 100m race.
- **Cycle count** The number of stroke cycles during the lap (one cycle = one arm stroke for fly and breast, and one cycle = two arm strokes for back and free).
- **Time** The official cumulative time in the race.
- **Tempo/rate** The frequency of swimming cycles during the lap measured, expressed in both cycles per minute, and seconds per cycle.
- **DPS** Distance per stroke, meters covered during one stroke cycle during the lap measured.
- **Velocity** Swimming speed in metres/seconds during the free-swimming portion of the length measured, i.e. without the start or turns.
- **Turn time** The time in seconds to execute each turn, usually measured from no more than 5m in and up to 10m out from the wall.
- **15m start time** Time in seconds from the starting tone to the 15m mark.
- **15m velocity** Average speed over the first 15m of the race.
- **7.5m finish** Time in seconds from the 7.5m remaining in the race to the finish.
- **7.5m velocity** Average speed over the last 7.5m of the race.

Fig. 80 gives an example of the kind of information provided by the race analysis system used at the 2006 European Championships in Budapest[1]. An analysis of the 2004 European Championship competition analysis data from Madrid indicated that the relationship between the quality of swimming performance and stroke length was not as significant as is commonly assumed. The average 'clean swimming' speed was significantly correlated to race results for all events, as expected.

The next most highly correlated variable with race performance was the turn time, which was significant in 91 per cent of all events. Start and turn times, along with clean swimming speed, were considered significant in butterfly, backstroke and breaststroke. This was similar to the freestyle events, but these races also showed that the finish time was an important part of obtaining a good race result.

The second half of the race was more strongly related to race performance than the first half of the distance races in all events. In the IM events, turn performance was significantly related to race performance. It was also found that the most significant individual stroke within the medley races was breaststroke, followed by backstroke, butterfly and freestyle.

In comparing the race analysis data of the 2000 and 2004 US Olympic Trials, sports scientists found that most of the men's events were consistent in their changes from 2000 to 2004, and almost all fields improved. The similar swimming velocities showed that actual speeds have stayed fairly consistent in the four-year Olympic quadrennial, but it is the way that races are swum that has changed the results. Stroke rates slowed down, DPS increased, and breakout distances increased. These changes reflect a greater focus on underwater swimming and race efficiency.

The women demonstrated some of the same qualities as the men, but overall they did not change nearly as much. Often they swam with slower stroke rates, greater DPS and longer breakouts. Several events were very

[1]The information on all events is available at http://www.swim.ee

Figure 80 Race analysis.

MEN'S 100 FLY FINAL	World record 20.07.03	A.SERDINOV	A.LEVEAUX	N.SKVORTSOV	S.PASTRAS	S.BREUS	T. COOPER	R.GOLDIN	M.NALESSO
1 Result	0:50.98	0:51.95	0:52.76	0:52.96	0:53.16	0:53.18	0:53.24	0:53.26	0:53.32
2 Start time 15m	5,6	6,06	5,98	6,22	6	6,22	5,92	6,06	6,2
3 Start speed 15m	2,68	2,48	2,51	2,41	2,5	2,41	2,53	2,48	2,42
4 Lap time 25m	10,88	11,42	11,26	11,7	11,32	11,42	11,32	11,38	11,56
5 Lap time 75 m	37,2	37,88	38,6	38,72	38,56	38,9	38,46	38,84	38,66
6 Swim speed first 25 m	1,89	1,87	1,89	1,82	1,88	1,92	1,85	1,88	1,87
7 Swim speed second 25 m	1,87	1,87	1,82	1,83	1,82	1,82	1,8	1,83	1,87
8 Swim speed third 25 m	1,86	1,86	1,79	1,74	1,79	1,79	1,83	1,77	1,79
9 Swim speed last 25 m	1,81	1,77	1,77	1,72	1,69	1,75	1,68	1,7	1,69
10 Frequency first 50 m	54	52	57	58	57	50	52	57	58
11 Frequency second 50 m	56	55	54	59	58	51	55	61	56
12 Stroke length first 50 m	2,07	2,16	1,93	1,9	1,93	2,19	2,09	1,94	1,94
13 Stroke length second 50 m	1,93	1,94	1,98	1,76	1,76	2,06	1,85	1,66	1,83
14 Turn time 15m	7,56	7,66	7,96	7,44	7,9	8,16	7,84	8,06	7,98
15 Turn speed 15m	1,98	1,96	1,88	2,02	1,9	1,84	1,91	1,86	1,88
16 Finishing time last 5m	2,7	2,75	2,86	2,64	2,78	2,84	2,9	2,64	2,84
17 Finishing speed last 5m	1,67	1,64	1,57	1,7	1,62	1,58	1,55	1,7	1,58
18 Ave. Swimming speed	1,86	1,84	1,82	1,78	1,8	1,82	1,79	1,79	1,8
19 Ave. Frequency	55	53	55	58	57	50	53	59	57
20 Ave. Stroke length	2	2,05	1,96	1,83	1,85	2,13	1,97	1,8	1,88

comparable to 2000, and though in many cases they did not match the winning 2000 times, they did consistently show greater depth in each field of eight. As examples of this, Figs. 81 and 82 show comparisons for men's 200m IM and women's 100m back-stroke respectively. The men's 200 IM final featured seven new faces, one of whom was the world record holder, and the event developed into a very high quality race. The top three finishers all posted times that would have won in 2000, as the field surpassed the standard set by the 2000 finalists.

Statistically, IM events are difficult to break down. Subtracted splits show that the 2004 field was more aggressive on all segments of the event. Swimming velocities were fairly similar, so most of the improvements were made up in other areas. Underwater break-outs, which were longer for fly, back and free in the 2004 field, appear to have made a difference. Also, stroke rates were lower and DPS was higher for all four strokes in 2004. In a trend opposite to that of the women's 100 fly, the 100 backstroke showcased a few extremely fast swims, but lacked the depth of the 2000 final. World record holder Natalie Coughlin broke 60sec again to claim the top

spot and eventually win the gold in Athens. The race was vastly different from that in 2000: smaller drop-off times, longer DPS, and slower stroke rates. Most notable were the far longer breakout distances, and the 2004 average exceeded even the longest breakout from 2000. Overall, the changes balanced out, produced similar swimming velocities and likewise similar average times.

COMPETITION ANALYSIS

The most common form of competition analysis in use today by coaches is the measurement of stroke rates and stroke lengths. Without using sophisticated equipment (most stopwatches have an in-built stroke rate function), instant information about stroke efficiency can be obtained. This can be used in competition and training, and is applicable from early competitive levels through to international events. Stroke rate is usually given as cycles per minute, but seconds per stroke or strokes per second can also be easily calculated. The simplest stroke length measure is to count the number of stroke cycles per lap. Fig. 83 shows the range of stroke rates and stroke lengths for international swimmers in each competitive event.

Figure 81 Race analysis: Men's 200m IM.

Event	Ave. Time 2000	2004	Ave Breakout (m) 2000	2004	Ave tempo (c/min) 2000	2004	Ave DPS 2000	2004	Ave speed (m/sec) 2000	2004
200 IM final time	2:03.36	2:01.11	n/a	n/a	n/a	n/a	n/a	n/a	n/a	n/a
FLY	0:26.44	0:26.23	10.94	11.25	53.38	49.55	1.99	2.14	1.77	1.76
BACK	0:31.28	0:30.72	6.75	8.75	42.45	41.47	2.26	2.33	1.60	1.60
BREAST	0:35.71	0:35.14	8.06	8.50	44.60	41.17	1.85	2.03	1.38	1.39
FREE	0:29.93	0:29.02	5.59	6.50	48.59	45.01	2.05	2.29	1.66	1.70

Figure 82 Race analysis: Women's 100m Backstroke.

Event	Ave time 2000	2004	Ave breakout (m) 2000	2004	Ave tempo (c/min) 2000	2004	Ave DPS 2000	2004	Ave speed (m/sec) 2000	2004
WOMEN 100 BACK	1:02.36	1:02.01	10.23	11.75	47.80	45.82	1.98	2.07	1.58	1.56

Figure 83 Stroke rate averages.

Average Stroke Rates from Finalists of European Swimming Championships, Madrid 2004

Stroke Rates: Men				Event	Stroke Rates: Women			
50				50 FS	**50**			
60.71					61.13			
50	**100**			100 FS	**50**	**100**		
52.50	50.00				53.38	51.50		
50	**100**	**150**	**200**	200 FS	**50**	**100**	**150**	**200**
45.25	43.63	42.63	44.63		47.13	43.75	44.63	44.63
100	**200**	**300**	**400**	400 FS	**100**	**200**	**300**	**400**
41.00	42.69	43.06	45.81		43.50	42.38	42.69	42.81
400	**800**	**1200**	**1500**	800/1500 FS	**200**	**400**		**800**
42.88	43.13	43.75	45.38		42.25	41.88	42.88	44.50
50				50 BK	**50**			
53.13					54.75			
50	**100**			100 BK	**50**	**100**		
48.25	45.50				48.50	46.38		
50	**100**	**150**	**200**	200 BK	**50**	**100**	**150**	**200**
43.63	40.38	40.25	40.88		42.38	40.38	39.88	40.00
50				50 BRS	**50**			
63.88					59.25			
50				100 BRS				
50.13	51.50				45.13	49.00		
50	**100**	**150**	**200**	200 BRS	**50**	**100**	**150**	**200**
40.00	36.33	37.83	43.83		34.88	33.00	34.50	37.25
50				50Fly	**50**			
63.75					63.13			
50	**100**			100 Fly	**50**	**100**		
56.25	55.88				57.25	55.50		
50	**100**	**150**	**200**	200 Fly	**50**	**100**	**150**	**200**
48.00	46.00	47.00	49.25		53.50	50.38	50.63	53.13

CHAPTER 11

Ergogenics

The recent developments in swimsuit technology are interesting from both an ethical and a fluid dynamics perspective. While there is little doubt that advancements from a clever application of fluid dynamics have improved performance in sports such as cycling and flat-water kayak racing (and despite significant amounts of marketing hype from the manufacturers), the 'scientific jury is still out' with respect to so-called 'hydrodynamically' designed swimsuits. At the Melbourne 2007 World Championships, medals were won with and without such swimsuits. Figs 84a & b illustrate a couple of swimsuits worn by international swimmers.

Progression through water depends on the interaction of propulsive and resistive forces. A swimmer can improve by increasing propulsive forces and/or reducing resistive forces that act on the body at a given speed. The physiological cost of any strategy must also be considered. When swimmers are not creating propulsive forces of sufficient magnitude, they slow down. It is frequently observed that some individuals seem to 'slip' through the water requiring less effort than others. Some swimmers look to be swimming well at slow speeds but when they attempt to increase speed they do not improve as much as others. One of the main reasons for these differences is the amount of resistance,

Figure 84a, b Swimsuit variations.

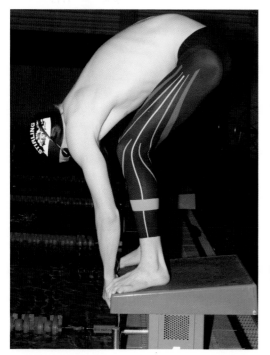

more commonly referred to as 'resistive drag', created by the swimmer.

An understanding of factors contributing to resistance is important in modern swimming and coaching. It is a topic of renewed interest and is now considered more important than previously thought. It appears that adjustments in technique to reduce resistive drag may be as beneficial as subtle adjustments to improve propulsive force. Keen observers of the changes in breaststroke styles at international level could not fail to have noticed how stark the style differences have become. Contrast the head and body positions of 1976 Olympic 200m breaststroke champion David Wilkie with that of 2004 victor, Kosuke Kitajima. We can only hypothesize as to the actual reasons for the 6sec improvement in winning times, but undoubtedly reduced resistance is a key factor. Despite aficionados believing that Wilkie was ahead of his time (his world record stood for six years), his stroke now seems almost primitive in comparison to the sleek, smooth, perpetual motion of today's stars such as Kitajima and current world record holder Brendan Hansen of the USA. This is testimony not to the fact that propulsion is so much better, but to the attention to detail paid to maximizing the benefits of reducing resistance by coaches and swimmers.

RESISTANT FORCES IN SWIMMING

As part of this discussion of the use of bodysuits, let us look briefly at the different types of resistant forces in swimming. There are three main types: (i) form drag, (ii) wave drag, and (iii) surface drag.

Form Drag

Form drag is the orderly flow of the water over the swimmer's body, and it may be disrupted at certain points depending on the shape, size and speed of the swimmer. Behind the disruption point, the flow reverses and may cause eddy currents. Consequently, a pressure differential arises between the front and the rear of the swimmer, resulting in forces termed 'form' or 'pressure drag'.

To minimize form drag, a swimmer seeks a 'streamlined' position – from the earliest days of 'learn to swim' this is emphasized. Thus, swimming with a 'head-up' position in backstroke increases form drag because the hips are forced to 'drop', thereby increasing the cross-sectional area presented by the body as it moves through the water. If a swimmer's body position or 'posture' in the water creates an increased cross-sectional area, then progress through the water will be resisted more than if the body is in a streamlined position.

Form drag is one of the easiest factors to control, and can be minimized by adopting a streamlined posture at every opportunity. A general concept for most strokes is to have the shoulder/chest area create a gap in the water and the hips and legs follow through that space: this usually translates into swimming with the body as level as possible. For example, the flat, streamlined body position adopted by Michael Phelps on butterfly contributes considerably to his outstanding performances in the pool. One factor that could affect streamlining, and thus form drag, is the buoyancy of the swimmer. This may seem obvious, but when we look at both the claims made for, and the properties of, the new swimsuits, this factor becomes a very important consideration.

Wave Drag

Speed at the water surface is constrained by the formation of surface waves. As a swimmer swims, water is pushed out of the way, creating a 'bow wave' not unlike that seen as ships move through the water. As speed increases, the bow wave, with increased size and inertia, cannot flow out of the way quickly enough and hinders velocity increases by the swimmer. Ultimately the limitations of each swimmer's technique will result in a 'speed limit', which for conventional ships with a fixed displacement hull is called 'hull speed'.

Wave drag results from the increased work required to climb the bow wave, and from the transfer of kinetic energy from the swimmer to the water. Wave drag increases steeply and becomes the dominant drag component as hull speed approaches. Exaggerated vertical movements increase wave drag – for example, excessive lifting of the head to breathe on fly. Any action that produces a force that is not directed along the longitudinal axis of the body in the direction of travel will cause lateral (rotational) movements of the body, hips, or legs, unless the motion is counter balanced by another action. Some experts refer to this as 'swimming the line'.

Unfortunately, the human anatomy does not permit all forces to be directed along the longitudinal axis. However, swimmers can improve techniques that minimize lateral movements and therefore reduce wave drag. In the context of this issue, it is unlikely that a bodysuit would have much effect on wave drag. It is gross movements, rather than the surface of the body, that cause any speed-reducing waves.

Surface Drag

Often called 'skin friction', surface drag is commonly attributed to the forces tending to slow the water flowing along the surface of a swimmer's body. The magnitude of the surface drag depends on the velocity of the flow relative to that of the body, the surface area of the body, and the characteristics of the surface. Skin roughness, body contouring, hair and swimsuit fabric are examples of the surface characteristics that create friction as a swimmer moves through water. In swimming, increases in speed cause a relatively small increase in surface drag as compared to form drag and wave drag.

There is some evidence that shaving hair off the body and legs can reduce surface drag. Research has shown that the reduced resistance causes a reduction in the energy per stroke when compared to an unshaven condition, and swimmers routinely 'shave down' for major competitions. Wearing a swim cap provides a smoother surface than does a head of hair, and thus reduces drag. Tight swimsuits of sheer fabrics with a structure that minimizes seams and edges may further reduce surface drag. And of course, the topic of this discussion, the recently developed bodysuits are supposed to generate less resistance than natural shaved skin.

> In summary, total resistance encountered during competitive swimming is the result of the summed effect of form drag, wave drag and surface drag.

BODYSUITS

Research involving bodysuits is, at best, very difficult. The number of factors that need to be controlled (for example the fit of the suits, the conditions of testing, placebo effect, maintenance of constant wetness, and so on) is intimidating, and few objective scientific studies have been conducted. Nevertheless, this hasn't stopped the swimsuit manufacturers from claiming a 'scientific' basis for their products, but they have failed to make such work available for peer review and/or independent evaluation.

A basic problem with researching the effects of bodysuits on swimming performances is the actual scientific approach to be used. Most academic, hydrodynamic models are based on static objects (for example, boat hulls, hydrofoils and so on), but swimmers do not meet this criterion as they are constantly moving. With arms and legs moving in all planes through four different swimming strokes, generalizing from static to dynamic models, and then across swimming strokes, would be flawed in every sense. Most abstract models would be inappropriate for swimming, as would be testing of materials in an environment other than competitive swimming itself.

Paul Bergen, coach of 2000 Olympic champion Inge de Bruijn, conducted a field-based practical test of the effects of Speedo's Fastskin suit on swimming performance. Without any statistical analysis, but simply by comparing the average times of groups of 25m sprint performances between Fastskins and conventional suits, he came to the following conclusions: the bodysuit had a significant advantage for underwater kicking and above-water swimming for both crawl stroke and butterfly; there was no advantage in wearing the suits for backstroke for either underwater kicking or above water swimming; and the bodysuit had negative effects on breaststroke underwater kicking and swimming.

The differences were only apparent when compared with a normal racing suit and with 'unshaved' swimmers. Physical and mechanical advantages are gained from shaving before important competitions, and it is possible that once shaved, a previously unshaved swimmer would equal or surpass the performance benefits from the suits; therefore the benefits of bodysuits might only apply to unshaved conditions.

Buoyancy: a Contentious Issue?

A further confounding factor that has not been controlled, is the wetness of the bodysuits. In a dry state, bodysuits float very well and take a long time to sink unless forced into and moved in water. Flotation, or buoyancy force, is provided by trapped air and surface bubbles. It is possible that early swims in any study could enhance bodysuit benefits through flotation. Swimmers do report a floating sensation when swimming with a bodysuit for the first time. As a research study progresses, and each trial begins with an increasingly wet bodysuit, the flotation effect would dissipate. It is possible that flotation could affect performance for one or only a very few trials when bodysuits are dry (as in a race).

Swimming researcher Rein Haljand of Estonia has investigated this in detail with a series of tests on the Adidas suit worn by Ian Thorpe. Professor Haljand's study examined the effects of the full bodysuit on starts, turns and swimming speed. There were positive influences on test parameters featuring starts, turns and swimming speed between the new suits and the old trunks. The tested swimmers felt that swimming with the new suits raised the legs higher and changed the body position to being more horizontal and flat for better propulsion. It is therefore possible that using the new suits, the swimmers' feelings are based on a faster speed of water moving under the body, and less water being 'carried' on their back. But what is clear is that the perceived (or actual) buoyancy gains are reported as significant.

Using buoyant materials in devices is against the rules of swimming, yet the international governing body for swimming, FINA, has 'approved' bodysuits for competitions, and has seemingly chosen to ignore the possibility that they may contravene the rules governing devices and buoyancy.

Measuring Active Drag

While manufacturers cite their own research to support claims that bodysuits improve swimming performance, independent assessment of that research will not be possible until it is made available for public scrutiny. Thus one cannot be sure that the manufacturers' research was conducted scientifically, objectively and with validity. Assuming bodysuits reduce resistive drag without affecting propulsion or increasing physiological cost, the best way to establish the effects of the suits is to measure active drag with and without a suit. Such a study has been conducted by Huub Toussaint in his aquatics laboratory in Amsterdam using an established method for the measurement of active drag[1].

Drag differences varied with velocity and swimmers, but in most instances, there was no clear reduction in resistance with the swimsuit being tested, Speedo's Fastskin. Indiana University's Joel Stager used an alternative method to evaluate the impact of bodysuits. At the 2000 US Olympic trials, all swimmers were issued with bodysuits, from several manufacturers but mostly Speedo. If these suits improved performance as manufacturers advertised, it would be reasonable to expect a 'step-like' improvement in all performances at the trials. Such sudden and noticeable improvements commonly occur when there is a rule change that advantages the swimmer.

Using data from US Olympic trials from 1968 to 1996, several regression equations were developed, and the power curve best-line-of-fit was used to predict 'normal progression' times for the 2000 trials. If the suits were as effective as proposed, most recorded times would exceed predicted times. Thus, Stager's work assessed whether bodysuits contributed to a better than expected level of performance. If there were no obvious improvements, the suits would be declared as not performance enhancing, and swimmers' performances would be in accord with reasonably expected progress.

Only two results differed significantly from predicted times: the women's 200m backstroke was significantly slower, and the women's 100m breaststroke was faster than predicted. Intriguingly, no improvement impact associated with bodysuits was evident.

Do Bodysuits Aid Performance?

At this stage it has not been empiracally proved that performance is improved by a bodysuit. Clearly, some believe that the suits do improve performance. Among those, the improvement is popularly attributed to the reduction of resistive drag. However, if the suits do aid performance, then there may be alternative explanations, one of which is increased buoyancy. In particular, when buoyancy is increased in the hips and legs, streamline is improved and frontal area is reduced. This could be a reason why the waist-to-ankle suits are popular with males, who tend to sink more in the legs than females.

Toussaint *et al* found that wetsuits worn by triathletes reduced drag by approximately 15 per cent. This was attributed to their effect of shifting the centre of buoyancy away from the head and towards the feet. So if bodysuits provide buoyancy, and the buoyancy is distributed to the rear of the swimmer, they may provide an advantage in a similar way. At the 2000 Olympic Games all male crawl-stroke gold medallists, other than Ian Thorpe (400m free), wore waist-to-ankle suits. Full bodysuits were shunned by Anthony Ervin, Gary Hall Jr, Pieter van den Hoogenband and Grant Hackett. However, in the other three competitive strokes, bodysuits and suits-to-ankles were not nearly as popular.

It would seem therefore, at least among male swimmers, that Coach Bergen's findings of assistance for freestyle and butterfly strokes is verified by the preferences of the best swimmers.

Scientific Opinion

The above review indicates that there remains much to be learnt about whether bodysuits provide an advantage. It is clear that the transfer of manufacturers' 'results' to competitive performances has not occurred. The claims have not been vindicated by the performances of moderate to highly skilled performers, and the advent of bodysuits has not resulted in a performance 'revolution' or any noticeable performance increase in any class of event. While there is a rationale underlying these suits, whether the suits are effective in a real swimming situation is not yet established.

The science underlying the design and production of bodysuits is particularly spurious. Similarly, the science refuting their value is, to say the least, sparse, and neither the case for or against has a solid footing. In general, scientists are sceptical of manufacturers' claims, and emerging studies seem to be siding with the scientists. However, as with many other contentious issues – land training, altitude training, lactate testing – coaches and scientists do at least seem to agree on some basic principles:

- When swimmers are unshaved and wear normal training swimsuits, freestyle and butterfly performances might improve in some individuals if they wear bodysuits.
- Once bodysuits become wet, they contain more water than do tight conventional suits, and are likely to cause a swimmer to go slower, rather than faster, particularly in races longer than 200m. For this reason, swimmers should not wear suits in training (bizarrely some do!) nor should they wear 'old' suits which do not have their original properties intact. Some bodysuits, because of coatings on their fabrics, will take longer to 'get wet' than others, but even they will eventually suffer the same problems as those that wet quickly.
- Particularly tight bodysuits could hamper the range of movement at important joints, such as the shoulders, hips and knees, and consequently, may hinder the correct execution of turns and dives.

> If you are a swimmer contemplating purchasing one of these devices, suit yourself, but think about it first and be sure that the bodysuit suits you.

THE WORLD HAS CHANGED!

All of which is fine and perfectly acceptable in the era pre-February 2008, but since the new Speedo LZR Racer (and subsequent versions from its main rivals TYR, Arena, and Diana) was unveiled, the sport of swimming has been turned on its head. At least the statisticians who keep track of world records would propose! In the six months leading up to the 2008 Olympic Games, countless new world marks have been established by swimmers wearing the new 'performance enhancing' bodysuits (twenty short course world records in the month of April 2008 alone!) and the controversy caused by this ergogenic technology has not been seen since the dark days of doping discussed in Chapter 2. Swimsuit manufacturers have been castigated for encouraging cheating and profiteering above sporting ethics; some manufacturers have been pursuing legal cases against others; and through it all the international governing body of swimming, FINA, have been keeping a watchful eye on the whole process while approving the suits amidst confusion and severe criticism from many sources.

As these words are being written, the 2008 US Olympic Trials are being broadcast online and almost every swimmer in every heat (that's more than 100 competitors in most events) is wearing the Speedo product or, occasionally, an equivalent. The inclusion of 'performance enhancing' materials either on/in or through these suits is undoubtedly contributing to improvements, but how and why is not yet clear. The suits themselves are not buoyant (or no more so that the Adidas suit tested by Professor Haljand), but they do appear to offer significant enhancements. Questions surround their compressive qualities – are they delaying or offsetting muscle fatigue? Is the design of the suit aiding core strength and thus body position and stroke mechanics? These and many other issues have been the subject of debate and discussion in official communiqués, legal depositions and internet blogs galore. Several former coaches (Carlisle, Daland and Colwin amongst them) have been campaigning to have the suits banned, or least much better regulated.

What is clear is that the sport of swimming has changed since February 2008. As journalist Craig Lord (*The Times*, London) so aptly put it, 'the genie is out of the bottle'. Whether any alterations to current rules and regulations will follow the Beijing Olympics is not known, but the swimmers, coaches, scientists and commercially interested parties will not be waiting for the genie to be put back in as they seek to obtain all possible advantages to improve performance.

---

[1]Toussaint, H. M., Beelen, A., Rodenburg, A., Sargeant, A. J., Groot, G. de, Hollander, A. P., and Ingen Schenau, G. J. van. (1988b) 'Propelling efficiency of front crawl swimming.' *Journal of Applied Physiology* 65, 2506–2512.

[2]Toussaint, H. M., Bruinink, L., Coster, R., Looze, M. de, Rossem, B. van, Veenen, R. van, and Groot, G. de (1989) 'Effect of a triathlon wet suit on drag during swimming' *Medicine and Science in Sports and Exercise* 21, 325–328.

PART 4: COMPETITION

CHAPTER 12

Mind Over Matter

'The mental capacity and strength of an athlete to produce their best physical effort under the most challenging conditions in the toughest previously unknown arena.' (Bill Sweetenham, former GB Swimming Performance Director)

This quote from Bill Sweetenham was his way of expressing the pressurized nature of high performance swimming. Having previously dealt with the physical and technical side of preparation for élite performance, it is now time to consider the mental aspects of matching up to the opening citation. Pre-competition strategies will be looked at first, followed by analysis of some of the key mental skills required for top flight competition.

PRE-COMPETITION STRATEGIES

Pre-race strategies contain all the thoughts and actions that need to take place to prepare a swimmer to start a race with the best form of race readiness. The main outcomes of these preparations are to minimize the effects of distractions on the swimmer's appraisal of preparations for racing, to focus the athlete's attention on the race, and to control the development of race readiness so that it will peak at the start of the race. Content is limited to actions on the actual day of a race, although it should be recognized that some élite athletes start their preparations as much as two days before important contests. When that is the case, the suggestions here should be extended and repeated to consume the total time period between the first instance of race awareness and the race start.

Research has shown that how one feels when waking in the morning markedly affects that person's perceptions and mood, and how they cope with that day's events. When waking on the morning of a race day, initial perceptions should be positive and enjoyable; if perceptions were negative, the rest of the day's events would be biased towards a negative appraisal, and that negative 'attitude' would have detrimental effects on race preparations and subsequent performance. Swimmers can learn to wake positively after a night's sleep or long rest. The aim of a wake-up procedure is to establish a positive mood in the athlete so that ensuing events will be interpreted positively. Features of a positive wake-up procedure are as follows:

- Wake slowly. Sudden changes in posture and activity levels have shock potential, and reactions to such a shock vary and may be inappropriate. Slow waking, lying in bed and controlling the sensations that are experienced, can be the basis for producing a positive mood.
- Engage in positive self-talk. The first thoughts that are recognized are important for mood-setting. Swimmers should self-talk with positive statements, such as 'I feel great', 'It's going to be a great day', 'The sleep felt good', and 'Now I am fully rested'.
- Do slow stretching. While still in bed, a slow stretching routine that exercises as many muscles as possible should be performed. The intensity of such activities should not be great: it should be at a level that produces relaxed, pleasurable feelings.
- Smile! The act of smiling is conditioned to pleasant feelings and associations.
- Make yourself feel good. The aim of the process is to feel good. Thus, the athlete

should continue the above activities until a positive attitude is achieved.

Waking and deliberately developing a positive attitude can be learned just like every other behaviour. Normally this can be achieved in around a week. To develop this control, swimmers should also develop the following habits:

- Place some unusual object next to the bed to serve as a signal to start the wake-up procedure as soon as it is noticed upon waking. It should be positioned so that it is likely to be the first object that is recognized (some of my swimmers have placed a photograph of themselves after a successful performance; this has a dual effect, as it reinforces positive thoughts and happiness).
- The first interaction of the day between the swimmer and another significant person should be for them to enquire about the adequacy of the wake-up procedure and what mood prevails (at big meets, this can become a very positive dialogue between room-mates).
- Use the wake-up procedure for both night sleep and extended rest periods – that is, between heats and finals as well as morning wake-ups.

This simple procedure influences an athlete's attitudes for the day by producing a positive approach to daily events. Although it may seem trivial, no event is too small to be considered and/or used if it will assist in producing the best performance of which a swimmer is capable. The major period of time between waking and racing should be devoted to following activities that avoid upsets. The most influential events are psychological in nature. Activities during this time should be planned and monitored; some of the major events of this period are discussed below.

Pre-Race Activities

What and when to eat: Prior to race day and when away from home, food service availability should be determined. Features such as rush times, length of lines waiting for service, service speed and extent of menu should be investigated. As a coping response, alternative eating places should be found. For very important races, it probably is wisest to take one's own food. This would place this potentially upsetting event under the athlete's complete control.

Rest or mild activities: A large proportion of the pre-race events are devoted to consuming time. Planned activities should be enjoyable and non-stressful. Minor diversionary activities should be tolerated. No matter what is done, the athlete should always have the upcoming race at the back of his/her mind. Impulsive or silly actions could produce distractions and possibly injury. Just consider these as examples from major league baseball: Milwaukee Brewers first baseman Richie Sexson pulled a muscle stretching a new cap; Atlanta Braves left-hander Mike Hampton, who strained his right calf in a treadmill accident, reinjured himself stepping out of the shower. And St Louis Cardinals minor leaguer Mike Crudale broke his toe answering the phone!

Equipment preparation and list: The swimmer should ritually attend to his/her equipment before leaving for the race site. This serves as a way of focusing the athlete's attention on the importance of the race.

When and how to travel to the race site: This should be scheduled, and adequate time planned in order for it to be achieved. An alternative route and mode of transport should also be determined. If a problem were to arise with the 'normal' transport (like missing the bus), a coping response would be to use alternative arrangements (hail a taxi, or hitch a lift with someone).

When to use performance-enhancement imagery: This assists the athlete to keep the principal purpose of the day in mind. If it is done periodically, it will focus the athlete on pre-race preparations and the assessment of their goals.

Group activities: Stress reactions are reduced in groups. If some athletes wish to participate in group activities they should be encouraged to do so. Group activities should be monitored, particularly if there is a potential for personality conflicts. The group atmosphere must be positive, light and active; for example fun quizzes, board or video games, and suchlike.

Psychological Problems

Two psychological problems often arise during this time: loss of confidence and an increase in tension.

Loss of Confidence

This causes a change in an athlete's appraisal of achieving race goals, and symptoms may be any or some of the following: reduced activity, lethargic movements, unhappy appearance, isolation from others, answers to questions that do not contain much information, a reluctance to talk to the coach or others, compliance but without enthusiasm, and a lack of attention to equipment.

As an attempt to overcome this problem, several actions can be followed. Use performance-enhancement imagery to rehearse sections of the race. Describe to others, or to oneself, what will be done in various scenarios that could occur in the race. Say out loud the positive self-statements that will be repeated during the race. Simulate parts of the race by using a longer-than-usual warm-up.

Once confidence is regained, the planned pre-race strategy should be recommenced at an appropriate stage. Some, or all of the above activities should be repeated until confidence is restored. It is helpful to include some of these actions in pre-race strategies to serve as 'insurance' against a loss of confidence occurring.

Increase in Tension

This problem is usually a precursor to the onset of anxiety, and results from becoming too aroused without appropriate mental control. Tension needs to be dissipated through diversionary activities that have some energy cost. Activities such as walking, easy running, table tennis, playing cards, or games in groups are useful. Activities such as reading, writing letters and watching television may be too passive to be of value. The level of activity has to moderate the level of tension in the athlete.

Avoiding Trouble

The main challenge for pre-race preparation away from the competition site is biding one's time so that no detrimental events occur. Little can be done at this time to enhance performance, but much could happen to detract from performance. Events should therefore be planned so that activities are purposeful – indeed, everything undertaken at the race site should be planned, because race performances can be dramatically affected by seemingly insignificant events. Initial activities after arrival at the race venue will 'set the stage' for the activities that follow, and undertaking deliberate activities immediately upon arrival will set the pattern for the remainder of the pre-race strategy.

A major task for achieving control over race readiness is to produce a constant reference point for preparations to occur, irrespective of the race site. One way of doing this is to perform enhancement imagery while moving around in the open air as the first activity; this produces a focus of attention on the race in the environment in which it is to occur. The scope of imagery in this early stage of preparation should encompass the whole race. This contrasts with what will be imagined later, because as the race approaches, the scope of imagery should narrow to the early segments of the race.

Some individuals prefer to start the real preparation for a race by completing a relaxation session with mental imagery immediately before leaving for the competition site. Others prefer to engage in relaxation as the first activity when they arrive at the race venue. The purpose behind these activities is to develop a consistent starting point for the planned routines that lead to the start of a race. It is good practice to have a consistent, comfortable activity as the first at the race site. From that consistent reference point, all planned activities should start on a predictable path.

The Warm-up

Warm-up should be as close as possible to the race start. If it occurs well before a race, it is possible that its benefits may dissipate before the event starts. There are three major effects to be achieved through a warm-up. First, the core temperature of the body should rise. Second, the neuromuscular patterns of the skill activities that will occur in the race should have been practised through some race-intensity-specific activity; this second feature means that the skill patterns exhibited in the warm-up should match those that are likely to occur in the race – that is, specific race segment pacing. Third, it is the first opportunity to focus on features of the physical and mental dimensions of the race. When deciding on warm-up activities, the swimmer must:

- justify the purpose behind each activity;
- work up the content, quality and intensity of the activities so that eventually they are the same as those of the race;
- perform some activities at an intensity that matches the highest effort levels that will occur in the race;
- have a warm-up that is open-ended; that is, it is not completed until the swimmer is 'ready'.

Once a warm-up is completed, the effects developed should not be allowed to wear off. Layers of clothing to preserve the elevated body temperature should be worn, and repeated precise-skill activity should occur in the period between the finish of the warm-up and the race start. There is no need to worry about expending energy that otherwise might be used in a race.

During this time fluid levels should be maintained. Drinks should be permitted, although some individuals should not take those with sugar in the last two hours before the start.

Coaches and parents should offer no new information or instructions, should elicit responses from the athlete by questioning him/her about some part of the race strategy, and should only focus on the early segments of the race. During this period it is also advisable for athletes to start to isolate themselves from others (well-wishers, competitors, media, agents); this makes it easier to focus on the upcoming race, and reduces distractions.

Stretching is another valuable activity that can be useful in the last phase of race preparations; however, it should not be overdone. Exercises should involve all joints to be used in the race, and each exercise should have a purpose to achieve some feeling of warmth and/or looseness. Stretching exercises should be performed alone so that there is no reliance upon another being. At this late stage of preparation, unnecessary second-party dependencies, such as massages, should be avoided.

As the race approaches, the content of the pre-race strategy should be such that the athlete relies more and more on events and actions over which he/she has total control. By keeping active and warm, and focusing on deliberate and practised activities, a state can be developed that is incompatible with psychological problem states such as anxiety, loss of confidence and increased tension. The warm-up signals that the 'race' has begun, and that the final preparations for racing have started.

Physical and Mental Build-up

At some designated time prior to race start, a swimmer should enter a phase of pre-race preparations that serve to heighten their responses and readiness to perform. This concerns a physical and mental build-up that will peak and coincide with the race start. A variety of activities are possible in a race build-up routine. The routine should start with the swimmer isolating themselves from all personal interactions, even with a coach. The role of a coach or adviser at this time is one of purely monitoring what the athlete is doing, and being a resource if required. This isolation allows the athlete to concentrate on planned physical and mental activities.

Physical activities should increase in their intensity as the race approaches. Bursts of activity become faster, but cover shorter distances. Stretching exercises become fewer, but faster and more dynamic. The amount of physical activity also increases over time so that just before the race, the swimmer is in constant motion. That motion will facilitate the control of physical arousal, which needs to be high if the swimmer is to start well. The swimmer should engage in positive self-talk. If it is difficult to concentrate on covert self-talk, then the positive statements should be muttered aloud. Muttering requires more concentration than thinking and may have better potential for self-control effects.

Task concentration changes as the race approaches: the closer the start, the greater the concentration on the start and the early race segments. The last thoughts before the start should be of how to do the best start possible. Thus as the race approaches, distant and final segments of a race strategy drop out of the swimmer's sphere of concentration.

Emotional Build-up

A procedure used by some of the greatest athletes in the world is called 'emotional build-up'. It consists of selecting some aggressive or assertive emotion – being furious or angry, hating some object, being wild or mad, wanting to attack the pool – which is deliberately imagined. It usually occurs quite close to the race start, possibly in the last 5 to 10min. As the race approaches, the intensity of the emotion is increased so that at the blocks, the swimmer controls optimum emotional and physical arousal through concentrating on perfection of the start. That state constitutes the development of a maximum race-readiness state.

Performance-enhancement imagery should be used frequently as a procedure for maintaining focus on the race. As the race approaches, segments rehearsed should increasingly be those of the early part of the race. Distant segments will lose their effect as the race start becomes imminent. The last imagery should be of the starting segment (*see* Fig. 85 for a swimmer focusing on the start).

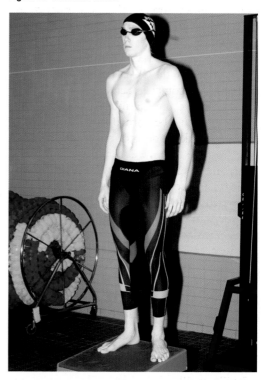

Figure 85 Swimmer focus.

Pre-race Strategy: Synopsis

A pre-race strategy requires an athlete to achieve certain outcomes:

- It should minimize the chances of distractions or problems occurring that might interfere with the production of a perfect race.
- Emotional control and intensity should peak in the seconds before the start.
- The swimmer should never lose deliberate control over the emotional states that are created.
- He should control thinking so that it is on the task of racing and proper preparations.
- Thought control should narrow to focus on the race as the race approaches.
- The highest physical arousal (developed through physical and emotional activities) should be timed to coincide with the narrowest focus of attention (the start) just as the race is to begin.

These features require a swimmer to perform a pre-race strategy that will produce the desired outcome of maximum race-readiness. Pre-race strategies should be developed on strategy planning sheets, and each item should be justified on the basis of its producing a desirable outcome; phases of the strategy should achieve predetermined goals. Pre-race strategies should be learned, and some training sessions should be devoted to the total practice of at least the race site activities.

The first pre-race strategy will serve as the basis for future strategies, and will be altered with each successive race as new elements are included and tried and others discarded. In time, precision and competence for developing the ideal race-readiness state will improve. Too much detail in a pre-race strategy is better than too little. Written strategies should always be taken to races. Should there be difficulty in concentrating on what should be done or thought, then the strategies should be read, and this will serve to focus the swimmer's attention on the task at hand. Much learning is involved in the development and deployment of strategies; however, practice at training and experience in races will contribute to the development of their desirable effects. They need to be worked on with the same intensity and importance as is given to any activity surrounding racing.

COMPETITION STRATEGIES

Race strategies contain all the behaviours and thoughts to be performed in a race. The preparation of a race strategy should develop sufficient information and mental activity to totally consume the duration of the race. Pre-planning competitive performances in this way reduces stress.

Segmenting the Performance

Segmenting a race is the best way to approach a complicated and extended event such as the majority of endurance races. A race should be divided into discrete units, each with its own challenges and content, goals, and evaluation criteria. The actual dissection of a race is a particularly individual process. The purpose of segmenting is to make the concept of a race one where the swimmer sequentially concentrates on and achieves short-term goals that are intermediate to achieving final race goals.

Segments constitute the basic units for mental rehearsal of endurance races. In a pre-race strategy, any mental rehearsal should attempt to focus on an entire segment, rather than isolated features taken out of context. Whether segment goals were or were not achieved should be evaluated at the end of each segment. If they were not, then a goal-recovery routine should be immediately implemented to recapture the features that should have been achieved.

This means that one of two things could happen at the transition stage from one segment to the next: first, if segment goals were achieved, a swimmer would proceed with the entire next segment. Second, if segment goals were not achieved, a goal-recovery routine would be implemented. After a recovery routine, the swimmer would enter the scheduled segment at the most appropriate place for the position in the race.

Segmenting a performance produces sustained, elevated performances. The swimmer should not think of the next segment until the current one is completed. Strategies should be developed around a segmented race plan.

Task-Relevant Thinking

At least two-thirds of the thought content of a race strategy should involve task-relevant thinking, because the latter is essential for maintaining form in a race. The technical aspects of swimming – for example pacing, intensity, breathing control, arm action, body position – contribute to the major improvements in performance that result from using strategies. Task-relevant thinking is stressed when increased speed is required, because an improvement in action speed should be attained through a technique change, not increased effort.

What types of task-relevant thoughts are used depends upon the stage of the race.

When a swimmer is not fatigued, such as in the first segment, specific technique should not be considered, as form that has been developed by training and is unhindered by fatigue will naturally emerge. If technique items were thought of early in a race, the phenomenon of 'cognitive interference' would occur, where thinking about doing automatic neuromuscular patterns while not fatigued actually reduces efficiency of function. It is only when fatigue is first recognized that thoughts should turn to specific technique features. Thus in the early stages of a race, task-relevant thinking should be general, such as focusing on pacing, positioning, or the clarity of thinking of the strategy.

If the swimmer 'runs out' of things to think of, or suddenly goes 'blank' while using a race strategy, this is called the 'dead spot' phenomenon. It indicates lost control of focus, and is a serious problem. It usually arises when too little strategy content is planned, and degrades performances. To avoid prolonged detrimental effects from this phenomenon, a swimmer should plan a dead-spot recovery routine. A popular approach is to prepare some task-relevant action with which the swimmer feels very safe and competent, and use that as the thought focus-point in order to recover and return to the strategy. That re-entry point will prompt concentration once again on task-relevant actions and thoughts.

To avoid dead spots or distractions, the manner in which task-relevant thoughts are used is important. The information that is planned should be cycled through a number of times. Constantly changing content keeps the information that is being considered fresh and vibrant. Developing different ways of thinking about each technical aspect is beneficial as it avoids monotony. This variety assists in keeping thoughts vital. Through variety and a constant change in control emphasis, the probability of 'dead spots' occurring is reduced.

The actual task-relevant content considered in a race strategy depends upon the individual. It should focus on producing the most efficient form of energy application and economical form of skill. Because of the complexity of swimming races one should never have difficulty in developing sufficient task-relevant content for a race strategy. Task-relevant thoughts sustain form and retard loss of efficiency. They also block the recognition of fatigue for extended periods of time.

Mood Words

Generally, two-thirds of a race strategy is consumed by thinking of task-relevant features; the other third is partly consumed by thinking of 'mood' words. Mood words set the mood of a performance. Language has certain 'basic' or primitive words which, when spoken or thought, have some movement or emotional component: they cause a physical reaction in the body. For example, the word 'crunch' conveys the feeling of strength more than does a sterile statement such as 'create force'.

Research has shown that when one thinks of words that produce a physical and/ or emotional component, performance is increased. It is therefore an advantage to think mood words that fit the mood of a performance. So when a swimmer wants to be strong, they should think mood words that generate strength; when they want to be quick, they should think speed words. How one thinks determines how one acts, therefore words that have an appropriate and direct action meaning should be used in strategies.

Mood words are differentiated from other words because of the physical/emotional reaction component: if a word or phrase does not produce that component, then it is not a 'mood' word. Fig. 86 lists some synonyms for various swimming-race capacities: individuals may select words that 'work for them' from this list, or they may add words from their own experience. The words should be interspersed throughout the strategy to match the variations in performance capacity demands. Thus the mid-section of a race should include some power words (such as 'pump', 'thump', 'rip', 'blast') that are spread throughout that segment. In a final segment, stability might be enhanced by concentrating on balance words such as 'solid', 'smooth' and so on.

Figure 86 Mood words.

Mood words - suggested synonyms for swimming-race capacities

Strength crush, squash, violent, solid, crunch, intense, muscle, haul, bear-hug, might, force, drive, grind, drag, press, push, lean

Power might, force, heave, impel, smash, snap, rip, blast, boom, bang, thump, thrust, explode, hoist, crumble

Speed fast, explode, alert, lunge, thrust, jab, rap, smack, brief, flick, whip, fling, pop, dash, quick

Agility nimble, move, dance, prance, brisk, alert, quick, shuffle, agile

Balance rock-hard, block, dead, solid, firm, rooted, anchored, set, rigid, hard

---

Mood words are used to embellish task-relevant thoughts, and to control actions and the mood (capacity) of a race.

The mood-word content that is used will comprise a 'sport language', as opposed to being a technical language. Thinking of pure technical statements, such as 'keep the elbow high' or 'finish off the kick', may interfere with performance because the processing of the sterile language components can be distracting, which causes performance to suffer. On the other hand, if the technical statement is translated into mood and primitive words that require no translation and are understood easily, performance will be enhanced.

The expression of a strategy must consider the language used. The language should be that of the swimmer and phrased in simple terms that do not require translation. Mood words should also be spread through a segment and said purely by themselves. The utterance of 'blast, blast, blast' can produce an increase in performance quality if power is required. A similar phenomenon occurs with other mood components, depending upon the capacity required at any particular stage of a race.

Mood-word utterances need to be added to a strategy. They can be used to break up sections of task-relevant thinking, and will consume some of the remaining one-third of the race thought content that is not used by task-relevant thoughts. The role of mood words is twofold. First, they are used to enhance performance capacities used in a race if they are uttered in concert with the appropriate capacity. Second, they make the language of a strategy more meaningful, being more expressive and effective than most of the bland technical state-

ments used by coaches. Mood words enhance performance, and they are an important feature of the content and expression of race strategies.

Positive Self-Statements

A critical feature of good race preparation and performance is positive thinking. The remaining race-strategy content, after task-relevant thinking and mood words have been developed, comprises positive self-state-ments. These three emphases of thought content constitute the total strategy. The statement of meaningful positive phrases helps maintain race effort, and swimmers should be encouraged to talk positively to themselves mentally, as if they were coaching themselves in the race.

Positive self-statements should not be meaningless, cheerleader-type expressions, for example 'go, go, go', and 'let's do it now'; rather, they should be meaningful phrases. Fig. 87 lists some examples of positive state-ments for four different situations in races: i) encouraging oneself, ii) handling effort, iii) evaluating segment goals, and iv) general positive self-talk. Positive self-talk should be spread completely throughout the strategy, and its inclusion should prevent any tendency to develop negative appraisals of perform-ance. As with task-relevant content and mood words, positive self-talk in swimming activi-ties has been shown to enhance performance.

The expression of positive self-statements and mood words is best if second person phras-ing is used. If that does not work, then first person expressions might be tried. Neverthe-less, the use of the second person appears to produce a perception of control over oneself,

Figure 87 Positive self-statements.

Self-encouragement
'You are doing great'
'Keep achieving those goals'
'This is the opportunity to dominate'

Effort Control
'It may hurt but concentrate on flowing movements'
'You have prepared for this so execute your strategy'
'Others are hurting just as much but they do not have a strategy'

Segment Goals
'The pace was dead-on. Now lengthen your stroke'
'Your split is just what you wanted'
'That segment improved your race time'

Positive Self-talk
'Great work'
'This will be even better than planned'
'This feels great. You really are stroking long'

and this is a consistent feature of the strategies that are formed by champions in many sports.

Coping Behaviours

Coping behaviours are important for race strategies because they govern the level of disruption when problems occur. For every preferred action an alternative action for achieving the same outcome should be planned; this allows the swimmer to cope with any problems that arise in a race. A number of general problems can occur in races, and these are different to when a deliberate planned activity does not work. Strategies should be developed for handling these general difficulties, even though they do not appear in the body of a race strategy. Rather, they are included as a general problem-solving capacity that should be developed, learned, and taken to every race.

If a swimmer develops a general appraisal or feeling of losing self-control with regard to executing the race strategy, a number of coping behaviours are possible that might assist in regaining self-control. For example:

- Return to basic fundamentals with which the swimmer feels very comfortable; engage in emotional positive self-talk; and/or concentrate on mood words that are appropriate for the segment being executed.

- Dead spots: the reactions to a loss of control are also appropriate for this problem. A re-entry point to the strategy should be at a very well learned and comfortable phase of the segment being executed.

- Distractions: dead-spot recovery routines are useful for regaining a focus of attention on the planned strategy. Another alternative is to analyze the situation and determine exactly where the strategy should be re-entered, and execute from there.

- Errors: execute planned coping behaviours. The major feature of coping behaviours and general coping strategies is that an athlete should never become rattled. The capacity to develop problem-solving behaviours for any race difficulty should be an aim of training and strategy development. With that capability, a swimmer should be able to race with confidence and certainty, and the race experience will be appraised as being a potentially positive happening.

Psychological Intensification

One of the principal aims of using strategies is to maintain control throughout a race. As a swimmer grows more tired during an event, fatigue symptoms emerge as a very strong distraction. However, there are methods to mask the detrimental effects of exercise fatigue, and the process of psychological intensification during a race is one method for coping with this problem. A major pain theory suggests that while an individual keeps his/her mind very busy and totally focused on some activity, the brain will not recognize a fatigue state. This means that if a swimmer can keep their attention totally involved with mental activity (strategy content), they will be able to control themselves in a fatigued state. The implication of this principle is that a swimmer should keep their mind totally occupied with thought content during a race. As the intensity of fatigue pain increases, thought intensity also has to increase in order to maintain control.

Psychological intensification is used to guard against the detrimental effects of fatigue. It stops complacency, loss of control, and dead spots. The procedure requires the volume of thought content and the intensity of thinking to gradually increase as fatigue develops.

In the early stages of a race when there is no fatigue, or the level of effort is in a 'steady state', a swimmer does not have to think too intently: the main aim is to control the performance and execute strategy content. However, with most swimmers there is a stage in a race where it is realized that increased effort is needed to continue, and this is when thought control needs to be intensified, otherwise performance will deteriorate. Intensification occurs by changing the nature of the thought content, and thinking 'harder' and 'faster'. There are some noteworthy features about the relationship of fatigue and thoughts in a race. During the initial part of the race and steady-state phase, the thought content is two-thirds task-relevant tactics and pacing rather than specific technique, and one-third mood words and positive thinking. The emphasis is on control and executing the planned strategy.

Just prior to the recognition of increasing fatigue, thought processes need to be altered: at this stage the swimmer introduces specific and detailed technique items that aim to keep the skill level as efficient as possible; they also make a deliberate attempt to think 'harder' by attempting to focus more intently on the changed task-relevant strategy content. The rate of thinking should increase and continue to increase for the remainder of the race in concert with increase in fatigue.

Towards the end of the race, subjective symptoms of fatigue become more intense. Before that stage, thought content should be increased even further through an even more deliberate focus on thinking, and a major emphasis on controlling the technical efficiency of movements. The ratio of mood words and positive thinking to task-relevant content remains the same; it is the volume and intensity of thinking that increases. That increase has to be sufficient to block the recognition of pain, because if the swimmer were to relax the intensification process during this latter phase, pain sensations would be recognized and performance would deteriorate markedly – and there is no chance of recovering the level of performance once that occurs.

Intensification relies heavily on the swimmer developing variety and different methods of thinking. If they were to concentrate too long on one item, it is possible that a rhythmical and monotonous form of thinking would develop. That monotony is similar to the chanting of mantras, and reduces sensitivity and even produces hypnotic states: therefore a lack of continual thought vitality is counter productive to good racing. This feature of race strategy development and its use in the intensification process cannot be over-emphasized.

Another feature of intensification is the relationship of changes in intensity to changes in fatigue. Thought intensity should increase before fatigue, as this prevents fatigue interrupting the conduct of the strategy. If a swimmer were to wait until fatigue sensations increased, then they would be coping with fatigue rather than masking it at critical stages in a race. By pre-empting fatigue sensation changes, the swimmer maintains a preferred-action orientation that is most desirable for producing maximum performance. Psychological intensification maintains concentration control, and that control will facilitate maximum levels of racing performance.

The Race Start

The race start warrants particular attention because it initiates strategy execution. It is important that races commence in the best possible manner because the first impression of the race will influence ensuing appraisals during the performance.

The start segment is the final focus of the pre-race strategy in the race build-up routine. At the starting line, the only goals considered should be those of the start segment. At that stage, to all intents and purposes, the swimmer should perceive the race as being a challenge to do a start as planned. Once the start is initiated, the swimmer focuses only on strategy content. If it has been learned well, it will unfold in sequence in much the same way as does a script in a play. The execution of the start segment should not require any settling-in phase, because all actions need to be self-controlled and aimed at producing the best start possible. The principal reason behind a start strategy is to introduce strategy concentration and performance levels with the utmost precision and effect.

Debriefing

One of the most significant opportunities for learning to occur is via the provision of immediate feedback. After a race, this is rarely considered; however, it is advocated that debriefing should become a part of race conduct. During the protocol (*see* Fig. 25) the swimmer should debrief the racing performance and race preparations independently of (and before speaking to) the coach or any others of significance.

Some Considerations

Some considerations that should be entertained are:
- Evaluate the goal achievements for each segment of the race.
- What can be improved in the strategy?
- How can concentration be improved?
- What content changes are required for task-relevant thinking, mood words and positive thinking?
- What was done but was not planned for?
- What was not done but had been planned?
- Are there any preparation improvements needed?
- Was the intensification adequate?
- Does anything need to be added to either the race or pre-race strategies?

Debriefing is a necessary feature of strategy development and learning. The effects of racing will be more influential on subsequent performances. The institution of this process will alter the nature of racing because it will focus the evaluation of racing on strategy execution. This in turn will probably produce a perception that *the goal of racing is to execute a race strategy.*

Learning Race Strategies

Learning race strategies is very similar to learning pre-race strategies. Some features that should be followed in the learning process are listed below:

- Practise race strategies and segments in a variety of competitions.
- Race-strategy segments should be the content of mental rehearsals for preparations.
- Around 20 per cent of strategy learning and rehearsals should be devoted to coping with alternatives as well as recovery routines.

The first attempt at strategies will probably be very detailed and lengthy. With time, practice, and the requirement to only refine previous strategies, development will become less time-consuming. After considerable practice, strategies will become a series of key words that trigger chains of thoughts. For very experienced swimmers, it may not be necessary to write strategies for every race. However, it is always necessary to prepare a strategy for serious races, and they should be recorded, even if they are of the form of a race plan indicating segments and salient features, and a series of words that initiate the proper thought focus for each segment. The detail, sequencing and alternatives of the race strategy must be learned.

No two races will have the same strategy. Adjustments to every swim, previous learning experiences, and racing conditions produce a continual refinement in strategy development and execution competence. This should result in continual racing improvements.

CHAMPIONS' CHARACTERISTICS

Coaches have often wondered if their swimmers behave in the most appropriate fashion to improve optimally. The characteristics that are universal across sporting champions and world

Figure 88 Champions characteristics checklist.

1. I make firm friends within the team who are serious about the sport.
2. I tolerate other athletes at all times.
3. I join fellow athletes in social functions.
4. I attempt to be liked by and friendly with other athletes.
5. I train with athletes who are cooperative.
6. I do not get upset when criticized by other athletes.
7. I offer constructive and positive advice to other athletes.
8. I accept advice from other athletes.
9. I help other athletes if asked to do so.
10. I am interested in team matters and projects.
11. I ask the coach why things are done in particular ways in my sport.
12. Unless I have other evidence, I trust that what the coach says is correct.
13. The coach and I together make decisions about my sport.
14. I usually do things as the coach says.
15. I let the coach know if I disagree with any decision or directive.
16. When asked to try new things, I apply myself fully.
17. I have asked the coach to tell me privately when I have done something wrong.
18. I can forget awkward social mistakes.
19. I calm down quickly after being upset by something involving my sport.
20. I do not brood over sporting problems or mistakes.
21. From my mistakes, I learn to do things better in the future.
22. I accept the blame for things that go wrong with me in my sport.
23. I prefer to know the training programme well in advance of the session.
24. I like training sessions which keep me busy all the time.
25. Slow-motion movies or videos help me to understand my sport better.
26. I always arrive early for training.
27. I never leave training early.
28. I try to do everything as well as possible at training.
29. I occasionally feel grouchy and want to work alone.
30. Feelings of ill-health, stomach upsets, and vague pains do not occur.
31. I organize my equipment well.
32. I have characteristics which are superior to other athletes.
33. I prefer to have someone plan trips and other forms of organization.
34. I am very enthusiastic about my sport.
35. My sport is the most important activity that I do.
36. I primarily compete for myself.
37. I could train by myself if the coach gave me adequate directions.
38. Watching my weight is important.
39. I seldom miss training through illness.
40. Before arguing on sporting matters, I wait until I am sure that what I will say is correct.
41. I do not break team rules.
42. I am conscientious about the details of my sport.
43. I make a point of not being absent-minded or forgetful of details concerning my sport.
44. I am as enthusiastic as possible about my sport.
45. I do not miss training even if some other interesting event comes up.
46. I tell the truth when I describe what I did in training.
47. I look for reasons, rather than for excuses, to explain what happens at training and in competitions.
48. Unfamiliar arenas do not affect my performance.
49. I enjoy training and competing.
50. I strive for better performances in training and competitions.
51. I keep my equipment well-organized and ready for use.
52. I make training challenging for myself.
53. I put more intensity into competing than I do into training.

Figure 88 (Continued)

54. I plan my preparations and competitions in detail.
55. I develop plans that tell me what to do if things go wrong at competitions.
56. I warm up by myself.
57. My warm-ups include things that will be done in the competition.
58. I do not let anyone bother me during warm-ups.
59. I do not worry about opponents.
60. I am nervous and tense before a competition.
61. If I am troubled before a contest, I can regain my composure.
62. I control my excitement by picturing what I will be doing in the contest.
63. I do not get distracted once my competition preparations begin.
64. I mentally rehearse my contest plan as often as possible.
65. I can maintain my concentration throughout the warm-up.
66. Just before the contest starts, I concentrate on how well I will start the competitive effort.
67. I set realistic goals for my contests.
68. Unusual events do not upset or distract me before a contest.
69. I do focus on the preparations for, and content of, the competition.
70. I start contests properly.
71. I am prepared to take a lead early no matter what the cost.
72. I do not save myself in order to make a good finishing effort.
73. When I am tired in a contest, I concentrate on my prepared plan.
74. I always do my best in competitions even though winning may not be possible.
75. Every competition is seen as an opportunity for me to improve.
76. I think only about my performance in a contest.
77. I do not get upset by officiating.
78. The more important the competition, the more enjoyable it is.
79. I use the information gained from a competition to modify and plan for the next contest.
80. I like the coach to tell me how well I am training and performing.
81. I like the coach to comment frequently on my techniques.
82. I like other athletes to notice and talk to me about my performances.
83. I like to compete and train with friends.
84. I like to train with athletes who are cooperative.
85. I like my parents to be interested in my sporting activities.
86. I like to be able to receive the outstanding athlete award in contests.
87. I like my friends from outside my sport to be interested in what I do.
88. I like training programmes to include a lot of variety.
89. I like each training session to be a challenge.
90. I like my skills to continually improve in training.
91. I like to know my progress and improvement in my sport.
92. I want to get as much information as possible about my sport.
93. I like the travel that is associated with my sport.
94. I like my name to appear in newspapers and on radio and TV.
95. I can compete well in every contest.
96. When my competition performances improve, I train harder.
97. I like to place frequently in competitions.
98. I like to qualify for at least one final at every competition.
99. Every training item and competition is a challenge to me.
100. I want to improve in all aspects of my sport, not just my speciality.

TOTAL SCORE OUT OF 100...........

record holders, irrespective of nationality, sport, or gender, have been described. There were a surprising number of features common to at least 75 per cent of the tested champions. It is now possible to assess athletes and let them determine the level of adequacy of their behaviours and attitudes toward swimming. The 'Champions Characteristics Checklist' (Rushall, 1987), as shown in Fig. 88 is reproduced for use by coaches to have their swimmers evaluate themselves on these critical factors. It is contended that an athlete cannot achieve his/her highest potential unless the vast majority of these features are evident.

Coaches should give the checklist to their swimmers and emphasize that only honest answering is of value. A characteristic should only be checked if it is absolutely certain that it is indicative of the swimmer. Young swimmers will normally score low because they have not had a chance to fully develop all the features that contribute to being a champion. Any missing features should be improved and/or developed. (A score of more than eighty would be a desirable initial target for young swimmers to eventually achieve.)

This checklist is part of the SPORT PSYCHOLOGY CONSULTATION SYSTEM (© Sports Science Associates, 1987) and is reproduced with permission by its author, Emeritus Professor Brent Rushall.

Instructions

This checklist contains characteristics and behaviours that have been shown to be consistent indicators of champion athletes. You are required to read each item and then decide if the item is something which is indicative of you. It is important that you answer honestly. If there is the slightest feeling that the item may not always be applicable to you, then do not respond. Answer the checklist by circling the number alongside the description that is true for you. After completion, count the number of responses you have made. That count is the percentage of thoughts and actions that you have that are required to think and act like a champion.

MENTAL SKILLS

Given the contention that there is a need to attend to psychological and behavioural deficiencies in high performance swimming, mental skills training exercises are proposed as a viable procedure for implementing constructive programmes. Exercises in a mental skills training programme are meant to assist coaches to embark upon a training programme with a minimum of inconvenience. They are constructed so they can be used by coaches with little training in behaviour modification, and should allow coaches to determine goals for mental skills training, to implement programmes by using appropriate exercises, and to evaluate the effectiveness of any devised programme.

The scope of the exercises is not all-encompassing. They are not related to every problem that arises in a swimmer, nor are they intended to develop every psychological characteristic important to sport. What should be included are those exercises which have proven to be beneficial, have developed essential characteristics and behaviours in very successful performers, and, if developed in the neophyte swimmer, will lead to an accelerated rate of performance improvement and an enhanced level of ultimate achievement.

There are some mistaken assumptions about altering behaviours and developing mental skills in athletes that first of all need to be dispelled.

First Misconception

It is a misconception that producing psychological effects is quick and easy. There is a general perception among coaches that altering psychological factors is a relatively easy procedure. The following are examples of common misconceptions of the involvement of psychology in sport: a single visit to a sports psychologist should correct all psychological deficiencies in an athlete; talking to a psychologist is all that is needed to 'correct' attitudinal problems; 'inspirational talks' are sufficient to alter a team's ability to win.

On the contrary, if mental skills are to be produced, the effort and time allocations that are required should at least be equated to that required to alter physical skills. Repetitions of mental skill elements, progressions towards a final global skill, feedback and reinforcement, and knowledge of progress, are essential features of the process required to develop mental skills. A swimmer must be prepared to apply his/her energies to all that is required to produce demonstrable changes in the psychological domain of sporting performance.

Second Misconception

Knowing what to do is the secret for effective psychology. It is a common belief that if a swimmer knows what they should be doing, then effective behaviour changes will result. Sport psychologists are often asked to give talks on what to do, how to behave, and what is necessary for effective motivation. In that arena knowledge is presented to both swimmers and coaches. However, knowledge or education alone is not a sufficient factor for producing behaviour change. Unless that knowledge is practised in simulated and real-life circumstances, coordinated with direction and the provision of feedback, and finally brought under the control of the swimmer, effective behaviour development will not occur. Knowing what to do does not guarantee that behaviours will change or occur. Knowing what needs to be done is not sufficient for mental skill or behaviour changes to occur. It is only when developmental practice procedures are followed that specific psychological changes can be effected.

Third Misconception

Mental skill development does not require the same amount of effort or time as do physical skill development and physiological conditioning. There is a common perception that psychological development programmes should be brief and not time-consuming. The tendency of coaches to give off-handed lip-service to what swimmers should be doing and thinking is evidence of this regard. The fact that when swimmers are not performing well, coaches turn to psychological reasons, such as 'bad attitudes', 'problem behaviours' and 'lack of desire', indicates a lack of understanding of what is needed to develop or correct mental skills.

To implement an effective mental skills training programme, swimmers have to perform even more sport-associated activities. Modern training programmes have realized the necessity for holding physical skill development practices and conditioning sessions on separate occasions. That need is based on the premise that if the two are mixed, there will be detrimental effects of each on the other so that the gains from practice are reduced to a less than optimum level.

The development of mental skills is a further requirement for the development of athletic excellence, and there is also a need for training programmes for specific mental skills. The resources that are required for psychological programmes have to be shared equally with physical skill and conditioning programmes.

One of the admirable features of mental skills training is that it does not always have to be conducted during scheduled training time. Much good work can be conducted in the form of away-from-training 'homework'. That possibility leads to the beneficial use of previously unproductive time. Thus it is not acceptable for coaches to contend that mental skills training cannot be implemented because there is no time at scheduled practices.

Having said that, as mental skills are developed, there is often a need to practise them during training sessions while skill and conditioning activities are being executed. Since many coaches rarely direct the mental activities of athletes, requiring athletes to execute mental skills in appropriate situations at training will fill an existing void and will not impose an excessive demand on them. A complicating feature of implementing a mental skills programme is the need for programming adequate mental skill practice trials in concert with physical practices. Once the organization for that integration is designed

Figure 89 Mental skills programme.

A. ESTABLISHING ATTITUDINAL AND MOTIVATIONAL BEHAVIOURS
Purpose: to increase the intrinsic positive value of the sporting experience.
Increasing the intensity of self-reinforcement
Positive interactions with others
Stopping negative thinking
Positive imagery

Purpose: to establish a goal-oriented focus for sporting activity elements.
Setting and evaluating personal activity goals
Setting group training goals

Purpose: to establish a constant orientation to the importance of sport participation.
Establishment of a daily positive focus
Daily positive recall
Periodic self-commitment

B. IMPORTANT SKILLS
Purpose: to learn imagery that will enhance performance.
Learning imagery control and vividness
Sensory recall training
Movement imagery training
Learning to relax: final stage
Relaxation and positive imagery for self-concept
Relaxation and positive imagery of an activity
Localized relaxation
Sleep, rest, and relaxation

C. COMPETITION PSYCHOLOGY
Purpose: to develop a basic competition strategy.
Segmenting a performance
Task-relevant thought content
Mood words content
Positive self-talk
Special considerations
Integrating a basic strategy
Competition goal-setting

Purpose: to develop competition preparation skills to facilitate
the use of competition strategies.
Waking with a positive attitude
Trouble-free planning
Establishing contest site mind-sets
Contest build-up routine
Learning and using pre-competition strategies

Purpose: to refine and embellish competition strategies.
Coping behaviors for competitions
Intensification skill
Start segment
Debriefing a performance

D. LONG-TERM ORIENTATION
Purpose: to establish a goal structure that will orient
performance and participation for a long time.
Setting sporting career goals
Setting relatively long-term goals
Setting performance goals
Setting performance progress goals

and implemented it will no longer impose an 'extra load' on the coach supervising the programme.

Mental skill development programmes require a similar amount of time allocation, effort expenditure, and practice in real-life situations as do the emphases of physical skill development and physiological conditioning.

It is not within the scope of this book to go into specific mental skills exercises in detail, but there are some general principles that can be followed, and many very good books and courses on the subject. There is also a growing network of accredited sports psychologists available to coaches and swimmers. Fig. 89 lists a suggested mental skills development programme: the content should be selected and then incorporated into a training plan. Mental skills need to be 'coached' with similar intensity and emphasis on importance, as are other factors in the training programme. Only concerted attention to the elements of any devised programme will produce desirable outcomes.

CHAPTER 13

Major Championship Meets

TRAVEL AND JET LAG

Jet lag occurs when your natural clock is not in time with the world around you, and although different individuals will be affected in different ways and to different degrees, everyone will be affected in some way. This short section is designed to make travel to competitions (and vacations) abroad easier by minimizing the impact of jet lag. The extent of any jet lag will be influenced by whether you are travelling east or west, and by how many hours of difference there are between your departure and arrival destinations; however, there are some general guidelines that will help.

Minimize the Impact of Travel

Pre-travel: Make sure you are well rested and have had sufficient sleep prior to departure.

Travel:

- Dress in loose and comfortable clothing – make sure you have enough options with warmer or cooler air cabins. Take some creature comforts, though don't weigh yourself down!
- Keep mobile during the flight by in-seat exercises and regular movement around the cabin.
- Drink fluid regularly, and avoid diuretic substances such as caffeine.
- Remove contact lenses before sleeping.
- If travelling overnight, sleep as much as you can on the plane.

You will need as much sleep in your destination as you do at home – once you have adjusted to local time, keep the same 'going to bed' and 'getting up' times, as this will help to ensure that you get adequate sleep. Remember that you may have lost some sleep through the flight, so you may need a bit more in the first few days. When you first arrive, if you wake in the night, try to remain in bed; but if you can't get back to sleep within 15–30min, it will probably be more productive for you to get up and do something relaxing, such as reading or listening to music (a relaxation CD might be helpful). When you feel sleepy, return to bed: hopefully you will then be able to get back to sleep.

Exposure to bright light during this time – such as that from a TV or computer screen – is likely to reduce the effects of your body's natural sleep hormones and make it even more difficult to return to sleep. Therefore avoid watching TV or playing computer games close to bedtime, or if you happen to wake in the night. It is probably prudent to avoid stimulating or exciting books, and TV series with 'cliff-hanger' endings, or computer games, as these will also act to disturb natural sleep processes.

Following travel, you are likely to be sleep-deprived, and this will result in your feeling sleepy during the day. Taking a nap for no more than 40min will help to repay some of the sleep debt, without impacting on your ability to acclimatize rapidly to the new time zone. Caffeine can be useful if used strategically to help you through periods of sleepiness. It generally takes 30min to work, and the effects last for about four hours. However, *avoid caffeine before bedtime*, as this will disrupt sleep. Despite some misleading claims to the contrary, there are no foodstuffs that improve or worsen jet lag, so you should aim to eat your usual diet at the equivalent local times to when you would normally eat at home.

TIME ZONE ACCLIMATIZATION

If your time zone acclimatization is left to chance and no interventions are used, your body will take around one day per time zone to adapt; this means that acclimatization for those travelling to the Beijing Olympics from Europe will take seven or eight days. However, if you use the correct strategy with appropriately timed sleep, light exposure and training, your internal body clock can be moved closer to Beijing time than 'home' time by the end of the second local night, and certainly the third.

Bright light is the most important factor in changing your body clock to the new time zone. Getting light exposure right in the first two days following arrival can be the key to adapting and acclimatizing quickly. The best time to seek natural, bright light during the first few days in the Far East is between 1pm and 7pm. By day three, the body should have adjusted enough to make light exposure at any time of day acceptable.

It is recommended to avoid daylight as much as possible in the first morning after arrival. To do this properly you may need to have your breakfast in your hotel room with the curtains still drawn. Try to eat at least something the evening before to help prevent you from waking early feeling hungry. Also take some breakfast-type snacks, along with some water, to your room, so that you can have something to eat without having to leave the room and expose yourself to bright sunlight on that crucial first morning.

THE SCHEDULING OF TRAINING

When exactly training is scheduled in the first few days will also have a major impact upon the time it will take you to acclimatize to the new time zone. Scheduling training at the 'wrong' time will slow down your acclimatization. Taking the 2008 Olympics example again, because the best time for light exposure in the first couple of days is between 1pm and 7pm, the training schedule should be modified in the first few days after arrival to reflect this. In addition, the early training sessions of a pre-Games camp should be less demanding than normal. The warm-up exercises, including the mobility and flexibility components of training, should be increased. However, the intensity of exercise, and particularly the level of difficulty or skill required, should be reduced to avoid injury. Interestingly for swimmers, the advice of experts is that morning training is best avoided until at least day three.

Top Tips for Keeping your Cool

Keeping cool in the heat is important all the time, and not just on competition/training days, and there are various ways this can be done:

- **Portable battery-operated fan:** A cooling breeze helps increase heat loss. If there is no natural breeze, then a fan can help.
- **A wide-brimmed hat**: Your head has a large surface area for heat absorption, and the wide brim protects your neck and shoulders from sunburn.
- **Mist spray**: A small atomizer/ mist spray of water can help you keep cool. Put a few ice cubes in the container and use when possible.
- **The 'cool collar':** A few ice cubes wrapped in a dampened towel and placed around the neck. This will help cool the blood flowing to and from your head (regularly replacing the ice is needed to maintain the collar's effectiveness).
- **Protective sunscreen:** Getting sunburned affects your body's ability to regulate temperature effectively and makes you more susceptible to the heat.

Top Tips for Keeping your Cool

- **Fluids:** Drink cool fluids at regular intervals – not only do the fluids help prevent dehydration, but they will also reduce heat illness. Cool fluids are absorbed well and help reduce body temperature.
- **Clothing:** Choose lightweight polyester fabrics that allow sweat to be wicked away and the skin to 'breathe'. Cotton fabrics are more likely to absorb sweat, which will reduce comfort.
- **Air-conditioning:** Buildings may have air-conditioning. Rather than staying outdoors and chatting after training/competing/meals and suchlike, move into the cooler environment.
- **Shade:** When you can't get into an air-conditioned environment, then find some shade. Direct sunlight increases body temperature as well as causing sunburn.
- **Cool showers:** Showering two or three times a day can help you stay feeling cool and refreshed. Removing dead skin cells and sweat build-up from the surface of the skin will also help you to sweat more efficiently. Perhaps try a cool shower at lunch and tea intervals.
- **Ice vests:** Ice vests can reduce the rise in the body's temperature during exercise in the heat, and prolong performance. The cooling vests can be worn for pre-cooling before exercise in the heat, or for recovery. There are now a number of different ice vests commercially available.
- **Hand cooling:** Hand cooling can be used as an effective way to reduce body temperature. You can achieve rapid cooling by placing you hands in a bucket of cold water because of the rich blood supply and wide connections between the arteries and veins in the hands. The principle is also the same for the feet and face, although these are less practical. Hand immersion in cold water can be effective and is a simple method, and the water doesn't have to be ice cold (between 10 and 20°C appears to be optimal) so it won't affect your dexterity.

Glossary of Technical Terms

Accredited meet A meet conducted with sufficient officials to certify conformance to the rules.

Admission Certain meets levy a charge for spectators, usually the larger, more prestigious events. Sometimes the meet programme (start sheet) is included in the price of admission.

Adverse analytical finding (AAF) Report from a WADA-accredited laboratory or other WADA-approved testing entity that identifies in a doping control sample the presence of a prohibited substance or its metabolites or markers (including elevated quantities of endogenous substances), or evidence of the use of a prohibited method. An adverse analytical finding does not necessarily lead to an anti-doping rule violation, since an athlete may have a 'therapeutic use exemption' for this particular substance. An adverse analytical finding may also correspond to a measurement performed on an athlete as part of a longitudinal study.

Age group swimming A programme through which a country provides competition for its younger members. Designed to encourage maximum participation, provide an educational experience, enhance physical and mental conditioning and develop a rich base of swimming talent.

Aggregate time Times achieved by four swimmers in individual events, which are added together to arrive at a relay entry time.

Anchor leg The final swimmer in a relay.

Anti-doping organization (ADO) Organization that is responsible for adopting and executing rules for initiating, implementing or enforcing any part of the doping control process. This includes, for example, the International Olympic Committee, the International Paralympic Committee, other major event organizations that conduct testing at their events, the World Anti-Doping Agency, International Sports Federations, and National Anti-Doping Organizations.

ASCA The American Swimming Coaches Association.

Axis An imaginary line from the top of the head through the spine to the toes, around which the body rotates.

Backstroke One of the four competitive racing strokes, basically any style of swimming on your back. Backstroke is swum as the first stroke in the medley relay and second stroke in the IM. In the backstroke the swimmer must stay on his or her back, except during the turns. The stroke is an alternating motion of the arms – much like the front crawl stroke – with a flutter kick. Since April of 1991, a swimmer is no longer required to touch the wall with his or her hand before executing the turn. The key to proper interpretation of the backstroke turn rule is the phrase 'continuous turning action', that is, a uniform, unbroken motion with no pauses. In a more technical interpretation, after the shoulder rotates beyond the vertical towards the breast, a continuous simultaneous double arm pull may be used to initiate the turn. There shall be no kick, arm pull, or flotation that is independent of the turn. The position of the head is not relevant. In all competitions, each swimmer's head must surface within 15m of the start of the race. This is a change from the 1988 FINA rule change which stated that a swimmer must surface within 10m of the start of a race. The rule was passed after US swimmer David Berkoff set a world record in the Seoul Olympics using a

35m underwater start. Backstroke race distances are 50m, 100m and 200m.

Blocks The starting platforms located behind each lane. Some pools have blocks at the deeper end of the pool, some have blocks at both ends. Blocks have a variety of designs and can be permanent or removable.

Breaststroke One of the four competitive racing strokes. Breaststroke is swum as the second stroke in the medley relay and the third stroke in the IM. Perhaps one of the most difficult strokes to master, the breaststroke requires simultaneous movements of the arms on the same horizontal plane. The hands are pushed forwards from the breast on or under the surface of the water, and brought backwards in the propulsive stage of the stroke simultaneously. The kick is a simultaneous thrust of the legs called a 'frog' or breaststroke kick. No flutter or dolphin kicking is allowed. Swimmers must touch the wall with both hands at the same time before executing their turn. Breaststroke race distances are 50m, 100m and 200m.

Bulkhead A wall constructed to divide a pool into different courses, such as a 50m pool into two 25m courses.

Butterfly One of the four competitive racing strokes. Butterfly (nicknamed 'the fly') is swum as the third stroke in the medley relay and first stroke in the IM. The most physically demanding stroke, butterfly features the simultaneous overhead stroke of the arms combined with the dolphin kick. The dolphin kick features both legs moving up and down together. No flutter kicking is allowed. As in breaststroke, swimmers must touch the wall with both hands before turning. The butterfly was 'born' in the early 1950s as a loophole in the breaststroke rules, and in 1956 became an Olympic event in Melbourne, Australia. In all US Swimming and FINA competitions, each swimmer's head must surface within 15m of the start of the race. This rule was passed at the 1998 FINA Congress in Perth, Australia. USA's Misty Hyman (Olympic 200m champion in Sydney 2000), among other swimmers, had utilized an extended underwater start prior to the restriction. Butterfly races are swum in 50m, 100m and 200m distances.

Cap The latex or lycra covering worn on the head of swimmers. The colours and team logos adorning these caps are limitless.

Carbohydrates The main source of food energy used by athletes.

Cards A card that may either be handed to the swimmer or given to the timekeeper behind the lane. Cards usually list the swimmer's name, competitor number, entry time, event number, event description, and the lane and heat number the swimmer will swim in. Backup times are written on these cards. Each event may have a separate card.

Centre of flotation A spot located within the chest near the sternum, which causes the body to float due to the buoyancy of the lungs.

Chain of custody Sequence of individuals or organizations who have the responsibility for a doping control sample, from its provision until it has been received by the laboratory for analysis.

Championship finals The top six or eight swimmers (depending on the number of pool lanes) who, after the heats swim, qualify to return to the finals.

Championship meet The meet held at the end of a season. Qualification times are necessary to enter the meet.

Chlorine The chemical used by most pools to kill the bacteria in water and keep it clear and safe to swim in.

Circle seeding A method of seeding swimmers when they are participating in a heats/finals event. The fastest eighteen to twenty-four swimmers are seeded in the last three heats, with the fastest swimmers being in the inside lanes.

Clinic A scheduled meeting for the purpose of education/instruction, for example officials' clinic, coaches' clinic.

Club A registered organization within the NGB.

Coach A person who trains and teaches athletes in the sport of swimming. Usually holds a recognized qualification.

Code of conduct An agreement signed by a swimmer prior to travel stating that the swimmer will abide by certain behavioral guidelines.

Code of ethics   A code of conduct that both swimmers and coaches are required to sign for certain events.

Copenhagen Declaration: The *Copenhagen Declaration on Anti-Doping in Sport* (Copenhagen Declaration) is a political document through which governments signal their intention to adopt the *World Anti-Doping Code* through the UNESCO International Convention against Doping in Sport. The Copenhagen Declaration was finalized by governments at the second World Conference on Doping in Sport in Copenhagen in March 2003.

Course   Designated distance (length of pool) for swimming competition. Long course = 50m / short course = 25m.

Court of Arbitration for Sport (CAS) Institution which is independent of any sports organization and provides for services in order to facilitate the settlement of sport-related disputes through arbitration or mediation by means of procedural rules adapted to the specific needs of the sports world. CAS is often referred to as 'sport's supreme court'. WADA has a right of appeal to CAS for doping cases under the jurisdiction of organizations that have implemented the World Anti-Doping Code.

Cut   US slang for qualifying time. A time standard necessary to attend a particular meet or event – 'he made the cut for Olympic trials'.

Deadline   The date that meet entries must be 'postmarked' by, to be accepted by the meet host.

Deck   The area around the swimming pool reserved for swimmers, officials and coaches.

Deck entries   Accepting entries into swimming events on the first day or later day of a meet.

Dehydration   The abnormal depletion of body fluids (water).

Development meet   A classification of meet or competition that is usually held early in the season. The purpose of a developmental meet is to allow all levels of swimmers to compete in a low-pressure environment.

Distance   How far a swimmer swims. Also used to describe events over 400m – 'he is a distance swimmer'.

Dive   Entering the water head first. Diving is not allowed during warm-ups except at the designated time, in specific lanes that are monitored by the swimmer's coach or designated personnel.

Diving pool   A separate pool or a pool set off to the side of the competition pool. This pool has deeper water and diving boards/platforms. During a meet, this area may be designated as a swim-down pool with proper supervision.

Doping control station   Location where the sample collection session is conducted.

Doping control   Process including test distribution planning, sample collection and handling, laboratory analysis, therapeutic use exemptions, results management, hearings and appeals.

DQ   Disqualified. This occurs when a swimmer has committed an infraction of some kind. A disqualified swimmer is not eligible to receive awards, nor can the time be used as an official time.

Drill   An exercise involving a portion or part of a stroke, used to improve technique.

Drop-off time   The differential between split times for both halves of a race.

Dry land   Training done out of the water that aids and enhances swimming performance.

Electronic timing   Timing system, usually with touch pads in the water, junction boxes on the deck with hook-up cables, buttons for back-up timing, and a computer type console that prints out the results of each race. At larger meets these systems are hooked up to a scoreboard that displays splits, times and overall results.

Entry fees   The amount per event a swimmer or relay is charged.

Event   A race or stroke over a given distance.

False start   When a swimmer leaves the starting block before the starting signal. One false start will disqualify a swimmer or a relay team.

Fastest to slowest   A seeding method used on the longer events held at the end of a session. The fastest seeded swimmers participate in the first heats, followed by the next fastest, and so on. Many times these events will alternate one girls' heat and one boys' heat until all swimmers have competed.

FINA The international rules-making organization for the sport of swimming.

Finals The championship heat of an event in which the top six or eight swimmers from the preliminaries compete, depending on the number of lanes in the pool.

Fins Large rubber fin-type devices that fit on a swimmer's feet. Used in swim practice, not competition, sometimes known as 'flippers'.

Flags Pennants that are suspended over the width of each end of the pool 5m from the wall to guide backstroke swimmers to the wall.

Freestyle relays There are two freestyle relays – 400m and 800m. In the freestyle relays, four swimmers each swim one fourth of the total distance. As in the medley relay, no individual may swim more than one leg of the relay.

Freestyle One of the four competitive racing strokes. Freestyle (nicknamed 'free') is swum as the fourth stroke in the medley relay, and the fourth stroke in the IM. In the freestyle, the competitor may swim any stroke he or she wishes. The usual stroke used is the front crawl. This stroke is characterized by the alternate overhand motion of the arms and a flutter kick which can be either a six-beat-per stroke or two-beat-per-stroke cycle rhythm. The slower two-beat kick is often used in distance races (i.e. longer than 400m), while the faster, six-beat kick is used in the sprint events and at the very end of the distance races. In all competitions, each swimmer's head must surface within 15m of the start of the race. This rule was passed at the 1998 FINA Congress in Perth, Australia. The freestyle is swum in 50m, 100m, 200m, 400m, 800m and 1500m distances at the Olympic Games. Women's events do not include the 1500m freestyle, while the men's schedule of events does not include the 800m freestyle.

Goal A specific time achievement a swimmer sets and strives for. Can be short- or long-term.

Goggles Eyewear worn by swimmers to keep their eyes from being irritated by the chlorine in the water.

Heats A division of an event when there are too many swimmers to compete at the same time. The results are compiled by swimmers' time swam, after all heats of the event are completed.

Hingeing or **unhingeing**: The relationships of the head to the spine, creating a balanced or unbalanced position in the water. Unhingeing results in the head being disconnected from the 'head/spine line', and loss of body balance.

IM: Individual Medley A swimming event using all four of the competitive strokes on consecutive lengths of the race. The order must be butterfly, backstroke, breaststroke, freestyle. Equal distances must be swum of each stroke. 'IM' is slang for the 'individual medley'. In the IM a swimmer begins with the butterfly, changes to the backstroke after one-fourth of the race, then the breaststroke for another quarter, and finally finishes with the freestyle. The 'no-touch' backstroke rule comes into play in the individual medley events in that the new turn may be used in the 400m IM (100m of each stroke) only in the middle of the backstroke leg. The new turn may not be used in the backstroke to breaststroke turn, however, and is therefore not allowed in a long course 200m individual medley race. The IM is swum in 100m, 200m and 400m distances.

Interval A specific elapsed time for swimming, or a rest used during swim practice.

Kick board A flotation device used by swimmers during practice for legs-only practices.

Kick The leg movements of a swimmer.

Lane lines Continuous floating markers attached to a cable stretched from the starting end to the turning end for the purpose of separating each lane and quieting the waves caused by racing swimmers. The specific area in which a swimmer is assigned to swim is called a 'lane'.

Lap One length of the course. Sometimes may also mean down and back (two lengths) of the pool.

Lap counter A set of plastic display numbers used to keep track of laps during a distance race. Also, the person who counts for the swimmer stationed at the opposite end from the start.

Leg The part of a relay event swum by a single team member or a single stroke in the IM.

Long course A 50m pool.

Long-axis strokes The freestyle and backstroke – those strokes in which the rhythm axis and rotation are along the head/spine line.

Lycra A stretch material used to make competitive swimsuits and swim hats.

Mark The command to take your starting position, 'take your mark'.

Marker Compound, group of compounds or biological parameters indicating the use of a prohibited substance or prohibited method.

Medals Awards given to the swimmers at meets. They vary in size and design and method of presentation.

Medley relay Swum as a 400m race. In the medley relay, all four strokes are swum by four different swimmers. No swimmer may swim more than one leg of the relay, which is swum in backstroke, breaststroke, butterfly and freestyle order. In addition it is possible to see a world record in the 100m backstroke (the first leg) in this race.

Meet director The official in charge of the administration of the meet.

Meet Competition programme in its entirety, designed to be a learning experience by implementing what has been learned in practice. The swimmer tests themselves against the clock to see how they are improving.

Metabolite Any substance produced by a biotransformation process.

Metres The measurement of the length of a swimming pool that was built per specs using the metric system. Long course metres is 50m, short course meters is 25m.

Missed test Conduct that may be relied upon to establish a failure by the athlete to be available for testing on any given day at the location and time specified in the time slot identified in his or her athlete whereabouts filing for that day.

NAGs National Age Group Championships held annually.

National Anti-Doping Organization (NADO) Entity designated by a country as possessing the primary authority and responsibility to adopt and implement anti-doping rules, as well as to direct the collection of samples, the management of test results, and the conduct of hearings, all at the national level.

Nationals National Championship held annually.

Negative split Referring to a swim paced with the second half faster than the first, for example 'he swam a negative 400, 2.02 and 1.59'.

NGB National governing body.

Nutrition The sum of the processes by which a swimmer takes in and utilizes food substances.

Nylon A material used to make swimsuits.

Official A judge on the deck of the pool at a sanctioned competition who is there to enforce the rules.

Olympic trials The accredited long-course swim meet held the year of the Olympic Games to decide which swimmers will represent the country at the Olympic Games.

Omega A brand of automatic timing system.

Open competition Competition that any qualified club, organization, or individual may enter.

Pace clock The electronic clocks or large clocks with highly visible numbers and second hands, positioned at the ends or sides of a swimming pool so that the swimmers can read their times during warm-ups or training sessions. Sometimes also known as a 'sweep clock'.

Paddles Coloured plastic devices worn on the swimmers' hands during training.

Pool The facility in which swimming competition and training is conducted.

Practice US slang for the scheduled training session/workout a swimmer attends with their swim team/club.

Prelims Session of a prelims/finals meet in which the qualification heats are conducted, otherwise known as 'heats'.

Prohibited list List identifying the substances and methods prohibited in sport. The prohibited list is one of the four WADA international standards and is mandatory for signatories to the World Anti-Doping Code.

Pull buoy A flotation device used for pulling by swimmers in practice.

Qualifying times Published times necessary to enter certain meets, or the times necessary to achieve a specific category of swimmer.

Race Any single swimming competition.

Ready room A room pool-side for the swimmers to relax before they compete in finals.

Referee The head official at a swim meet in charge of all of the 'wet side' administration and decisions.

Relay Swimming event in which four swimmers participate as a relay team, each swimmer swimming an equal distance of the race. There are two types of relay:

• Medley relay: One swimmer swims backstroke, another breaststroke, another butterfly, and another freestyle, in that order.

• Freestyle relay: Where all swimmers comply with the rules for freestyle. Normally swimmers will swim front crawl, but the rules permit them to use any style as long they enter the water from the blocks.

Sample/Specimen Any biological material collected for the purposes of doping control.

Scratch To withdraw from an event in a competition.

Senior meet A meet that is for senior level swimmers and is not divided into age groups. Qualification times are usually necessary and will vary depending on the level of the meet.

Session Portion of meet distinctly separated from other portions by locale, time, type of competition, or age group.

Set A group of drills put together to form a complete practice.

Shave The process of removing all arm, leg, and exposed torso hair, to decrease the 'drag' or resistance of the body moving through the water. Used mainly by senior swimmers at very important (championship) meets.

Short course A 25m pool.

Short-axis strokes Breaststroke and butterfly – those strokes in which the rhythm axis and rotation occur on a line drawn *across* the body along a fulcrum that is located at the centre of mass.

Split A swimmer's intermediate time in a race. Splits are registered every 50yd or meters, and are used to determine if a swimmer is on record pace. Under certain condi-

tions, splits may also be used as official times.

Sprint Describes the shorter events (50m and 100m). In training, to swim as fast as possible for a short distance.

Start The beginning of a race. The dive used to begin a race.

Starter The official in charge of signalling the beginning of a race, and ensuring that all swimmers have a fair start.

Stations Separate portions of a dry-land or weight circuit.

Streamline The position used to gain maximum distance during a start and/or push-off from the wall in which the swimmer's body is as tight as it can be.

Stroke There are four competitive strokes: butterfly, backstroke, breaststroke, freestyle.

Stroke judge The official positioned at the side of the pool, walking the length of the course as the swimmers race. If the stroke judge sees something illegal, they report to the referee and the swimmer may be disqualified.

Suit The racing uniform worn by the swimmer, in the water, during competition. The three most popular styles/types of suits worn are nylon, lycra and fastskin.

Swim-down Low-intensity swimming used by swimmers after a race or main practice to rid the body of excess lactic acid and to gradually reduce heart rate and respiration.

Swim-off In a heat/finals-type competition, a race after the scheduled event to break a tie. The only circumstance that warrants a swim-off is to determine which swimmer makes a final.

Taper The final preparation phase prior to major competition. An older, more experienced swimmer will shave their entire body to reduce resistance and heighten sensation in the water.

The 'T' An imaginary 'T', with the cross member drawn from armpit to armpit and the stem drawn down the centre of the body from the extended chin to the lower sternum.

Time trial A time-only swim which is not part of a regular meet.

Timekeeper The volunteers sitting behind the starting blocks/finish end of the pool, who are responsible for getting watch times on events and activating the backup buttons for the timing system.

Touch Pad   The removable plate (on the end of pools) that is connected to an automatic timing system. A swimmer must properly touch the touchpad to register an official time in a race.

Unofficial time   The swimmer's time displayed on a read-out board, or read over the intercom by the announcer immediately after the race. After the time has been checked, it will become the official time.

Vitamins   The building blocks of the body. Vitamins do not supply energy, but are necessary for proper health.

WADA: The World Anti-Doping Agency (WADA) is the international independent organization created in 1999 to promote, co-ordinate and monitor the fight against doping in sport in all its forms at the international level. The agency is composed and funded equally by the Olympic movement and governments of the world. Its key activities include scientific research, education, out-of-competition testing, development of anti-doping capacities, and monitoring of the World Anti-Doping Code.

WADA-accredited laboratory   Anti-doping laboratory accredited by WADA in compliance with the International Standard for Laboratories, applying test methods and processes to provide evidentiary data for the detection and, if applicable, quantification of a threshold substance on the prohibited list in urine and other biological samples. WADA has been responsible for accrediting and reaccrediting anti-doping laboratories since 2004.

Warm-up   Used by a swimmer prior to a main practice, set or race. Gets muscles loose and warm, and gradually increases heart and respiration.

Watch   The hand-held device used by timers and coaches for timing a swimmer's races and taking splits. Stopwatches are used to time swimmers during a competition by coaches, parents and officials. When totally automatic timing equipment is used, watches serve as a back-up method.

Weights The   various   barbells/benches/ machines used by swimmers during their dryland programme.

Yardage The distance a swimmer races or swims in practice. Total yardage can be calculated for each practice session.

Useful Addresses

United Kingdom

British Swimming
Harold Fern House
Derby Square
Loughborough
LE11 5AL
Tel: 01509 618700
Fax: 01509 618701
email: cserv@asagb.org.uk

BSCTA – British Swimming
Coaches & Teachers Association
Brian McGuinness, Secretary
Will Thorne House
2 Birmingham Road
Halesowen
West Midlands
B63 3HP
Tel: 0121 550 4888
Fax: 0121 550 4272
email:brian.mcguinness@gmb.org.uk

English ASA
Harold Fern House
Derby Square
Loughborough
LE11 5AL
Tel: 01509 618700
Fax: 01509 618701
email: cserv@asagb.org.uk

**ISTC – Institute of Swimming
Teachers & Coaches**
Dennis Freeman-Wright
Chief Executive
41 Granby Street

Loughborough
Leicestershire
LE11 3DU
Tel: 01509 264357
email: istc@swimming.org.uk

Scottish Swimming
National Swimming Academy
University of Stirling
Stirling
FK9 4LA
Tel: 01786 466530
Fax: 01786 466521
email: info@scottishswimming.com

Welsh ASA
Wales National Pool Swansea
Sketty Lane
Swansea
SA2 8QG
Tel: 01792 513636
Fax: 01792 513637
email: secretary@welshasa.co.uk

Worldwide

Australia (AUS)
Australian Swimming Ltd
Unit 12, 7 Beissel Street
Belconnen Act 2617
PO Box 3286
Canberra
Australia
Tel: 61-2 6219 5600
Fax: 61-2 6219 5606
email: swim@swimming.org.au

FINA – Federation Internationale De Natation Amateur
Avenue de L'Avant – Poste 4
1005 Lausanne
Switzerland
Tel: 41 21 310 4710
Fax: 41 21 312 6610
web: www.fina.org

Irish ASA
House of Sport
Longmile Road
Dublin 12
Eire
Tel: 00 353 1 450 1739
Fax: 00 353 1 450 2805
email: webmaster1@swimireland.ie

LEN – Ligue Europeenne de Natation
c/o CONI
Stadio Olympico
Palazzina Bonifati
00/94 Roma
Italy
Tel: 3906 3685 7870
Fax: 3906 3237058
email: lenoffice@tin.it

New Zealand (NZL)
Swimming New Zealand
Level 3, Booth House
202–206 Cuba Street
PO Box 11 115
Wellington
New Zealand
Tel: 64-4 801 9450
Fax: 64-4 801 6270
email: sport@swimmingnz.org.nz

South Africa (RSA)
Swimming South Africa
Johannesburg Athletic Stadium
124 Van Beek Street
North Wing, Ground Floor
2094 New Doornfontein
Johannesburg
South Africa
Tel: 27-11 404 2480
Fax: 27 11 402 2481
email: gensec@swimsa.co.za

Swimming/Natation Canada
2197 Riverside Drive
Suite 700
Ottawa
Ontario
K1H 7X3
Canada
Tel: 613 260 1348
Fax: 613 260 0804
email: natloffice@swimming.ca

United States Swimming, Inc.
1 Olympic Plaza
Colorado Springs
CO 80909
USA
Tel: 719 866 4578
Fax: 719 866 4761
email: webmaster@usa-swimming.org

Index